Advance Praise for Abortion to Abolition

"This critical reading offers insight into Canadian histories of reproductive health access and the manifold violence of Canada's carcel system, while communicating the vital hope embedded in politics and action at the intersection of reproductive justice and abolition."
— Dr. Catherine Bryan, Dalhousie University

"In *Abortion to Abolition*, Martha Paynter unflinchingly names the carceral state as the foremost threat to reproductive justice in so-called Canada. Paynter takes great care to expose prisoners' experiences of carceral maternity, demonstrating that incarceration (particularly of Indigenous women) enables the continued separation of parents from their children, a fundamental design element in any colonial project. After decades of frontline nursing and advocacy, Paynter deftly illuminates that fight for reproductive justice doesn't end with abortion access and must include the fight to abolish the violence of prisons."
— Meenakshi Mannoe, Vancouver Prison Justice Day Committee, Pivot Legal Society

"This book sews together all of the various threads of reproductive justice work in the medical professions, academia, and advocacy into one comprehensive and accessible collection. The stories that are told throughout remind us of our shared humanity and demonstrate clearly the impact that interlocking systems of oppression have on our society. This book is a comprehensive, powerful, and essential resource for all of us working toward liberation."
— Emilie Coyle, Executive Director, Canadian Association of Elizabeth Fry Societies

ABORTION TO ABOLITION

ABORTION TO ABOLITION

Reproductive Health and Justice in Canada

MARTHA PAYNTER

ILLUSTRATED BY JULIA HUTT

Fernwood Publishing
Halifax & Winnipeg

Development editor: Fazeela Jiwa
Copyediting: Erin Seatter
Text design: Brenda Conroy
Cover design: Emily Davidson
Printed and bound in Canada

Published by Fernwood Publishing
32 Oceanvista Lane, Black Point, Nova Scotia, B0J 1B0
and 748 Broadway Avenue, Winnipeg, Manitoba, R3G 0X3
www.fernwoodpublishing.ca

Fernwood Publishing Company Limited gratefully acknowledges the financial support of the Government of Canada, the Canada Council for the Arts, the Manitoba Department of Culture, Herit-
age and Tourism under the Manitoba Publishers Marketing Assistance Program and the Province
of Manitoba, through the Book Publishing Tax Credit, for our publishing program. We are pleased
to work in partnership with the Province of Nova Scotia and Arts Nova Scotia to develop and pro-
mote our creative industries for the benefit of all Nova Scotians.

Library and Archives Canada Cataloguing in Publication

Title: Abortion to abolition: reproductive health and justice in Canada /
by Martha Paynter.
Names: Paynter, Martha, author.
Description: Includes bibliographical references and index.
Identifiers: Canadiana (print) 20210353961 | Canadiana (ebook) 20210362928 |
ISBN 9781773635149 (softcover) | ISBN 9781773635255 (EPUB) |
ISBN 9781773635262 (PDF)
Subjects: LCSH: Reproductive rights—Canada—History.
Classification: LCC HQ766.5.C3 P39 2022 | DDC 363.9/60971—dc23

CONTENTS

For every person in this book who fought for change.
We got this far because of you. We will keep going.

BEYOND ABORTION

The state of abortion access in Canada is unlike anywhere in the world. The 1988 *Morgentaler* decision resulted in complete decriminalization. A person cannot be charged for having or providing an abortion for any reason, at any gestational age. With few exceptions, medication and aspiration (surgical) abortion are funded by taxpayers, and patients do not pay for care out of pocket. Almost every primary care provider in the country, including family physicians and nurse practitioners, can prescribe medication abortion. And bubble zone laws or hospital policies in many cities protect patients from antichoice protestors at clinic entryways, so people can access care without fear of physical harassment or violence. Importantly, these provisions reflect the unconditional support of a vast majority of people in Canada for the right to abortion.

A few persistent access barriers remain. Canada does not have enough competent, confident abortion providers, especially outside large urban centres. The need to travel to access abortion services remains a huge burden, the cost of which is often privatized. Allowing more people, like midwives and nurses, to participate in procedural abortion care and training more providers to do procedures at later gestational ages are both critical steps to improving access. Many noncitizens are currently excluded from publicly funded care, but everyone should be eligible regardless of status. Temporary foreign workers, international students and migrants deserve access to abortion. Contraception should be covered under medicare. Finally, birth control remains a private expense, which ignores the gendered experience of managing reproduction and the gendered consequences of unplanned pregnancy.

Everyone needs to talk openly and often about abortion. Everyone needs to expand their understanding of abortion — not only health care providers but all people who could get pregnant or cause pregnancies. One-third of people who can get pregnant in Canada will have an abortion in their lifetimes, and complications are extremely rare. Abortion is common, normal and safe. It is basic reproductive health. It is self-care.

As a nurse educator, I noticed that even students in nursing school are not familiar with the processes of aspiration or medication abortion, even though most of them are women and people with a uterus and in an age group where abortion is particularly common, and they could be assumed, based on their academic focus, to know about

1

clinical issues. They are interested, forthright and enthusiastic. But the information is not in their standard curriculum. I am working to change that. Meanwhile, I wanted to write a book about abortion that was approachable and reassuring for my nursing students and the general public alike — one that pushed understanding and action for reproductive health and justice further.

I hope this book prompts more forward momentum for those aspects of reproductive justice that demand action and resolution beyond abortion, which has been the focus of white feminist discourse and activism for decades. White feminism and neoliberal feminism centre the needs and concerns of white and middle-class women, such as the right to abortion or to career advancement (Zakaria 2021). The dominance of white feminism in colonial worldviews results in neglected or worsening conditions for other groups of women, trans people and nonbinary people, such as state interference in the family and police violence. Improved conditions for white women do not "trickle down" to create improvements in conditions for all women. Rather, white women can make gains on the backs of others (Loreto 2020; Phipps 2020).

I am a white bisexual cisgender woman working as a clinician, researcher and advocate in Atlantic Canada in the field of reproductive health and criminal justice. This book reflects the beliefs and understandings I have come to from that very privileged position, informed by the feminism and prison justice activism of many writers and organizers who identify as Black, Indigenous and trans. This book sketches a broad background to the current state of reproductive rights in Canada in the context of systemic colonialism, racism, classism, homophobia and transphobia. The chapters move from bodily autonomy to abortion to the right to parent and to parent in safety — the key tenets of reproductive justice, developed by women of colour in resistance to the myopia of the white feminist focus on abortion. The term "reproductive justice" — a merging of reproductive rights with social justice (Ross 2017) — speaks to the intersecting oppressions Black people, Indigenous people and people of colour experience along with gender discrimination, as well as the complex changes in power needed for reproductive liberation. The book closes with stories about parenting in prison and an argument that prison abolition, another movement led by people of colour, is a necessary step towards reproductive freedom. Twenty years of engagement in reproductive health and justice work has confirmed this necessity in my mind and informed how I chose and told the stories here.

My work in abortion has spanned three Atlantic provinces, each with its own tumultuous and restrictive history of abortion access. When I worked in management for the New Brunswick Department of Health in 2007, I negotiated to have every Tuesday morning off, paid, so I could volunteer at the Fredericton Morgentaler Clinic a block away from my office. At the time Dr. Henry Morgentaler was in a legal dispute with the Department of Health over its refusal to pay for care at his clinic, an issue continuing today. An antichoice organization owned the building next to the clinic, and on Tuesdays, when the physician came from out of town to perform the procedures, the clinic would be surrounded by protestors. We had a little team of "escorts" identified by blue cotton aprons we wore over our coats, and it was our job to huddle around patients, talk over the sounds of the protestors and make sure every patient made it inside safely. I found these few hours of volunteering per week to be much more fulfilling and purposeful than any paid work I was doing at the time. For several years I fundraised for Dr. Morgentaler's legal battles in Fredericton, organizing a live event called Arts Auction for Choice. Despite the conservative nature of the city, the arts scene is vibrant. Prominent painters and ceramicists would contribute to the cause, and the auctions were startlingly successful. The money raised went straight to Morgentaler's legal defence fund, managed by the Abortion Rights Coalition of Canada.

After Morgentaler died in 2013 and the clinic lay empty, I was part of the group that came to be called Reproductive Justice New Brunswick. As a collective, we crowdfunded nearly $200,000 towards a down payment on the clinic building. This was before platforms like GoFundMe became commonplace. A single supportive column by Elizabeth Renzetti (2014) in the *Globe and Mail* instantly and exponentially buoyed public support. We did not take on ownership of the property; instead, we gave the funds to Dr. Adrian Edgar, a young family physician, and supported him in leading the clinic's reincarnation. He opened Clinic 554, a general family practice with a specialization in trans health care, and once a week was able to provide abortion services, just as the Morgentaler Clinic had for twenty years. I still feel pride in our role in the launch of Clinic 554 and disappointment it was forced to close in 2020, which I discuss in Chapter 2.

Once the transition to Clinic 554 was sorted out, I shifted focus to the crisis on Prince Edward Island (PEI). Abortion services had been unavailable in PEI since 1982. I strategized with a team of activists that took the government to court over its unconstitutional ban on abortion services in 2016. The fight was won before a trial ever started, and a full-service clinic was established in Summerside the next year. More details about this battle are contained in Chapter 2.

After medication abortion (in the form of the mifepristone pill) was approved by Health Canada in 2015, I pushed for public funding for the drug in Nova Scotia as chair of the Halifax chapter of Women's Legal Education and Action Fund (LEAF). Eventually, public coverage of mifepristone became policy not only in Nova Scotia but in nearly every province and territory in the country. My nursing career led me to frontline abortion care in Nova Scotia, one of the only provinces with a nurse-led, toll-free, centralized self-referral phone line to arrange for aspiration or medication abortion. With clinical and academic colleagues at Dalhousie University, I co-created the first interprofessional health education course in Canada devoted to the subject of abortion. Abortion is, to me, one of the most captivating aspects of Canadian history. But abortion is only one part of reproductive health and justice.

I started working in advocacy for reproductive health for people in prison in 2012. While listening to CBC Radio one morning, I heard Julie Bilotta's story, and it immediately shifted the course of my life. Bilotta was forced to give birth in a solitary confinement cell at the Ottawa-Carleton Detention Centre in September of that year. She was taken to the hospital and separated from her baby, then returned to prison, unable to touch him, nurse him or parent him. When I heard about Bilotta, I was holding my first baby, safe, at home. I felt the same rage about Bilotta's mistreatment I felt about denied access to abortion: it was the same problem of gendered control and oppression. I reached out to friends and colleagues — doulas, nurses, lawyers — and we started an organization in Nova Scotia called Wellness Within: An Organization for Health and Justice, committed to safeguarding the reproductive rights of people experiencing criminalization.

Our first project was to gain security clearance at the provincial jail and federal prison in Nova Scotia to provide volunteer doula support. Doulas are nonclinical support people who provide companionship, advocacy, information and comfort to people in pregnancy, labour, birth and postpartum. Perhaps, we thought, if Bilotta had had a doula, she would not have been so mistreated. There are doula programs in prisons in several US states, and research has found the presence of doulas improves clinical outcomes (Shlafer et al. 2021; Stanley et al. 2015). We believed the doula role in our organization had to be unpaid, nonprofessional volunteer work, an act of solidarity and humility, not an act of charity or paternalism. We did not want to receive financial compensation from or be helpful to the prison system; we morally opposed it.

Through this work, I went from being a volunteer escort at an abortion clinic to a companion for pregnant people in prison — this transition made sense to me, like following along a continuum. What I saw in the prisons directed me towards more intentional prison abolition work. I shifted my career from health policy and management to clinical nursing practice and research and began writing about how nursing could contribute to abolition (Paynter, Jefferies and Carrier 2020; Paynter et al. 2021). Like abortion, prison abolition is a critical element of reproductive justice.

Abortion has long been a white feminist project, dominating discussion about reproductive rights and crowding out concern for other violations, including the rights of incarcerated parents and their children, who are disproportionately Black, Indigenous and people of colour. Women of colour developed the concept of reproductive justice to encompass the breadth of social issues that must be addressed to safeguard reproductive freedom, and to actualize reproductive rights as human rights, when racism and other types of intersecting oppressions fiercely control and limit opportunity (Ross 2006a; Silliman, Fried and Ross 2016). Women of colour also lead the work of prison abolition. Exposing and dismantling racism is foundational to these two movements. Feminism would gain relevance and effectiveness by addressing and dismantling the racism of (white) feminist discourse and its centring of abortion above all else. As Black feminist Mikki Kendall (2020, 6) critiques, "There's nothing feminist about having so many resources at your fingertips and choosing to be ignorant."

The term "reproductive justice" was first coined in summer 1994 by twelve "founding mothers": Toni M. Bond Leonard, Reverend Alma Crawford, Evelyn S. Field, Terri James, Bisola Marignay, Cassandra McConnell, Cynthia Newbille, Loretta Ross, Elizabeth Terry, "Able" Mable Thomas, Winnette P. Willis and Kim Youngblood (Bond 2001; Black Women for Reproductive Justice 2012a, 2012b). These Black leaders of the reproductive rights movement were attending a conference in Chicago co-hosted by the Illinois Pro-Choice Alliance and Ms. Foundation for Women where a President Clinton proposal for universal health care was presented. The reform package inadequately covered issues of reproductive health and failed to address Black women's needs. A few months prior, many of these leaders had attended the United Nations International Conference on Population and Development, where a Programme of Action was adopted connecting reproductive rights, sustainable development, migration, health and international cooperation (Ross 2006b; United Nations Population Fund 2014). They envisioned US health care reform that addressed inequity and included full access to sexual and reproductive health services.

Having raised $40,000 and collected 836 endorsements from prominent Black women, the Women of African Descent for Reproductive Justice, as the group was known, published full-page ads in the *Washington Post* and *Roll Call*, and held a press conference in Washington, DC, to launch their counterproposal for reform. They demanded that reproductive freedom be recognized as "a life and death issue for many Black women" deserving "as much recognition as any other freedom" and that reform to health care include not only abortion funding but a full spectrum of sexual and reproductive care (Williams 2019, 1). Their statement shifted the discourse forever after, cementing reproductive justice as integral to human rights and social justice movements.

Like the Black feminist theory of intersectionality (Crenshaw 1989; Collins and Bilge 2020), reproductive justice recognizes how intersecting oppressions including racism and sexism affect how rights are experienced — or denied. In 2005 Asian Communities for Reproductive Justice published a visionary treatise on reproductive justice that expanded its meaning:

> We believe reproductive justice is the complete physical, mental, spiritual, political, economic, and social well-being of women and girls, and will be achieved when women and girls have the economic, social and political power and resources to make healthy decisions about our bodies, sexuality and reproduction for ourselves, our families and our communities in all areas of our lives. (2)

Many of the founding mothers, Asian Communities for Reproductive Justice and other grassroots organizations would go on to found SisterSong Women of Color Reproductive Health Collective in 1997. Based out of Atlanta, Georgia, SisterSong remains the leading voice internationally in reproductive justice work.

Moving far beyond the right to abortion, contraception and reproductive health care services, reproductive justice includes rights to bodily autonomy, to participate in safe and fairly compensated sex work, to live free from sexual violence, to self-define our gender identity and express our gender freely, to determine the size and makeup of our families, to not have children, to have children and to parent children in safe and sustainable communities without fear of colonial and racist state violence (Ross and Solinger 2017).

This latter part is specifically how prison abolition is connected to reproductive justice. Incarceration is an enduring institution of colonial and racist state violence (Lumsden 2016; Palacious 2016). While the Indian Residential School regime in Canada ended in 1996 (Truth and Reconciliation Commission 2015; Union of Ontario Indians 2013), the contemporary prison system is a continuation of cultural genocide (MacDonald 2016; Puljak 2015). In Canada, although Indigenous people make up less than 5 percent of the population in the country (Health Canada 2020), one-third of people in prisons are Indigenous. The disproportionality is higher still for Indigenous women, who make up nearly 50 percent of women behind bars (Office of the Correctional Investigator 2021).* Indigenous people are incarcerated at earlier ages, receive harsher sentences, are classified at higher levels of security and experience more harms, including solitary confinement, than white people in prison (Cardoso 2020; Native Women's Association of Canada 2017).

Black people are also disproportionately incarcerated. Although race-disaggregated data collection in the justice system is decidedly lacking, what data is available is striking. A research team led by Dr. Akwasi Owusu-Bempah found that 12.8 percent of men and 7.1 percent of women incarcerated in Ontario in 2010 identified as Black (Owusu-Bempah et al. 2021), despite Black people comprising only 4.7 percent of the Ontario population (Statistics Canada 2019b). Black people in Ontario are also remanded more often to pretrial custody and spend longer periods in remand in comparison to white people (Mehler Paperny 2017). In Nova Scotia the situation is even worse: Black people make up 11.1 percent of admissions to provincial corrections (Mark Furey, personal communication, October 3, 2018) but only 2.4 percent of the population (Statistics Canada 2019b). At the federal level, Black people make up 7.2 percent of people in prison (Public Safety Canada 2020) but comprise 3.5 percent of the general population in Canada (Statistics Canada 2019b). Disproportionate and longer periods of incarceration obviously affect reproductive rights and the ability to create a family and care for children.

As US political scientist Rachel Roth (2017, 1) has described, "Every dimension of reproductive justice is negatively affected by imprisonment —from access to abortion and basic medical care to maintain one's health and fertility to the ability to form and maintain relationships with one's children." All people experiencing criminalization face threats to reproductive justice. Incarcerated people experience strip searches (Shakur 1988), sexual assault and trauma, restricted health services, delays and interruptions in creating their families, and separation from their babies and loved ones (Hayes, Sufrin

---

* In this book I have endeavoured to use gender-inclusive language; however, available statistics are often specifically collected and published as pertaining to women.

and Perritt 2020). These harms are all amplified by racism and the disproportionate incarceration of Black and Indigenous people. There can be no reproductive justice or racial justice while incarceration persists.

Prison abolitionists recognize the prison system is ineffective and nonrehabilitative. It perpetrates violent harm, including physical assault and injury, emotional torment and mental illness, malnutrition and eating disorders (Davis 2003; Ling 2021). Harm cannot be remedied through more harm (Kaba 2021). Prison is exploitative and fundamentally unfair (Prison Research Education Action Project 1976; Gilmore 2007). Prisoners work for poverty wages and face inflated prices for phone calls and canteen items. Prison is also exceedingly expensive for the public: it costs over $80,000 per year to incarcerate one woman. Keeping someone in solitary confinement costs half a million dollars per year (Office of the Parliamentary Budget Officer 2018). Those are tax dollars that could be invested in a host of positive social programs, including education, housing, income support and health care.

Prison abolitionists acknowledge the rootedness of incarceration in racism and colonialism, and the intergenerational cycle of trauma the prison system perpetuates. They advocate for the destruction of prisons and the creation of compassionate, evidence-based, community-led solutions to the drivers of criminalization: poverty, trauma and white supremacy. As Dr. Angela Davis (2003, 106) wrote, "The first step, then, would be to let go of the desire to discover one single alternative system of punishment that would occupy the same footprint as the prison system." Prison abolitionists urge imagination and complexity in thinking about alternatives.

Just one part of prison abolition, a part I can play a useful role in as a reproductive health nurse, is advancing sexual and reproductive health care and education, prioritizing people who experience criminalization. In the fall and winter of 2019–20, before the pandemic hit, I was hired by the Canadian Association of Elizabeth Fry Societies (CAEFS) to facilitate workshops about reproductive health in each of the federal prisons designated for women across Canada. The workshop project started with a call from Senator Dr. Yvonne Boyer. In 2017 Senator Boyer, a Métis nurse, lawyer and professor, and Dr. Judith Bartlett, a Métis physician, wrapped up an external inquiry into allegations of forced sterilization of Indigenous people in Saskatoon. Senator Boyer was concerned that incarcerated people may have missed the opportunity to provide testimony to the inquiry because of their incarceration, the cost of calling her office from prison, they had not received word the inquiry was happening or they did not know what sterilization was. In collaboration with Senator Boyer, CAEFS staff and Indigenous Elders from several Nations, we developed a workshop covering the issue of sterilization but also, more generally, reproductive justice for people in prison.

While Canada has an extensively chronicled history of abortion, the scholarship about reproductive health for incarcerated people is thin. To create the workshops, I drew on the Canadian health research of Dr. Fiona Kouyoumdjian, Dr. Claire Bodkin, Dr. Ruth Elwood Martin, Dr. Jessica Liauw and Dr. Allison Carter Ramirez and legal-criminology scholars including Dr. Adelina Iftene, Dr. Gillian Balfour, Dr. Jennifer Kilty, Dr. Justin Piché, Jessica Hutchison and Kaliyah Miller. I incorporated theoretical work on reproductive justice and prison abolition in the United States from Critical Resistance (2004) as well as Dr. Angela Davis, Loretta Ross, Dr. Rachel Roth, Dr. Dorothy Roberts, Dr. Ginette Ferszt, Dr. Rachel Hardeman, Dr. Chenelle Jones, Alexa Kolbi-Molinas, Dr. Jamila Perritt, Dr. Renita Seabrook, Dr. Rebecca Shlafer, Dr. Carolyn Sufrin, Andrea Ritchie and Dr. Ruth Wilson Gilmore, among many others. I juxtaposed these theories and movements with legal cases from Canada and human rights law. The workshops became about sharing the stories that made a difference in reproductive health, rights and justice.

Participants in the workshops deeply understood reproductive justice and abolition and described the relevance of the movements to their lives. They named the injustice of generations of their families experiencing state interference in family life, from residential schools to foster care to imprisonment. As one participant said, "The water in First Nations, that's about to reproductive health — it's impossible to enjoy the idea of having children and raising them in a safe way when the water is brown" (Paynter 2021, 17). They felt their bodies under constant threat and surveillance in the prison system. They required permission for everything. Their bodies were not theirs to govern. They felt the reproductive injustice of being denied the right to hug and hold. For the same reason abortion is central to feminism — it is a necessity for bodily autonomy — feminism should include prison abolitionist ethics. Incarceration is incompatible with the right to bodily autonomy.

Workshop facilitators travelled to each of the five federal English-language institutions for women: Truro, Nova Scotia; Kitchener-Waterloo, Ontario; Maple Creek, Saskatchewan; Edmonton, Alberta; and Abbotsford, British Columbia (BC). We facilitated workshops with over two hundred people. When the project was finished, I wrote a report for CAEFS with recommendations for action based on what participants had shared (Paynter 2021). The workshop tour was one of the most important experiences in my life. I saw prison spaces infrequently seen by the public and I learned so much from the people inside.

The legal cases we shared in the workshop were stories of resilient, everyday individuals who pushed major changes in public attitudes and formal changes to the law. Told like stories, these cases reached people, making reproductive justice relatable and accessible. After the workshop tour, I wanted to write a book to share the same kinds of stories with the public. I think of each of the twenty-three stories in this book as enough to change a reader's perspective about current priorities for reproductive rights activism, to ensure it includes queer parenting, fertility treatment, environmental sustainability and abolition of the carceral systems of child protection and prisons. All the stories here have a legal conflict, but there is much more to the stories than the litigation — and there is so much more to progress than legal decisions that favour reproductive rights. To me, these stories shift the very meaning of reproductive freedom in Canada from abortion access to complete autonomy over one's body and decisions about child-bearing and parenting.

Those of us working in reproductive health, as activists, teachers, lawyers, health care professionals, policy-makers or even voters, should be using reproductive justice to identify and examine how reproductive freedom is supported and constrained in Canada. Canada has a deep history of reproductive oppression, most evident in the persistent control of Indigenous communities. Reproductive oppression erases the person, their sovereignty over their body, their life and their future. This country also has a strong history of reproductive liberation. The Constitution Act enacted in 1982, and in particular the Charter of Rights and Freedoms contained therein, advanced and affirmed human rights, including bodily autonomy and gender equality. Criminal law in Canada is under federal jurisdiction, and it is not easily or arbitrarily changed when an antichoice politician is elected. Canada has no laws limiting access to abortion. And the Canada Health Act of 1985 made health services, with some troubling exceptions, a public responsibility to fund and organize. These laws provide a resilient base for defending reproductive rights.

For all this strong foundation, the key moments and people in Canada's reproductive health history are not commonly known. People in Canada are bombarded by US news, and many people will know exactly what pundits mean when they talk about *Roe v. Wade*, but similarly critical court cases in Canadian history do not roll off the tongue. Even those of us who are deeply engaged in abortion work are unlikely to make connections between the reproductive health care we provide and fights to defund the police and child protection services, to preserve freshwater supplies and to end discrimination against noncitizens. But making those connections will make us better at our work; it is a best practice for organizing. In her landmark abolitionist text *Golden Gulag*, Dr. Ruth Wilson Gilmore (2007, 7) wrote, "It is not only a good theory in theory but also a good theory in practice for people engaged in the spectrum of social justice struggles to figure out unexpected sites where their agendas align with those of others." Building relationships between movements for social justice amplifies our likelihood of success and nourishes us through interconnectedness in struggle and support.

The cases that have shifted reproductive justice and prisoner rights in Canada are often fought by anonymized and marginalized people in court, then written up in opaque case law that is inaccessible to the general public and those who need to know it most, including youth, students and marginalized and criminalized individuals. These stories and the people involved in them are fascinating, enraging and radicalizing. They need to be known. Canada needs a repertoire of content affirming how reproductive rights got to where they stand now, laying bare what is missing and directing future action towards substantive reproductive freedom. In this book I have placed the legal cases in context with broader discussions about human rights, racial justice, economic justice, environmental justice and gender equity — because reproductive health and freedom are far more complex than the outcomes to be found in case law alone.

This book tells just some of the stories behind some of the changes to reproductive health and justice in Canada. It is beautifully accompanied by images created by Nova Scotia artist Julia Hutt. Sometimes the protagonists in these stories collaborated with Julia in the designs. I know some of these people personally, but I have tried to only use public information in crafting this book. All these stories have previously been written about by scholars, journalists and even the protagonists themselves, whom I cite directly and aim to amplify. All these stories can be explored in greater depth by examining publicly available sources in the reference list. This is the first time these stories have been collected together to show the connections between them and to argue they have shaped the trajectory of reproductive health and justice in Canada.

This book is not by any means a complete picture of reproductive health law or cases in Canada. These stories shook me and direct what I do and how I do it: research, teaching, advocacy and clinical practice in abortion care, prison abolition and reproductive justice. I hope I did justice to the people I write about, and I dedicate this book to them.

Chapter 1

BODILY AUTONOMY

Bodily autonomy is the first principle of reproductive rights. It has long been synonymous with choice (SisterSong n.d.): you should have the right to choose what happens to your body. For decades "choice" was the rallying cry of abortion activism — the fight to be able to choose not to continue a pregnancy. But choice implies a menu of equivalent, or at least acceptable, options, and "the privilege to exercise discrimination in the marketplace among" them (Solinger 2013, 157). It skips over the problem of not having options. The rhetoric of choice is individualistic, but available options are the products of broad social contexts and systemic structures of inequality. It is not a person's fault to be met with no choices, or so-called bad choices; it is the result of a social algorithm of privileges and oppressions. "Choice" sounds easy, even flippant. The reality of reproductive decision-making is much more complicated. Contraception fails, relationships become abusive, jobs are precarious. The environment is in catastrophe. The police are killing children.

As described in the introduction, Black feminist leaders in the United States, including the founding mothers of Women of African Descent for Reproductive Justice, rejected the simplicity of second-wave feminism's language of "choice" and the false equivalency of abortion and reproductive liberation. In the early 1990s they developed the framework of reproductive justice with consciousness of the complexity of people's lives, including intersecting experiences of racism, sexism, ableism, homophobia, transphobia, xenophobia, class inequality and other oppressions and how these constrain opportunity and rights, even when such rights may exist on paper. As reproductive justice scholar Dr. Kimala Price (2010, 46) describes, "Although the 'choice' message tactic may have worked in the short run in response to the actions of the conservative antiabortion countermovement, many reproductive rights activists, especially women of color, believe that choice should not be the long-term or sole goal of the reproductive rights movement." Rather, substantive access — and the complete social, political and economic freedom required for access — is the cornerstone of reproductive justice.

The complexity and robustness of reproductive justice is widely appreciated and the framework has been adopted by organizations and individuals working in the field of reproductive health (service delivery; Planned Parenthood 2021) and rights (law; LEAF n.d.). The language of reproductive justice has now broadly replaced the movement's rallying cry of "choice" and tunnel vision focus on abortion rights: "Instead of focusing on the means — a divisive debate on abortion and birth control that neglects the real-life experiences of women and girls — the reproductive justice analysis focuses on the ends: better lives for women, healthier families, and sustainable communities" (Ross 2006c, 14–15). The fight does not stop at the right to abortion; the social transformation required for reproductive freedom is vast.

The canonical principles of bioethics are nonmaleficence (minimize harm), beneficence (amplify welfare), justice (aim to be just) and autonomy (support patient governance over clinical decisions). As bioethicists Dr. Carolyn McLeod and Dr. Sue Sherwin (2000) have theorized, threats to a person's autonomy include not only information they are lacking or even the coercion they may face, but also the oppression they endure. Racism, sexism, ableism, homophobia, transphobia, xenophobia, class inequality — these are oppressive realities determining what is possible. It is naïve at best and punitive at worst to suggest that the person experiencing their impact could easily change them.

Abortion is not so much a choice as a necessary service in society. Without access to abortion, people who can get pregnant — women, trans people and nonbinary people — cannot determine their own paths. They may not be able to complete their educational goals or obtain a safe, fulfilling job. They may not be able to share their life with partners who treat them with kindness and care. They may instead face poverty, violence and exclusion. Without abortion, people who can get pregnant cannot fully participate in social democracy. The need for abortion is not up for debate.

However, the overreliance on access to abortion as a sole metric of reproductive freedom crowds out the complexity of securing bodily autonomy. Bodily autonomy is determined by our ability to govern ourselves, our bodies, our sexual lives and our reproduction in relation to structures of oppression. Reproductive freedom is determined not just by our access to and consent to abortion or pap smears or prenatal care or hormone replacement therapy. It is not transactional, a measure of services received (although if these services are denied, then so is reproductive health). It is not sufficient for rights to be stipulated by law if they are not supported in real life. But it is also unlikely we will experience these rights if they are excluded from legal frameworks.

In 1982 Canada enacted the Charter of Rights and Freedoms, which is fundamental to the country's organization. Section 7 of the Charter reads, "Everyone has the right to life, liberty and security of the person" (Canada, Department of Justice 1982). In other words, you have the right to sovereignty over what you do and what happens to you. Section 15 reads, "Every individual is equal before and under the law and has the right to the equal protection and equal benefit of the law without discrimination and, in particular, without discrimination based on race, national or ethnic origin, colour, religion, sex, age or mental or physical disability" (Canada, Department of Justice 1982). Public policy cannot discriminate against you: you have the right to be free from the intersecting oppressions that violate reproductive freedom. Charter rights are the backbone of the Canadian Human Rights Act.

Surprisingly, learning about the Charter of Rights and Freedoms is not standard in Canadian public-school curricula or even university programs for health professionals. As a practising nurse and an instructor for nurses in training, I believe it is important to teach and know the Charter. The public should also expect health professionals to work to advance human rights as part of compliance with their professional codes of ethics. We must know where things stand to know where we are to go next.

The stories in this first chapter are, in my mind, critical to a conceptualization of bodily autonomy in Canada. The most basic tenet of bodily autonomy is the right to be who you are —to be and not be punished for being. Gendered violence against women, girls, trans and nonbinary people is an attack on the very right to be.

This chapter begins with the Montreal massacre, which, until April 18–19, 2020, when twenty-two women, girls and men were murdered in Nova Scotia by a man impersonating an RCMP officer, was the largest mass killing of women by a single person in Canadian history. The mass murders of December 1989 and April 2020, both of which were extreme acts of gender-based violence, are horrific. Yet these events are small in comparison to the extended and expansive genocide against Indigenous women, girls and Two-Spirit people, ongoing in Canada since this land was first occupied by colonial settlers. Bodily autonomy should always be considered with recognition of how the colonial project of Canada relies on subjugation of Indigenous Peoples.

All violence is made more lethal when guns are present. The first section of this chapter describes how *Heidi Rathjen,* a survivor of the massacre at École Polytechnique, has clawed at the limits of gun control law for three decades to gain some semblance of reparation for herself and her murdered classmates. Background checks, gun registration and assault rifle bans do not eradicate the ideology of white male supremacy, but they do reduce harm.

The story of *Justice Claire L'Heureux-Dubé,* in the second section of this chapter, shows the constraints of sexual assault law when its adjudicators are steeped in misogynistic anachronisms, and how transformative the voice of feminist dissent is in that context. In Canada, sexual assault includes all unwanted sexual touching, not only penetrative acts. Consent must be freely given, continuous and conscious. Intoxicated people or people who are asleep cannot consent, nor can people subject to the authority of another because of employment or other power structures. Sexual assault and gendered violence deny bodily autonomy, cultivate fear and self-alienation and groom stereotypical thinking. Once sexual assault cases reach the courtroom, it is far too late to prevent harm. Prevention is the constant work of fostering reproductive justice and dismantling misogyny.

Dismantling misogyny must include dismantling transmisogyny. To experience bodily autonomy, you must be able to govern your own gender identity and expression. Gender is socially constructed, and should be yours to determine. But enduring cisnormativity and transmisogyny in health systems and the institutions they interact with marginalize and oppress (Bacak, Bright, and Wilson 2020; Boe et al. 2020). The third section shows how the late *Synthia Kavanagh* faced transphobic restrictions to her gender expression not only in general society in 1980s Canada but also in one of the most binary-enforcing institutions there is: the prison. Forbidden from being housed in a facility designated for women and from seeking gender-affirming surgery, she endured extreme sexual violence and emotional and physical attacks while incarcerated for over ten years. In 2000 her complaints before the Canadian Human Rights Tribunal were finally heard. Her activism changed the circumstances of her life, but it took seventeen more years before transgender rights were added to the Canadian Human Rights Act. Prison systems remain one of the most threatening regimes with respect to freedom of gender identity and expression.

Bodily autonomy includes the right to have sex and feel love. Powerful LGBTQ+ activism over decades has driven Canada to largely remove sexuality as a criminal matter and to reverse exclusionary family law legislation. In 1969 homosexuality was removed from the Canadian Criminal Code. In 1996 sexual orientation was added to the list of protected grounds under the Canadian Human Rights Act. That same year, BC became the first province to legalize same-sex adoption (it took until 2011 for the last of the provinces and territories, Nunavut, to do the same). In 2005 same-sex marriage became legal across Canada, only the fourth country in the world to make the shift. Internationally, Canada is positioned as a leader in the protection of LGBTQ+ rights, and yet the changes that have been made took decades to be fully realized in practice. For example, conversion therapy, the discredited and harmful practice of psychological manipulation to try to manifest heterosexuality and cisnormativity, was only banned in 2021 (Canada, Department of Justice 2021).

How Canada deals with sex work is a glaring anomaly in a landscape of progressive law-making on bodily autonomy. If your body is yours, you should be the governor of what labour you engage in. The state should protect workers from violence and wage theft, and it should safeguard children and other vulnerable people from exploitation. But laws in Canada continue to inaccurately merge sex work with human trafficking and confuse exploitation with autonomy, thus criminalizing sex work. These laws place people at greater risk of surveillance, violence and harm. In the colonial project of Canada, this harm is unequally borne by Indigenous people, particularly Indigenous women, girls and Two-Spirit people. The fourth section of this chapter recounts how *Terri-Jean Bedford* and her colleagues, Valerie Scott and Amy Lebovitch, took the country to court for the right to do their jobs as sex workers. Despite their win under Section 7 of the Charter, the federal laws refashioned after their 2013 case continue to violate bodily autonomy and endanger women, trans people and nonbinary people.

Freedom from gendered violence and sexual assault, freedom to express your gender and freedom to work autonomously in the sex trade are foundational to self-sovereignty. So is safety from state violence. In the final section of this chapter, the 2020 story of *Santina Rao* and her public assault by Halifax police officers shows how gender stereotypes and racism intersect and the police — public servants — fail to protect the public. "Although the role of law enforcement in policing lines of race and class is generally recognized, until more recently their role in constructing and enforcing racialized borders of gender has been less visible," explains lawyer, organizer and author Andrea Ritchie (2017, 127). "Gender represents a central axis around which policing takes place." Reproductive freedom for everyone requires the most marginalized in our society to be safe — in this case, a young Black mother in a Walmart in a historically racist city must be safe to do her shopping without interference, and her children must be safe from the trauma of witnessing their mother being assaulted. Policing, in its function to protect property and control class, race and gender, is an irreconcilable threat to bodily autonomy.

In 1974 Marc Lalonde, then Canada's minister of health, published a landmark report, *A New Perspective on the Health of Canadians*, critiquing the health system's focus on treatment over prevention. The report was one of the first times a government acknowledged the importance of social determinants of health. Health professional schools teach about social determinants of health now, but far too little acknowledgement is made of how power regulates those determinants. Poverty, one of the most important determinants of health, sounds alterable but can only change if social structures shift to redistribute wealth (Health Canada 2020). Every year Canada spends $266 billion on health care services (Canadian Institute for Health Information 2021), $20 billion on prisons (Office of the Parliamentary Budget Officer 2013), and $15.7 billion on police (Conor et al. 2020). Only $177 billion is spent on social protection (Statistics Canada 2017), although it has been acknowledged for forty years that social and economic inequality is the most pressing need to address to improve the lives of people in this country. There is still so much work to do to remove the oppressive social structures limiting choices and, consequently, reproductive freedom.

Bodily autonomy is a vast concept, and just five critical cases out of thousands of possibilities are discussed here. Importantly, this autonomy is not a matter of individual will alone or of legal limitations. It is in the centre of complex social realities — privileges and oppressions — that cannot be ignored in fighting for reproductive justice.

Heidi Rathjen

Dr. Teresa Sourour's coroner report about the Montreal massacre opens with a definition of the concept of avoidable death (Quebec Coroner's Office 1991). This refers to the extent to which emergency medicine responsiveness could have reduced the mortality rate among those injured. There were significant problems with the emergency response to the massacre — but the massacre could have been avoided had the perpetrator not been allowed to buy the gun in the first place. Heidi Rathjen has dedicated her life to advocacy for gun control to prevent any recurrence of the deadly violence she survived on December 6, 1989.

At 5:10 p.m. in the evening, a twenty-five-year-old man in blue jeans entered room C-230, where an engineering class was in progress on the second floor of École Polytechnique de Montréal. He fired a shot at the ceiling, then ordered the girls on the left, the boys on the right. The students thought he must be joking, firing blanks. A very odd joke, but a joke. He repeated the order, and the students bungled it a bit, mixing themselves up, but he ordered them to sort it out, directing the women to the back left corner. He told the men to leave. He said the women were "une gang de féministes" [a bunch of feminists] and "J'haïs les féministes" [I hate feminists] (Paradis 2018, 1).

He said he was "fighting feminism" and fired thirty shots, killing six people. He moved throughout the building, firing, wounding, missing, reloading, moving again. He killed a woman through the glass of the door to room C-218. He then took the escalator to the first-floor cafeteria, where a hundred people were gathered. He killed one woman, and everyone else dispersed. He found two women in a storage cupboard and killed them. He continued his rampage, killing five more women on the third floor in room B-311. In total, twenty-eight people were shot. At about 5:28 p.m., he shot himself.

Calls to 9-1-1 began at 5:12 p.m., but there were delays in routing the calls to the police and emergency medical services. The first caller was asked for the exact address of Polytechnique, a well-known building on the University of Montreal campus. The coroner's report reads, "It must be noted that initially, Urgences-Santé [emergency medical services] did not regard the event as a disaster" (Quebec Coroner's Office 1991, 18). No disaster protocol was followed. Police arrived at 5:21 p.m. Ambulances started arriving at 5:24 p.m., one by one, each set of paramedics calling for reinforcement as they realized they were not enough. Police officers accumulated outside the building, erected a perimeter and instructed the emergency medical workers to stay put. At 5:35 p.m. police received information the killer was dead and finally entered the building. It was not until 5:45 p.m. that medical emergency services personnel had access to the interior. Once inside, they lacked equipment to communicate, guides to show them where to go, means to identify the victims and a clear process for triage. They were surprised to encounter both armed police and plain-clothes police in the halls. It took until 6:41 p.m. to get the injured out of the building and into ambulances. The last two of the dead were not found until 7:15 p.m.

The event would come to be called the Montreal massacre. Fourteen women died. Their names are Geneviève Bergeron (born 1968), Hélène Colgan (born 1966), Nathalie Croteau (born 1966), Barbara Daigneault (born 1967), Anne-Marie Edward (born 1968), Maud Haviernick (born 1960), Maryse Laganière (born 1964), Maryse Leclair (born 1966), Anne-Marie Lemay (born 1967), Sonia Pelletier (born 1961), Michèle Richard (born 1968), Annie St-Arneault (born 1966), Annie Turcotte (born 1969) and Barbara Klucznik-Widajewicz (born 1958). Laganière was a clerk in the school finance office and Klucznik-Widajewicz was a nursing student. The twelve other victims were studying engineering.

Heidi Rathjen was in her fourth year of studies. When she first heard the gunshots, she and several classmates hid, lights out, door shut, in the student lounge. They heard shot after shot and moans. One called 9-1-1. They stayed put for forty-five minutes, until they heard the boots and baritone voices of "the cavalry" (Rathjen and Montpetit 1999, 2). Finally, help had arrived. Only after she was evacuated from the building did she understand the massive extent of the violence and that only women had been targeted, including two women she knew well, Lemay and Daigneault. Within days, Rathjen and a large group of Polytechnique students and staff launched into action, beginning with a petition for new laws prohibiting Canadians from owning assault weapons.

The shooter had legally purchased his firearm, a high-powered semiautomatic Sturm Ruger Mini-14 .223 calibre, two weeks prior. Analysis of mass shooters has found most use semiautomatic weapons in their attacks. They are nearly always men between the ages of seventeen and forty-nine. They nearly always act alone, and most kill themselves (or are killed by police). Most are in a type of crisis in the period before the massacre, such as job loss, marriage breakdown or escalation of domestic violence (Peterson and Densley 2021).

The campaign No Notoriety (n.d.) recommends against sharing details about shooters, because one common factor among mass killings is that the perpetrator studies the actions of others and plans fastidiously. The Montreal shooter visited the Polytechnique campus several times in the fall of 1989 to acquaint himself with the layout. Without affording him excessive attention, it is worth noting a few facts. He had three notes on his person, characterizing his actions as a drawn-out suicide mission driven by antifeminist hate. His father abused him and his mother when he was a child, and after his parents' separation his father ceased contact with him (CTV News 2006). His applications to Polytechnique and the Canadian Armed Forces had been rejected.

The petition from Rathjen and colleagues received widespread media attention. She brought it forward to the Congress of Canadian Engineering Students, who endorsed it after they heard her speak about what she went through. Soon Rathjen was working more on amassing signatures for the petition than on anything else, including her studies. "I had no regrets. I would have taken charge of the petition project no matter what," she later said (Rathjen and Montpetit 1999, 3). The petition generated 560,000 signatures. Then an encouraging letter from Dr. Wendy Cukier, a professor at the Ryerson

Polytechnical School, sent Rathjen in a new direction. The two joined forces to create the Coalition for Gun Control. Rathjen worked for about six months as an engineer before moving full-time into a role as the Coalition's executive director.

In 1991, stemming in large part from the coalition's efforts, the Conservative federal government enacted Bill C-17, which made changes to the Firearms Acquisition Certificate system (RCMP n.d.). Since 1977 the system had required Canadians to apply for a certificate for gun ownership; however, there were few restrictions to certification. Handguns have been restricted since 1934 and universally required registration. Bill C-17 added a requirement that applicants provide photo identification and two references, participate in safety training, wait at least twenty-eight days to receive the certificate and be subjected to increased background checks.

Firearms are not just a feminist issue because one was used in an antifeminist massacre. Firearms place women, trans people and nonbinary people at risk in many ways (Canadian Women's Foundation 2018). Firearms are used to threaten and control. Every year in Canada approximately 100,000 women and their children seek shelter from abuse, and much of the abuse involves firearms (Coalition for Gun Control 2018). Women comprise 80 percent of those killed by their intimate partners in Canada, and having a firearm in the house increases the risk of homicide and homicide-suicides. Gun control laws like the long-standing handgun registry make a difference, as is evident in the stark difference between gun violence in the US and Canada generally. Bill C-17 had an impact: Researchers found the 1991 legislation was associated with a decrease in the rates of homicides and suicides involving guns (Bridges 2004). From 1996 to 2006, spousal homicides involving a firearm fell by 50 percent (Canadian Centre for Justice Statistics 2008).

However, Bill C-17 was not nearly enough. The Coalition for Gun Control wanted assault weapons banned. In 1993, a majority Liberal federal government was elected, and Rathjen and Cukier arranged to meet with the new minister of justice, Allan Rock, to present their proposal for phased implementation of gun registration. In the book *December 6: From the Montreal Massacre to Gun Control* (Rathjen and Montpetit 1999), Rathjen describes Rock as insisting they needed to provide more evidence. Both she and Cukier felt despair. They endured ruthless harassment, including abusive phone calls and threats in the mail, and worried it was all for nothing. But most of the Canadian public supported them, despite the media attention the opposition attracted. Four weeks after their meeting, Minister Rock announced plans for more gun control. Bill C-68 passed in December 1995, although it took many years to come into force. The bill included harsher penalties under the Criminal Code for firearms offences, the creation of the Firearms Act and a new firearms licensing system to replace the Firearms Acquisition Certificate System. Perpetrators of domestic violence could lose their gun licences, and licensees would be subject to a renewal process every five years. The legislation was not a panacea, partly because it took thirteen years to bring its aims to fruition (McPhedran and Mauser 2013). The bill was introduced in 1993, but an amnesty period stretched until 2006, when registration of all guns finally became required to be compliant with Bill C-68.

There are a lot of guns in Canada. In 2007, there were 1.8 million valid firearm licences and 7.2 million registered firearms, of which 91 percent were nonrestricted long guns (Gonzales and Mandelman 2009). Basically, there is one registered gun for every four people in Canada. Gun owners are a powerful lobby, and from its inception the gun registry faced political opposition. It was criticized as overly expensive, overly invasive and subject to corrupt lobbying. The Conservative government of Stephen Harper, elected in 2006, pushed hard for its dissolution.

In 2009 the twentieth anniversary memorial for the Montreal massacre victims was overshadowed by rhetoric against the gun registry. Rathjen was quoted as saying the Conservative effort to tear down the registry was a "slap in the face of the victims of Polytechnique, as well as all the other victims of firearms" (Delacourt 2009, 1). In 2012 the Conservatives' Bill C-19 passed, removing long guns (nonrestricted firearms) from the registration requirement and allowing for the destruction of all the data related to long gun ownership already entered.

There were several attempts to overturn Bill C-19. The Quebec government filed for an injunction, ultimately unsuccessfully, to preserve the data. In 2014 the Barbra Schlifer Clinic in Toronto, dedicated to addressing legal issues involving violence against women, appealed to the Ontario Superior Court to halt the removal of the requirement to register long guns. The clinic's counsel argued that Bill C-19 failed to protect women's life, liberty and security of the person, Section 7 rights in the Charter of Rights and Freedoms, and to prevent sex and gender discrimination under Section 15, the equality provision (Barbra Schlifer Commemorative Clinic v. Canada 2014). The presiding judge disagreed.

Despite the hurdles they encountered, Rathjen and Cukier led a necessary conversation about gun violence in Canada after what was then the worst shooting massacre in Canada's history. Gun violence is male violence. Women hold only 12 percent of gun licences in Canada and own only 4 percent of the restricted firearms still requiring registration (Gilmore 2019). The guns used in domestic violence against women are largely long guns (Burke 2020b), and the use of guns in domestic violence is more common in rural areas, where guns are used for hunting (Gonzales and Mandelman 2009). Guns are a common weapon in domestic violence femicides, and women are two times more likely than men to be "sexually assaulted, beaten, choked or threatened with a gun or a knife" (Statistics Canada 2018, 1). A woman or girl is killed by a man every other day in Canada, and once per week a man kills a woman in a domestic violence homicide (Canadian Femicide Observatory for Justice and Accountability 2021).

In 2020, in the early months of the COVID-19 pandemic, Canada experienced a far deadlier massacre than the one in Montreal. Over the April 18–19 weekend, a fifty-one-year-old denturist tore through rural Nova Scotia, shooting and burning buildings, killing twenty-two people, including twelve women, one of whom was pregnant, and a teenage girl. The rampage happened after his domestic partner, Lisa Banfield, who had long endured his abuse, escaped from a particularly brutal attack. As with the Montreal massacre, the emergency response was characterized by delay, miscommunication and poor conceptualization of the scale of the disaster — another failure to prevent avoidable death. A Mass Casualty Commission was created for an independent public inquiry into the Nova Scotia killings, with findings set to be released in late 2022.

The Canadian Femicide Observatory for Justice and Accountability counts instances of femicide in Canada. Its findings for 2020 show that 160 women and girls were killed by violence. Thirteen of those were from the Nova Scotia massacre. One in five were Indigenous. Of note is that women are more likely to be killed in nonurban settings and to be killed by a firearm there, to be killed by an intimate partner or a family member, to be "collateral" victims and to be killed through excessive violence (Canadian Femicide Observatory for Justice and Accountability 2021). Femicide in Canada is a product of enduring misogyny intersecting with colonialism, racism and other types of oppression. Violence against trans and nonbinary people is poorly tracked and there is no corresponding data.

In spring 2021 the federal Liberal party of Justin Trudeau proposed yet another iteration of gun control legislation, tabled as Bill C-21. The bill includes a buy-back program for assault weapons like the one used at Polytechnique. It would allow municipalities to ban handguns. For survivors, the bill is a far cry from what they need and could be easily reversed by future governments (Bronskill 2021). In August 2021 a federal election was called, halting the bill's progress into law.

The work Rathjen started in response to the Montreal massacre is a shared responsibility for all Canadians and necessary to honour the victims and prevent future gun deaths, and it continues. Reproductive justice starts with the right to live in safety.

Justice Claire L'Heureux-Dubé

Freedom from sexual violence is a fundamental reproductive right. You cannot be healthy, mentally and physically, if your body is at risk of or experiencing sexual violence. The 1999 Supreme Court of Canada decision in *Regina v. Ewanchuk* was foundational to the legal protection of freedom from sexual violence in Canada. The complainant was a formidable but unnamed seventeen-year-old woman. The response of Supreme Court Justice Claire L'Heureux-Dubé to the case catapulted it into the canon of reproductive rights history. L'Heureux-Dubé was renowned as a champion of battered women in family law, the first woman jurist on the Quebec Superior Court and only the second woman called to serve on the Supreme Court of Canada. She clearly condemned misogynistic tropes in the prior decision of the appellate court regarding the case and wanted to go one step further than the official written decision by her colleague, Justice John C. Major. This section focuses on her archetypal response in *R v. Ewanchuk* and the meaning of the final verdict as it relates to reproductive justice.

First, the story behind the case. In 1994 a seventeen-year-old woman arrived at forty-four-year-old Steve Ewanchuk's workplace in Edmonton for a job interview, which he conducted in a van. Ewanchuk had come across the young woman the day prior, walking through the mall, and he had proposed to her at the time that she work for him selling his woodworking (Barretto 2009). After a brief interview, Ewanchuk invited the young woman into his trailer to "see some of his work" (R v. Ewanchuk 1999, 340). Once inside, he shut the door behind them, and she believed he had locked it. His inappropriate touching began immediately. He hugged her and asked for a massage. Feeling scared and trapped, she complied (Backhouse 2017). Ewanchuk then proceeded to intensify the assault, which the young woman objected to repeatedly. Every time she objected, he would stop briefly, then he "increased the level of sexual activity" (R v. Ewanchuk 1999, 370). Only when he was rubbing his bare genitals against the young woman did he finally heed her objections, and she was able to leave. Ewanchuk hugged her again and gave her $100 "for the massage" (R v. Ewanchuk 1999, 342).

When the young woman reported the assault to police, they were unsurprised, as Ewanchuk already held four convictions for sexual assault (Backhouse 2017). Under Canadian law, sexual assault includes all unwanted sexual touching, not just penetrative acts. At trial the judge acknowledged the young woman had clearly not consented, but acquitted Ewanchuk anyway on the defence of his mistaken belief in consent. The case then went to the Alberta Court of Appeal, which upheld the acquittal in a 2–1 decision. Justice Catherine Fraser dissented, arguing the acquittal relied on a misinterpretation of consent. To her, the young woman's periodic silence and failure to express her fear verbally could not be mistakenly understood as communicating consent. Consent must, after all, be continuous and freely given, not selectively pulled from the moments when the young woman was not objecting, in a room she believed she could not escape from. The majority opinion, however, found merit in the defence of mistaken belief; in his decision, Justice John McClung notoriously wrote the case was less a criminal matter than a "hormonal" one (R v. Ewanchuk 1999, 374). He said the young woman should not have worn shorts to the interview and "did not present herself to Ewanchuk or enter his trailer in a bonnet and crinolines" (R v. Ewanchuk 1999, 372). He emphasized the young woman already had a baby and lived with her boyfriend, further implying she was not innocent in matters of sex.

When the case made its way to the Supreme Court of Canada, L'Heureux-Dubé tore into the stereotypes and myths McClung had relied upon. Accepting the defence of implied consent ignores the repeated times the young woman said no; it "denies women's sexual autonomy and implies that women are in a state of constant consent to sexual activity," wrote L'Heureux-Dubé (R v. Ewanchuk 1999, 336). She ridiculed McClung's need to mention the young woman's baby and boyfriend, as if he wanted it on court record that she was "not a virgin" (R v. Ewanchuk 1999, 372) — as if her sexual history would make any difference in her lack of consent during the altercation with Ewanchuk. She cited the Declaration on the Elimination of Violence against Women (United Nations General Assembly 1993), which Canada signed in 1993 and which condemns gender discrimination, including the very same discriminatory beliefs used in the Alberta Court of Appeal decision.

Ewanchuk's behaviour was acceptable to McClung in much the same way that sexual violence is often dismissed as "boys will be boys." A forty-four-year-old man could not be held responsible for controlling his impulses, yet a seventeen-year-old woman was expected to claw her way out of a locked trailer if she were to be believed about refusing his advances. L'Heureux-Dubé found "stereotypical assumptions lay at the heart of this case," wrote Justice Beverly McLachlin in agreement, and "these stereotypical assumptions no longer have a place in Canadian law" (R v. Ewanchuk 1999, 336).

In February 1999 the Supreme Court threw out the acquittals of the two lower courts and convicted Ewanchuk of sexual assault. L'Heureux-Dubé's scathing criticism of McClung's old-fashioned, sexist values wrought a deluge of critique. Newspaper editorials decried her response as a disgraceful, political, feminist manifesto, inappropriate for her position on the bench. A conservative women's organization sent a complaint about her to the Canadian Judicial Council (Backhouse 2017). McClung issued a public statement in the *National Post*, accusing her of nurturing a personal vendetta against him and, absurdly, indicting her for the growing number of suicides among men in Quebec. Unbeknownst to McClung, L'Heureux-Dubé's husband had died by suicide two decades prior. His letter was widely denounced, and a week later he issued a public apology in the same newspaper (McClung 1999). As feminist theorist Sara Ahmed (2014) has written about extensively, when you expose a problem, you become the problem. What L'Heureux-Dubé exposed was how heavily McClung's reasoning rested on misogynistic myths. Instead of renouncing his bias, he slandered her.

Despite the immediate vilification she endured, L'Heureux-Dubé's decision came to be praised internationally. *R v. Ewanchuk* and L'Heureux-Dubé's meticulous critique of

McClung's reasoning went on to form the basis of many legal education programs, including that of LEAF, the Canadian organization for feminist litigation, law reform and public education. LEAF was an intervenor in *R. v. Ewanchuk* and, as this book describes, many other critical cases pertaining to gender equality. L'Heureux-Dubé stepped down from the Supreme Court in 2002 (Makin 2002).

In 1999, the year of the *Ewanchuk* decision, the rate of self-reported sexual assault in Canada was 21 per 1,000 people per year, not terribly different from the rate fifteen years later of 22 per 1,000 people (Statistics Canada 2019a). Women are seven and a half times more likely than men to report sexual assault, and 82 percent of sexual assault victims are, like the young person in *R. v. Ewanchuk*, under eighteen years of age (Canadian Women's Foundation n.d.). Most of the time, the perpetrator is known to the victim, not a stranger who attacks suddenly. Unlike in *R. v. Ewanchuk*, most sexual assaults are not reported: it is estimated only 5 percent are reported to police. From there proceeds a rule of halves: in just over half of cases an accused is identified; half of those identified are charged; half of those charged are prosecuted; half of those prosecuted are convicted; and half of those convicted receive a custodial sentence (Rotenberg 2017). Police and court systems antagonize victims, discouraging reports and prosecutions, and pervasive gender stereotypes result in acquittal after acquittal (Craig 2018). With outcomes like this, it is important that people who experience sexual assault know, at the core, they are right to feel wronged — their bodily autonomy was violated. A very unambiguous case like Ewanchuk, where the victim clearly and repeatedly said no, should not have prompted a protracted debate about consent.

But misunderstandings about consent and judicial reliance on misogynistic stereotypes continue. In 2014, in another sexual assault case in Alberta, Justice Robin Camp asked the complainant why she "couldn't just keep [her] knees together" (*Toronto Star* 2015, 1) and why had not she screamed if she was frightened (Craig and Woolley 2015). He concluded that "young women want to have sex" (Willingham and Hassam 2016, 1) and acquitted the accused, Alexander Wagar. He warned the complainant she ought to tell her male friends "to protect themselves, they have to be careful" (Willingham and Hassam 2016, 1).

Camp's archaic and insulting comments to the complainant were met with criticism and ridicule internationally. Complaints were made against him, and the Canadian Judicial Council called an inquiry to determine his suitability to remain on the bench. At the hearings he said he had spent his formative years in South Africa and was unversed in Canadian criminal law, including the meaning of consent. He even referred to the complainant as "the accused" (Fine 2016, 1). She told the council his statements had caused her to feel suicidal. The five members of the inquiry committee voted unanimously to remove Camp from his position.

The Camp inquiry overlapped with the case against Jian Ghomeshi, one of the highest profile and most controversial sex assault trials in Canada's history. Following months of intensifying allegations with varying levels of verifiability, the CBC fired the radio host in fall 2014. Ghomeshi turned himself in to police and was arrested on four charges of sexual assault and one charge of physical assault for choking. For the next year, the case against him dominated the news, including the damning findings of an external investigation led by lawyer Janice Rubin. After conducting ninety-nine interviews with CBC employees, she found ample evidence of inappropriate and sexual misconduct and said that CBC management condoned Ghomeshi's behaviour (Houpt 2015).

The criminal trial did not begin until winter of 2016. Ghomeshi's lawyer, Marie Heinen, intensely questioned the credibility of the complainants, including well-known actors Lucy DeCoutere and Sarah Dunsworth. Because the witnesses had exchanged texts, Heinen accused them of colluding. Sexual assault is a deep blow to self-esteem, and it is sensible and likely that two people who experienced the same thing would communicate to support each other. DeCoutere had written intimate notes to Ghomeshi after the alleged assaults, so Heinen accused her of lying about the acts being nonconsensual. But it is a common pattern for survivors to offer assailants love and kindness after the violence in an effort to ignore the trauma they have experienced and avoid becoming a victim (Chapin 2016). When Justice William Horkins delivered his verdict, he found Ghomeshi not guilty on all charges. Advocates across the country erupted in rage and mourning. In October 2017 celebrity allegations against movie producer Harvey Weinstein flung the world into a massive and ongoing conversation about sexual assault, but Canadians had already spent recent years in public reckoning over the Camp and Ghomeshi cases.

Despite the promise of *R. v. Ewanchuk*, sexual assault is common and commonly tolerated. The criminal justice system fails to bring resolution and healing to those who are harmed. Lamentation of its failings can lead one to lose sight of how the court case comes after an assault has already happened. The person who was assaulted already feels the physical and emotional pain of the violation, and the reporting process intensifies the scrutiny of and potential harm to survivors. It is retraumatizing to call the police, to face an interrogation, to be a complainant in court, to endure cross-examination. Because the reporting process is so intimidating and violating, most survivors simply do not report. Of those who do, many are doubly defeated by their aggressor's acquittal, showing more clearly why it's important to prevent harm in the first place. The court does not prevent harm. Ewanchuk's four prior sexual assault convictions did not protect the young woman in 1994. Evidence shows incarceration does not reduce risks, as prison itself is a site for extreme sexual violence (Just Detention International n.d.).

Reproductive health and justice require prevention of sexual assault, so it does not occur in the first place. This will not happen by excusing hormonal impulses like Ewanchuk's or ignorance like Camp's but by amplifying understanding of body sovereignty. This must begin early. Instead of pressuring little children to accept unwanted hugs from family members, which grooms them to feel powerlessness when they are inappropriately touched, salute their boundaries. Instead of enacting dress codes in schools, which inevitably police girls' clothing and lay blame for boys' distractions on the exposed skin of girls, encourage kids to wear whatever they feel comfortable in. If someone shows up in a shirt with hateful messaging (Currie 2021), talk about how words can hurt and the difference between promoting discrimination and supporting freedom of expression. Use real words to talk about sexual body parts and sexual activities, so people are specific about what they consent to and what they do not. Create environments where consent is possible by addressing social inequalities jeopardizing safety. Talk about what sexual assault is, expose it and condemn it. Recognize that the trauma of sexual assault affects survivors' memories and responses. Listen to and believe survivors.

28

Synthia Kavanagh

Self-sovereignty includes freedom of gender expression. Born in 1962 in BC, Synthia Kavanagh knew as a young child that she was a girl. Her childhood was a difficult one, dominated by institutionalization. She was placed under the care of the Children's Aid Society in elementary school, and from ages eleven to sixteen she was held in a juvenile detention centre. As a young teenager, she began hormone therapy after receiving a diagnosis of gender identity disorder, which was then required to access treatment. She changed her name legally at age 19 to Synthia.

Like many trans youth, Kavanagh experienced early criminalization. US data shows that trans youth represent 13 to 15 percent of criminalized youth, and most of these are racialized individuals (Hunt and Moodie-Mills 2012). While Statistics Canada only began asking about gender identity on the census in 2021, the department estimates 0.35 percent of people in Canada identify as transgender or nonbinary (Statistics Canada 2020). Trans and nonbinary people are indisputably at greater likelihood of experiencing criminalization than cisgender people. This may be because they face disproportionate vulnerability to family abandonment and homelessness, are misunderstood, are punished and excluded from school, face barriers to employment, experience high rates of poverty, and are more likely to engage in sex work and to develop substance use disorders. The 2019 Trans PULSE Survey of three thousand Canadians identifying with a gender other than the one assigned to them at birth found 31 percent had thoughts of suicide in the past year, and only 16 percent characterized their mental health as excellent or very good (Bauer, Scheim, and Churchill 2020).

At age twenty-two Kavanagh was charged with killing another trans woman named Lisa Black. They had lived together as roommates, and both worked in the sex trade. In 1989 Kavanagh was convicted of second-degree murder and sentenced to life imprisonment with no chance of parole for fifteen years. Although she had previously sought approval for gender-affirming surgery (at the time referred to as sex-reassignment surgery), she had not yet received the surgery at the time of sentencing and Correctional Services Canada (CSC) refused to allow her to be placed in an institution designated for women.

The social construction of gender as a binary enforces the division of prisons into "for men" and "for women," but the construction of prisons as "for men" or "for women" also reciprocally enforces the construct of a gender binary in greater society (Pemberton 2013). This may sound like an overstatement, but prisons play a major role in society. Federal prisons are an expensive public service, costing upwards of $110,000 per prisoner per year (Office of the Parliamentary Budget Officer 2018, 4) and employing over seventeen thousand people, with the provincial and territorial systems employing many more. How prisons define and regulate gender matters, and Kavanagh's fight against gender regulation and control is a critical moment in Canada's reproductive justice history.

From 1990 to 1993, when Kavanagh first filed a complaint with the Canadian Human Rights Tribunal, CSC denied her access to the hormonal therapy she had been taking continually for over a decade. For many years she was forbidden from wearing "feminine" clothes and was disciplined for possessing lipstick, which was considered contraband. She was also barred from proceeding with gender-affirming surgery. This severely impacted Kavanagh's emotional and physical health. She endured strip searches from male guards, sexual harassment and observation while urinating (Findlay 1999). She was also beaten and raped (Kavanagh v. Canada 2001). She believed had she not participated in these forced sexual acts, she would not have survived Millhaven Institution, a federal prison in Ontario. To "keep people safe," prisoners who are targets for physical and sexual violence are often placed in "protective custody" — effectively solitary confinement — which Kavanagh endured for extensive periods (Vancouver Prison Justice Day Committee 2007).

Kavanagh resisted. She went on hunger strikes and "acted out" in protest of her treatment. She engaged in self-harm, attempted genital self-mutilation and attempted suicide. Even without imprisonment, trans people generally experience high rates of mental illness and suicide stemming from harassment, violence and the failure of those around them to affirm their gender (Centre for Suicide Prevention n.d.). As Égale Canada (2020) explains,

> It is vital to understand that these sobering statistics are a direct result of inadequate access to affirming care and that these issues stem from LGBTQI2S people's experiences of ongoing systemic oppression, erasure, and exclusion. LGBTQI2S communities have led a long battle against medicalization and pathologisation —where the medical system and categorization of sexual difference or gender diversity have caused an immense amount of harm.

Prisons compound the risks and are known to be sites of elevated rates of self-harm. The rate of suicide in federal prison in Canada is seven times higher than the rate in the general population (Kouyoumdjian et al. 2016). Incarcerating trans people subjects them to layers of risk of self-harm and suicide.

Health care, including hormone therapy, supportive mental health counselling and surgical care, is an important part of supporting gender expression for trans people. Health care providers have the power to define the need for and determine access to gender-affirming care, thus acting as gatekeepers (Ashley 2020a). But beyond this problematic power, people in prisons face barriers to health care, period. They cannot use the internet and phone access is restricted and expensive, blocking their access to health information. Health care is the most common issue in complaints about conditions of confinement made by prisoners to the Office of the Correctional Investigator. Health care staff are employed by the same body that employs correctional officers, compromising the duty of care, and health care concerns can easily be deprioritized in the name of security.

After ten years of incarceration in eleven facilities for men — including the Don Jail and the Millhaven maximum-security federal institution in Ontario, and the Mission medium-security federal institution, Kent maximum-security federal institution and Mountain medium-security federal institution in BC — Kavanagh's complaints reached the Canadian Human Rights Tribunal. Kavanagh argued she was discriminated against in three ways: (1) she was forced to be incarcerated in a prison designated for men because she had yet to undergo gender-affirming surgery; (2) she was denied access to her hormonal treatment, an issue that was resolved by the time her case was heard; and (3) she was denied access to gender-affirming surgery. Gender-affirming surgeries can include "vaginoplasty, phalloplasty, metaidioplasty, chest reconstruction, breast augmentation, hysterectomy, penectomy, orchiectomy, vaginectomy, salpingo-oopherectomy and electrolysis" (Égale Canada n.d.). They are also called top surgery and bottom surgery, genital reconfiguration surgery and transitional surgery, or they can be referred to by the specific surgical procedure (Ashley 2020b).

Although the federal Canada Health Act sets out the principles of hospital-based and physician-provided health care across the country — requiring it be universal, comprehensive, publicly administered, accessible and portable — health care delivery is a provincial responsibility. Pharmaceutical treatment, outside of what is provided in hospital, is not included in the Canada Health Act, and therefore medications are paid for privately or covered through personal insurance plans. Health care for people in federal custody is funded by the Canadian government. At the time of Kavanagh's incarceration, gender-affirming surgery was not considered a medically necessary procedure for which CSC would pay, and it was not an allowable elective procedure that she could pursue at private expense.

Prior to Kavanagh's activism, the federal corrections policy was to "freeze" a transgender person's transition (Findlay 1999, 20). At the time, the CSC commissioner's directive from governing health care stipulated that prisoners with gender identity disorder could continue taking hormones if they had already been taking them before incarceration, but gender-affirming surgery was completely unavailable even if a person were able and willing to pay on their own (Findlay 1999). The Clarke Institute's Gender Identity Clinic in Toronto, now a part of the Centre for Addiction and Mental Health, supported the "freeze" policy. It required that patients pass a two-year "real life test" to qualify for surgery, and as prison was not "real life," prisoners were considered ineligible. Trans health writer Justin Cascio (2003) describes the language of the "real life test" as originating from a 1974 set of guidelines published by a trans man named Reed Erickson, likely under the guidance of his physician James Lorio, and not based on any scientific research. Effectively, the test requires trans patients to demonstrate dysphoria so acute it harms their mental health while also showing they have the stability to live for a period without accessing physical health care. Passing this convoluted test would supposedly provide evidence of readiness for medical transition.

"Unless sex reassignment surgery has been completed, male inmates shall be held in male institutions," specified CSC's directive (Kavanagh v. Canada 2001, n.p.). Legal scholar Barbara Findlay (1999, 20) described the catch-22 that trans prisoners faced: "The result for almost every trans [person] is that s/he must spend her entire prison term in a facility designed for people of the gender that s/he is not." CSC argued the housing policy was to protect women. But it is obvious that Kavanagh, a woman, experienced untold violence and sexual assault as a result of the policy.

In the tribunal hearing, there was no debate that Kavanagh's incarceration in prisons designated for men violated Section 15 Charter protections against discrimination based on sex and disability. What was up for debate was whether it was justifiable given the carceral context. The judges recognized that transgender identity is at odds with the gender binary of prison operations at a systemic level but found CSC's rationale for housing Kavanagh in facilities for men did not pass muster. They ruled that CSC had to develop policy to attend to the vulnerability of trans prisoners and that each case be individually assessed to determine the most suitable housing placement. They concluded CSC's blanket policy against gender-affirming surgery was plainly discriminatory.

Kavanagh's case was successful. She received surgery in 2000 and was transferred to Joliette Institution for Women in Quebec in 2001. A line was added to CSC policy suggesting prisons conduct individual assessments for trans prisoners and consider their vulnerability when making housing decisions. However, placement of trans prisoners remained subject to a CSC (2017, 1) policy that "pre-operative male to female offenders with gender dysphoria will be held in men's institutions and pre-operative female to male offenders with gender dysphoria will be held in women's institutions."

In 2017 the Liberal federal government passed Bill C-16, An Act to Amend the Canadian Human Rights Act and the Criminal Code. Bill C-16 added gender expression and gender identity to the Canadian Human Rights Act as prohibited grounds for discrimination and to the Criminal Code in Section 318, which prohibits promotion of genocide of identifiable groups. As a result of Bill C-16, CSC adopted a policy to place prisoners in institutions according to their gender identity, not their anatomy. Fallon Aubee was the first trans woman to be placed in an institution designated for women in accordance with the new policy. She said, "Despite all the stigma, the discrimination, the harassment, the abuse, the sexual abuse, I believe it was a worthwhile journey because I can stand tall and proud today and say, I'm a woman and I'm going to be recognized as a woman and I'm going to live in a woman's prison" (Harris 2017, 1). In a space that routinely violates the basic bodily autonomy of everyone, Aubee eked out the right to at least be acknowledged for who she was.

The range of gender-affirming surgeries and related medical procedures that are publicly covered varies by province and territory. The plan recently unveiled in the Yukon has been described as the most comprehensive and a gold standard for the country (Taylor 2021). In the late 1990s, all but two provinces, Ontario and PEI, covered what was then called sex-reassignment surgery. Ontario covered the cost for nearly twenty years until 1998, when the Conservative government of Premier Mike Harris delisted it without consulting experts in the field. Musician Michelle Josef initiated a Charter challenge against the province in 1999 because the surgery would have cost her $22,000 (Josef v. Ontario Minister of Health 2013). Delay after delay in her case ensued, and even after a change in government to the Liberals, the province fought back. Then, just as Josef's case was about to be heard by the Ontario Superior Court, the government reinstated coverage for the surgery. Josef was awarded $200,000 for her extensive legal costs.

Kavanagh's and Josef's cases advanced important legal protections; however, trans and nonbinary people continue to face sexual and physical violence, discrimination and exclusion. They are overpoliced and overcriminalized, underserved by health systems and erased in data collection related to reproductive health. Inclusion and support for trans and nonbinary people are priorities for reproductive justice action. People fighting for sexual and reproductive rights, including the rights of trans and nonbinary people, must consider how prison abolition fits into this work.

Prisons are violent and unhealthy for everyone, and especially dangerous to the safety and autonomy of trans and nonbinary people. Although a person's placement in a facility corresponding with their gender is affirming, imprisonment is linked with a host of health problems and reduced life expectancy (Kouyoumdjian et al. 2016). In March 2021, reportedly while out on parole, Synthia Kavanagh died (Serving Life 25: One Guard's Story 2021). The period after prison release is one of elevated vulnerability, particularly to overdose. Bodily autonomy requires safety from the cycle of subjugation found in the revolving door of the prison system. I discuss the intersections between reproductive justice and prison abolition in greater detail in Chapter 5.

34

Terri-Jean Bedford

Sex work is one area where a successful constitutional challenge arguably made things worse for rights to bodily autonomy. In 2007 Terri-Jean Bedford, Valerie Scott and Amy Lebovitch filed a lawsuit against the federal government, then led by Conservative prime minister Stephen Harper, arguing three sections of the Criminal Code violated their Section 7 right to security of the person as sex workers. Sex work itself was legal, but the Criminal Code made it difficult to safely engage in legal work and put relationships and housing at risk.

First, the "communicating law" prohibited communication about sex work. Instead of being able to take the time to screen clients and negotiate rates and terms, outdoor workers were forced to get into clients' cars immediately. This law effectively drove sex workers into unlit, unpopulated areas to protect themselves from interference from police or prohibitionist groups.

The second law, the "bawdy house law," stipulated that it was illegal to be in or keep a space for the purpose of sex work. The law effectively kept sex workers from reporting assaults that happened at home or in shared dwellings. A conviction for keeping a bawdy house could lead to seizure of a person's assets, and future discrimination could bar a person from ever being able to rent or own a place to live.

The third law, the "living on the avails law," prohibited anyone from making a living from sex work, or even being with someone who did. Sex workers' spouses or children could be in trouble. The law also made it difficult for sex workers to hire support such as security guards and administrative staff.

Bedford, professionally named Madame De Sade in her work as a dominatrix, had worked in the sex trade for over a decade before the lawsuit. She owned a bawdy house nicknamed the Bondage Bungalow just outside of Toronto. She found the laws made work indoors much safer than outdoors. She knew the challenges of keeping herself safe: as a child she was placed in foster care and experienced routine abuse, and during her career she had frequent experiences of assault. She was also fined and imprisoned for violations of the bawdy house law. In 2007 she enlisted the support of two colleagues, Scott and Lebovitch, and lawyer Alan Young in a fight to strike down the three laws placing her at risk.

Bedford and her colleagues brought an intersectional analysis to their approach. Not only were most sex workers women, trans people and nonbinary people, but they were also disproportionately young and Indigenous, racialized or newcomers to Canada. They faced layers of marginalization, and seeking state help when they were in danger was next to unthinkable. The police did not offer protection.

Bedford, Scott and Lebovitch's first fight took three years. During the trial in 2009, their defence team brought forward twenty-one expert witnesses with lived experience and academic backgrounds to testify to the danger the three laws presented. Justice Susan Himel reviewed twenty-five thousand pages of evidence (Abdul 2014).

In September 2010 she issued a decision in full agreement with Bedford and her colleagues: All three laws infringed on their rights and were overbroad, arbitrary and grossly disproportionate. They produced the opposite result of what was intended and increased the risk of sex workers experiencing violence and harm.

Without even taking a breath, the federal government appealed Himel's ruling. Singularly funny and righteous, Bedford was forthright with her exasperation: "The laws [Harper] seeks to preserve are impermissibly vague in giving us answers. That means unelected officials for arbitrary reasons will decide when people's private consenting behaviour is not legal" (Bedford, Lebovitch and Scott 2015, n.p.). The Ontario Court of Appeal upheld most of Himel's decisions, finding however that the communication law was constitutional in its purpose to prevent street solicitation. Scott said the Court of Appeal's decision made her feel like she was finally "a person" (Bedford, Lebovitch and Scott 2015, n.p).

Upon final appeal, the Supreme Court of Canada ruled on December 20, 2013, in a 9–0 decision, that all three laws were inconsistent with the Charter. The court recognized that "the regulation of prostitution is a complex and delicate matter. It will be for Parliament, should it choose to do so, to devise a new approach, reflecting different elements of the existing regime" (Canada v. Bedford 2013, 1107). Rather than declare the three laws immediately invalid, the court gave Parliament one year to deal with the situation. Failure to respond would result in the complete decriminalization of sex work.

This is where things went sideways.

The Conservative government put forward Bill C-36, Protection of Communities and Exploited Persons Act (Canada, Department of Justice 2017b). In effect as of December 2014, the new law criminalized the purchase of services, if not the provision. Section 286.1 of the Criminal Code now reads, "It is an offence to obtain for consideration, or communicate with anyone for the purpose of obtaining for consideration, the sexual services of a person." The bill also criminalized the advertisement of sex work, "receiving material benefits from the purchase of sex" (Section 286.4) and "procuring a person for the provision of sexual services" (Section 286.2). These provisions, which sound like they are protecting sex workers from exploitation, replicate the so-called Nordic model, which aims to decrease demand for sex work by criminalizing the purchase of sex. But as Scott said, "Being forcibly rescued is the same as being kidnapped" (Bedford, Lebovitch and Scott 2015, n.p). In other words, this attempt to protect sex workers denies them autonomy over their work and is effectively coercive.

Bill C-36 acknowledged the evidence put forward in the Bedford case, referring to the physical danger of sex work and how it is largely women and girls, and disproportionately Indigenous women and girls, who sell sex. But in order to catch the buyers, sex workers are put under increasing surveillance, which inevitably drives sex work into hiding, with all the risks associated with being in the shadows. Then there are the economic consequences. Reducing demand reduces the pool of clients, so workers have less income and are forced to be less selective about which clients they take on. Further, sex workers can be charged for the offences supposedly designed to target the people who are presumed to be exploiting them (Ham 2011). For example, one sex worker could be charged for helping another find clients or for renting an apartment specifically for sex work. Finally, criminalization makes the industry even harder to track, muddying the evidence about the impact of the law on it and the harm experienced within it. There was already shockingly little research about sex workers, their clients, their experiences and long-term outcomes before Bill C-36 (Canada, Department of Justice 2015) and almost no accounting for trans and nonbinary sex workers in Canadian statistics.

Instead of prohibition, Bedford, Scott and Lebovitch urge complete decriminalization of sex work. In 2003 the New Zealand Prostitution Reform Act resulted in just that. In New Zealand, sex work is legal, communicating about it is legal and "bawdy houses" or brothels are legal. Four years after the Prostitution Reform Act came into force, an external review examined the state of the industry through extensive interviews and surveys (Abel, Fitzgerald and Brunton 2007). The review found that people entered into sex work mainly because of financial, social and identity factors. Decriminalization of sex work did not increase entry into the field. Most workers explained that they stayed in the industry to pay for household expenses. Half had children, and many reported appreciating the flexibility in working hours to accommodate childcare needs. The workers reported having more money, more friends and more independence than they had prior to decriminalization. The main disadvantages they reported were stigma and public harassment as well as the physical and mental stress of the job. Half of respondents had left the industry at some point but returned for financial reasons. They had strong access to health services, as 87 percent reported having a family doctor. Most responded that after decriminalization they were more likely to refuse a client with whom they felt uncomfortable. All respondents reported they always used condoms for vaginal and anal sex because they could safely refuse to take on a client who asked for services without them (Abel, Fitzgerald and Brunton 2007). All of New Zealand's legislation protecting workers' rights applies to sex workers as well. For example, sex workers have won cases against brothel managers for sexual harassment (Lim 2020). Decriminalization improves worker safety.

The most vocal opposition to the Prostitution Reform Act came from mainstream feminist organizations. Support for sex workers has long split feminist organizations. In Canada many feminist organizations opposed the *Bedford* ruling and supported the Nordic model. This is another example of white feminism in action, as pearl-clutching white saviourism, inattentive to the realities of economic survival in a racist, classist, homophobic, transphobic, ableist and xenophobic society. Without question, women, girls, trans and nonbinary people are exploited and endangered in the sex trade. Between 1991 and 2014, 294 sex workers in Canada were murdered, and one-third of these cases remain unsolved (Rotenberg 2016). Feminism should champion substantive equity and transform society to improve the lives of women, girls, trans and nonbinary people. Criminalization of sex work simply does not do that.

The same year Bedford, Scott and Lebovitch launched their lawsuit, pig farmer Robert Pickton was tried for the serial murders of women in BC. The investigation into his violence was the largest in Canadian history. He targeted sex workers and women who used drugs in Vancouver's Downtown Eastside. Indigenous women accounted for a high proportion of the victims. Concerns about women going missing from the area had circulated for some time, but systemic racism in the Vancouver Police Department and the stigmatization of sex workers and people who use drugs allowed Pickton to go years without arrest. He was convicted for killing Sereena Abotsway, Mona Wilson, Angela Joesbury, Brenda Wolfe, Georgina Papin and Marnie Frey. He faced charges for the murders of twenty others, but after the first trial these charges were stayed. The names of these women are Jacqueline Michelle McDonell, Dianne Rosemary Rock, Heather Kathleen Bottomley, Jennifer Lynn Furminger, Helen Mae Hallmark, Patricia Rose Johnson, Heather Gabrielle Chinnock, Tanya Marlo Holyk, Sherry Leigh Irving, Inga Monique Hall, Tiffany Louise Drew, Sarah de Vries, Cynthia Dawn Feliks, Angela Rebecca Jardine, Diana Melnick, Debra Lynne Jones, Wendy Crawford, Kerry Lynn Koski, Andrea Fay Borhaven and Cara Louise Ellis.

After the Pickton trial, BC's lieutenant governor ordered a public inquiry into how so many women could have gone missing in Vancouver with so little public response. The inquiry, which wrapped up in 2012, was widely criticized for failing to include grassroots voices and dismissing the critical role of sexism and racism in the Vancouver Police Department's response or lack thereof (Oppal 2012). It replicated the silence it was intended to question (Collard 2015). The inquiry did acknowledge the criminal regulation of sex work contributed to the marginalization of the people Pickton preyed upon: "The VPD pursued a strategy of containing the women into more remote and unsafe parts of downtown Vancouver.… The unintended consequence was that police created a space for the survival sex trade to exist where the women were violated, often with impunity" (Oppal 2012, 66). Advocates in Vancouver say the results of the inquiry made a difference locally, and arrests related to sex work have fallen (Ling 2018), although police mistreatment of sex workers persists (Lindsay 2021). Police surveillance and consequent endangerment of sex workers continue throughout Canada, and no major political party is prioritizing work to repeal Bill C-36.

With increased recognition that police fail to protect marginalized communities, including Indigenous and racialized people, sex workers and people who use drugs, public attitudes are changing in favour of sex work decriminalization. In 2014 the Canadian Public Health Association denounced Bill C-36 for failing to address the health considerations faced by sex workers and the increased workplace violence the new laws would subject them to. In 2019 a statement in solidarity with sex workers seeking decriminalization was signed by 150 organizations in Canada (Action Canada for Sexual Health & Rights 2019). Many feminist organizations that previously took positions that criminalization would help sex workers have reversed course and issued public apologies (e.g., WAVAW Rape Crisis Centre 2018).

Bodily autonomy means having the right to protect yourself from harm, and criminalization of sex work does more harm than good. Sound social infrastructure, like a national childcare program, pharmacare and affordable housing would increase sex worker safety far more than the arrest of their clients. Addressing stigma, misogyny and transphobia is far more likely to prevent violence against sex workers than is the criminalization of their work (Johnson, Burns and Porth 2017).

Santina Rao

She placed the produce items in the canvas storage basket under the baby's stroller as she made her way through the Halifax Walmart with her two children. She had just made a purchase in the electronics department, but there was no scale to weigh the produce, so she set off to find a cash register elsewhere in the store (Rao 2020). As she did so, she spoke on the phone with her mother, who was offering encouragement because she was deeply depressed and navigating the process of pressing charges against her ex-boyfriend. In the toy aisle she stopped to put together a bottle of formula for her baby. Her toddler was selecting a toy.

Suddenly, five security guards and police officers surrounded her. Santina Rao, a twenty-three-year-old Black mother, did not know what was happening. They accused her of concealing items and asked for her identification. She said they could look through her things and see her receipts. They refused. They took the identification and asked her if she still lived at the same address. At this point she became scared and upset. Why would they need to know her address in the toy aisle? They then cuffed her for being "aggressive." The toddler reached for her mother and was blocked by an officer. Another man held Rao back. As her terror escalated, she swore at the officers to get off her. At least three men pushed her to the ground. In the fight, Rao's arm was broken and she was punched in the face. She was left bruised and concussed. The January 2020 altercation was caught on a shopper's cell phone camera.

Police charged Rao with assaulting an officer, resisting arrest and causing a disturbance. She was left in a police car, separated from her children, while medical personnel attended to an officer's injuries (McNamara 2020). When she sobbed, asking to know where her children were, she was told to stop, that she was embarrassing herself.

Due to her injuries, she was unable to care for her children for weeks afterwards, and she needed prescription glasses and therapy. The trauma of her children witnessing the violence shook her most. "That's the hardest thing, it really, really dwells on me the hardest and the biggest," she said (Ryan 2020). The official line from the police was that officers were responding to a theft in progress. A theft of approximately $6.50 in produce?

While most research on violence against mothers and its impact on children in Canada focuses on domestic violence, the impacts are likely to be similar when police perpetrate the violence. The exposure of children to woman abuse is defined as "seeing a mother assaulted or demeaned, hearing loud conflict and violence, seeing the aftermath (e.g., injuries) [and] learning about what happened to a mother" (Cunningham and Baker 2007, 6). As Black feminist Robyn Maynard (2017, 84) has written, "Black life has been so effectively stigmatized that even highly spectacular forms of state violence are largely unrecognized as such, and go uncontested by mainstream society."

While the COVID-19 pandemic would later usher in a whole new level of policing in Canada and around the world (McClelland and Luscombe 2020), Halifax was already reckoning with this issue of policing people just for being present in public. What Rao experienced was an example of the long-discussed Halifax Regional Police practice of "street checks." Formally, a street check is a record of an interaction between a police officer and a member of the public. They are commonly understood, though, as "getting stopped randomly by the police. Random stops where they ask you questions for no reason" (Wortley 2019, 3). This had become such a problem in the city that in 2017 the Nova Scotia Human Rights Commission hired Dr. Scot Wortley, a criminologist from the University of Toronto, to analyze what was going on. He conducted community meetings and processed twelve years of police street check data from 2006 to 2017.

Wortley's report, released in spring 2019, found Black people were vastly overtargeted by police. The rate of street checks for white people without a prior criminal charge was 136 per 1,000 people; for Black people it was almost four times higher, at 437 per 1,000. But for those who had a criminal charge history, the disproportionate street check rate was several times higher: 169 for white people compared to 1,443 for Black people (i.e., some Black people experienced more than one street check). The outcome of a street check is that — forever after — you are a data point entered in the police information system. This does not prevent crime, but it does change how you are perceived by law enforcement and the public. Think of what comes to mind when a news report labels someone as "known to police."

Although African Nova Scotians are the largest "racially visible" group in the province (Nova Scotia, African Nova Scotian Affairs n.d.) and have resided there for hundreds of years, the Black population of Halifax remains very small at about 15,000 people out of 450,000. Of the 6,790 Black men in the city, more than half — 3,724 individuals — were subjected to street checks during the study period (Wortley 2019, 131–32). It was well understood a year later, when Rao was arrested in 2020, that Halifax police had a racism problem. Wortley's report concluded street checks did not produce information of value for public safety and were harmful to the people who got "checked." Wortley also called for an independent opinion as to the legality of street checks.

Research lawyer Jennifer Taylor and former Supreme Court of Nova Scotia justice Michael MacDonald published a legal opinion on street checks in October 2019. They found the Nova Scotia Police Act did not actually permit street checks and that street checks interfered with two Charter rights — Section 8, the right to be free from unreasonable search and seizure, and Section 9, the right to be free from arbitrary detention. They concluded, "The common law does not empower the police to conduct street checks, because they are not reasonably necessary. They are therefore illegal." (Taylor and MacDonald 2019, 9). In November 2019, the chief of the Halifax Regional Police, Dan Kinsella, issued a public apology for street checks and their inherent reliance on racial profiling (Fraser 2019).

What happened to Rao, a young woman without a criminal record stopped and threateningly questioned about her identity in the middle of a department store in the presence of her children, arguably met the definition of a street check even though it occurred indoors. On a frigidly cold January evening two days after she was assaulted, 150 protestors staged an hour-long rally in the Walmart parking lot and then several dozen led a walkthrough of the store (Devet 2020). They held cardboard signs saying "Support Black Mothers" and "End Racial Profiling." The protest, the proximity of her arrest to the release of both the Wortley and MacDonald–Taylor reports and the video clearly showing police brutality spurred public concern about the incident. It also mattered that Rao was a mother. While she endured plenty of abuse on social media, and victim-blaming calls for "hearing from both sides," many supporters could see themselves in her shoes and imagine themselves making the same fight-or-flight trauma response to a perceived threat to their children.

Individual members of the public and numerous organizations enthusiastically wrote to and called the Public Prosecution Service in Nova Scotia to demand the charges against Rao be dropped. In July, they were. Facing a group of supporters outside, COVID-19 precautions in place, Rao said, "I had no idea that actually so many people would have cared" (Quon, Al-Hakim and Thomas 2020, n.p.). She disclosed how the experience haunted her family. Her daughter sometimes said to her, "Mommy, I'm going to protect you from the police" (Quon, Al-Hakim and Thomas 2020, n.p.).

The Serious Incident Response Team (SIRT), the internal affairs investigation unit for the Halifax Regional Police, was enlisted to investigate the officers' violent conduct against Rao. It hired Tony Smith as an observer to represent the African Nova Scotian community in the proceedings. In October 2020 SIRT concluded the police officers were justified in their use of force against Rao, "given the aggressiveness of the female" (Chiu 2020, 1). Smith accused the unit of excluding him from the process and denying him input into the report. Former lieutenant governor of Nova Scotia Mayan Francis, a Black woman, stated publicly that the incident and SIRT's response made her fearful of police for the first time (McMillan 2020).

The violence police perpetrate against women, trans people and nonbinary people is one reason why carceral feminism, the belief that gendered violence can be remedied with more policing, prosecution and prison, meets justified critique (Press 2018). Policing has gendered consequences, and more policing in a sexist society puts women, trans people and nonbinary people at greater risk. Arrests traumatize children, and women are more likely than men to be caring for children when they face arrest. After a parent's arrest, children may be sent to foster care. Arrest places women, trans people and nonbinary people in an extreme position of vulnerability, and officers are known to sexually assault people under arrest. For instance, Constable Carl Snelgrove, an officer in Newfoundland, has three times faced trial for sexually assaulting a woman while on duty and was convicted in May 2021 (Smellie 2021). As discussed earlier in this chapter, there is also the issue of how police revictimize people who report sexual assault through interrogating questions and insensitivity (Moore 2020).

Being held in police custody is differently experienced by women, trans people and nonbinary people than cis men, with more potential for harm. Consider Lillian

Desjarlais, a young Indigenous woman in Saskatoon, who spent three days in a police cell block in February 2016 (CBC News 2016). At the time she was exclusively breast-feeding her four-month-old baby. She was denied access to the baby or even a breast pump, had no privacy, was given no extra clothes, experienced excruciating pain from engorgement and developed mastitis. The baby was without breastmilk the whole time, and after the disruption the mother and baby were unable to continue breastfeeding —a clear violation of the mother and baby's connection and their bodily autonomy (Allen 2017).

Police terrorize women, trans people and nonbinary people adjacent to crimes. Consider how police treated Debbie Bushie, another Indigenous woman in Saskatchewan, moments after informing her that her son Colten Bushie had been killed by a white man. Officers yelled at her to "get it together," accused her of intoxication and even went so far as to smell her breath (Coletta 2021, 1). A grieving, shocked, terrified mother of a dead young son was grilled in her own home.

Police also commonly perpetrate violence in their own domestic relationships. In the past nine years, fourteen police officers in Nova Scotia have faced charges of domestic abuse (Burke 2020a). Survivor Ellen Doyle had two black eyes after her boyfriend, a member of the Halifax Regional Police, smashed her face into a tile floor. Although the issue has not been well studied in recent years, older studies have found domestic violence occurs in up to 40 percent of police officer households (Friedorsdorf 2014). Just as SIRT investigations involve police investigating police and rarely find officers at fault, people in intimate relationships with violent police officers fear calling for help because they expect police will undermine any investigation against a colleague (Burke 2020a).

Policing, then, is not a solution to gendered violence, nor is it an effective way to respond to the racist violence of police. Yet, in 2021, the Halifax Regional Police budget increased to include funding for, among other things, a study of body cameras and more police staff to manage complaints against them (Berman 2021). Footage of Rao's assault did not protect her from the assault, and funding police to support more complaints against the police for more violence by police is a circular logic indeed.

To experience bodily autonomy, there must be freedom from sexual violence, from gendered violence and from state violence. Reproductive justice requires the liberty to shop, to talk on the phone with your mom, to walk along the sidewalk and to just be unbothered. Just be left alone. Violence against women, trans people and nonbinary people is pervasive in our society, and policing mirrors that violence — police cannot be the solution. "Defund the police," a call heard round the world in response to police violence, has feminist implications.

In April 2021 Canadian media was full of reactions to the conviction of police officer Derek Chauvin for the 2020 murder of George Floyd in Minneapolis. Hundreds of thousands of Canadians had marched in the streets to demand accountability for his death. In 2020 the deaths of Chantel Moore, a member of the west coast Tla-o-qui-aht First Nation, in New Brunswick, and of Regis Korchinski-Paquet, a Black and

Indigenous woman, in Ontario, among others, prompted widespread protests and calls for an end to police violence in Canada. Yet from January to the end of November in 2021, police in Canada shot sixty-four people, killing half (Malone 2021). Most of those killed were Black or Indigenous.

Everyone that police injure or kill is someone's parent, someone's child or both. Police brutality is an obvious and yet often overlooked indicator of reproductive injustice in this country. Reproductive justice is freedom from police violence.

Chapter 2

NOT HAVING CHILDREN

Reproductive justice, as described in the introduction, includes the right to choose to have children or not, and to parent any children you choose to have in safety (Ross and Solinger 2017; SisterSong n.d.). It captures the complexity of reproductive freedom when the intersecting implications of racism, colonialism, classism, homophobia, transphobia and ableism further circumscribe choices and opportunities. As Dr. Angela Davis (1981, 355) wrote, "During the early abortion rights campaign it was too frequently assumed that legal abortions provided a viable alternative to the myriad problems posed by poverty. As if having fewer children could create more jobs, higher wages, better schools, etc." Abortion is not a replacement for a social safety net and a just society.

Although now widely adopted by organizations and individuals in the reproductive rights movement, the term "reproductive justice" is often misused as a less stigmatizing stand-in for abortion rights. This erases how the concept was developed in response to the white feminist hyperfocus on abortion rights, to the exclusion of concerns about other types of reproductive oppression, such as coercive sterilization, state removal of children from families and the criminalization of substance use by pregnant people. A key objective of this book is to bring together stories about these types of legal battles in Canada to discuss how they made an impact on reproductive justice in this country. Still, abortion is essential to reproductive justice, and this chapter highlights some important abortion and contraception rights cases that advanced the right to choose not to have children in Canada.

Abortion rights in Canada are unlike anywhere else in the world. Abortion in Canada is completely decriminalized. Like any health care service, there may be access challenges related to geography or a lack of willing and capable providers in certain areas, particularly rural and remote settings, but there is no risk of criminalization. This is a truly unique approach. Although over sixty countries in the world have legalized abortion on demand, this usually comes with legal limits, such as maximum gestational age. No law limits abortion based on gestational age in Canada; it is governed by the practice norms and preferences of abortion care providers.

The path to decriminalization was long and started with a lengthy path towards criminalization. New Brunswick was the first province to adopt a law that limited abortion, in 1810, long before Confederation. The law mirrored what was in place in Britain, criminalizing provision of abortion after "quickening," when fetal movement becomes detectable, around sixteen weeks. PEI, Newfoundland, Upper Canada and Nova Scotia followed suit with laws of their own. In 1841 the quickening distinction was removed in Upper Canada, and the next year New Brunswick did the same. Then in 1849 New Brunswick specifically criminalized patients seeking abortions, and in 1864 the province criminalized provision of "poisons" to cause abortion, regardless of whether there was proof of pregnancy (Backhouse 1983). In 1869 the various provincial laws were consolidated into a federal one, based on the restrictive model presented by New Brunswick. As described in this chapter, New Brunswick has been (and is) a stalwart antagonist in the long fight for abortion access. The consolidated law established a maximum punishment of life imprisonment for a conviction for abortion.

This chapter opens with the case of *Dr. Emily Stowe,* who is best known as one of the first women to become a licensed medical doctor in Canada, and less known as the defendant in a well-publicized abortion trial in 1879. Spoiler alert: she was acquitted, but her acquittal did not shift how the justice system approached the crime of abortion. She was one of many people tried for illegally performing abortions at the time, but as a rare female doctor she was both a high-profile and unusual defendant. Emblematic of white feminism, her priority was her own professional success: Dr. Stowe did not vocally support reproductive autonomy for all, or even the privacy and dignity of her low-income patients. This case sets the stage for reckoning with white feminism as conflicting with the advancement of reproductive justice in Canada. Shortly after her acquittal, Canada, as a united colonial federation, enacted its first federal Criminal Code in 1892. The Criminal Code criminalized the procurement of abortion, distribution of contraceptives and several other gendered experiences.

The next section in this chapter covers the great Eastview Birth Control Trial of 1936–37, a six-month affair to prosecute *Dorothea Palmer* for sharing information about contraceptives in the small town of Eastview, Ontario. Her defence was financed by the white industrialist, eugenicist and rubber factory owner A.R. Kaufman. Over forty defence witnesses were called to the high-profile, theatrical trial. Palmer's acquittal loosened public attitudes and understanding of birth control forever after, but the scrutiny and sacrifices of the court experience drove her into a type of exile, and her case did not change the law.

While it would be false to paint all illegal abortion as inherently unsafe, and there are certainly access concerns associated with regulation of care, many of these procedures did result in serious complications. There were reportedly four thousand to six thousand deaths from illegal abortion from the 1920s to 1940s alone (Pro-Choice Action Network n.d.). In 1964 Lottie Leanne Clarke, a thirty-four-year-old mother of three, developed sepsis and died following an illegal abortion. Dr. Morton Shulman, an independently wealthy physician and politician, had been appointed chief coroner of

Ontario in 1963. Shulman was known for meticulously applying himself to the coroner role, and one of his many controversial stands was to call for an inquest into each death associated with abortion. Around this time, an estimated 33,000 to 120,000 illegal abortions were performed every year in Canada (Pro-Choice Action Network 2007).

Clarke's case caused Shulman to draw a line in the sand: too many women were dying from illegal abortions. Shulman recommended abortion be legalized for cases where a woman's physical or mental health was at risk, for cases of rape and incest and for cases where the baby was expected to be born with anomalies (Edmonds 1965). In 1967 the Canadian Medical Association, representing physicians across the country, called for legalization. That year, Liberal Prime Minister Pierre Elliott Trudeau tabled bills to ease restrictions on abortion, divorce, homosexuality and contraception. The so-called Omnibus Bill passed in 1969, including amendments to Section 251 of the Criminal Code governing abortion. From then on, abortion was legal if a Therapeutic Abortion Committee comprised of physicians determined the pregnancy posed a risk to health.

To activists on the ground, the amendment did not go nearly far enough. What if hospitals chose not to appoint a Therapeutic Abortion Committee? (Many did not.) What if there were delays in seeking committee approval? (There were many.) What if committees refused requests? (They did.) While legal, abortion became an overly bureaucratic process and access remained highly unequal across the country. Immediately following the Criminal Code amendments, action for better access amplified. The Abortion Caravan, started by seventeen women in the grassroots Vancouver Women's Caucus, crossed the country in 1970 to call out the continued access barriers. Their van carried a coffin filled with coat hangers, representing the thousands of people dead from illegal or inadequately legal abortion. They performed a skit in communities along the way, enacting a Therapeutic Abortion Committee as it heard pleas from a series of patients. Their committee turned down all of the requests save one, from a woman costumed in furs with a silver spoon in her mouth.

Clever, antiauthoritarian and dogged, the caravan attracted surveillance from the RCMP. The police suspected Marxism was behind the project and connected the participants to the antiwar, left-wing radicalization they were tasked with investigating at the time: "Each day the caravaners would 'drive three hundred miles, do guerrilla theatre, eat and have a public meeting.' RCMP spying was a part of this routine" (Sethna and Hewitt 2009, 468).

Having reached Ottawa in time for Mother's Day in May, the caravanners hosted a giant rally with allied liberation groups on Parliament Hill, marching from there to the prime minister's residence on Sussex Drive. He was away at his summer cottage, so instead of meeting with him, the marchers installed the coffin on his front lawn (Wells 2020). Two days later they tried again to meet with Trudeau, donning suits and purses and using forged passes to enter the House of Commons, where they then locked themselves to their seats using borrowed bicycle chains. The RCMP surveillance failed to prevent the remarkable and conspicuous direct actions of the caravanners, who drew attention to the cause of abortion access with unprecedented success.

The next few decades of action were dominated by the legal disputes generated by Dr. Henry Morgentaler, a Holocaust survivor based in Montreal. He flouted the 1969 Criminal Code restrictions by performing abortions in his private clinics without anyone's approval, on demand, for any reason. He was charged multiple times and imprisoned for ten months. No jury would convict him. In 1982 the federal government enacted the Charter of Rights and Freedoms with the equality provision coming into force in 1985. Section 7 of the Charter guaranteed all people in Canada the right to life, liberty and security of the person. Section 15 granted protection from discrimination based on sex. Restrictions on abortion, which forced people to remain pregnant when they did not want to be, violated both Charter provisions. In 1988 the Supreme Court of Canada struck abortion from the federal Criminal Code in the landmark *R. v. Morgentaler* decision.

The *Morgentaler* ruling stands out as an international anomaly for how profoundly and broadly it shifted the legal meaning of abortion, and nothing of such magnitude is easily accepted. Individuals, some religious organizations and patriarchal provinces fought hard against it. The third section of this chapter describes the ordeal that *Chantal Daigle* endured in 1989, facing an abusive, controlling ex-boyfriend who wanted to bar her from accessing abortion and a province that refused to support her sovereignty. She resolutely resisted them both, permanently shifting the legal conceptualization of fetal and maternal rights through her persistence. In Canada, the fetus is not a person.

The next game-changing moment came in 2015, when Health Canada approved mifepristone for medication abortion. "Mife," or simply "the abortion pill," had been used for decades outside of Canada, and why it took so long to be approved in Canada is a story unto itself. The regulatory hoops in place when it first came on the market, such as the need to be observed ingesting the medication and having a physician hand it to a patient in person, were soon stripped away. Canada is now one of the only places in the world where any prescriber can provide medication abortion to any patient up to nine weeks gestational age. In the few years of its wide availability, the proportion of abortions procured through medication has risen to nearly 30 percent. Although medication abortion has limited effectiveness after nine weeks of pregnancy and several serious contraindications, and a sizable group of people would prefer an aspiration abortion for clinical or personal reasons, access to medication abortion has clearly led to very significant changes.

After 2015 Canada's most stubborn provinces on abortion, New Brunswick and PEI, were finally forced to reckon with their anachronism and expand access in important ways. The fourth section of this chapter describes *Clinic 554* in Fredericton, New Brunswick, as a protagonist in the overdue legal fight for equitable abortion funding across the province. The final section recounts how anonymous PEI artist *iamkarats* turned an image of the province's iconic Anne of Green Gables into an emblem representing the right to abortion access, just in time for the tide around the island to finally come in.

Three main issues remain on the horizon for abortion activists. First, the sheer size of Canada makes access always conditional on location and ability to travel. Having more competent, confident providers will improve this situation, so promoting abortion in health professional education is critical. Second, abortion care is not universally available to people in Canada. The cost of abortion, whether it be aspiration or medication, is covered by public health insurance (medicare). People without a health card, such as temporary foreign workers, international students and other newcomers, may not have the means to cover the costs privately. The third issue is access to contraception. It does not make any sense to have public funding for abortion and not for birth control. Pharmacare is critical for reproductive justice.

For two centuries, abortion in Canada has sat in the middle of a power struggle between the medical profession, the legal profession, public policy-makers, religious organizations and the antichoice lobby, abortion providers, activists and supporters and pregnant people themselves. There are likely hundreds of richly researched comprehensive chronologies about how abortion law and policy changed in Canada over the years, but these five stories capture the complexity, courage and relentlessness central to the history of abortion in this country. They are unforgettable.

Dr. Emily Stowe

Contemporary discussion about reproductive health and justice in Canada often starts with January 1988 as ground zero, when the *Morgentaler* decision by the Supreme Court of Canada resulted in the complete decriminalization of abortion in the country. But Canada did not arrive at that marker without decades, indeed centuries, of work — often two steps forward, one step back.

Dr. Emily Stowe is now commemorated as the first woman to practise medicine in Canada and for her leadership in the suffragette movement at the turn of the century. There is a public school named after her in Courtrice, a small town in Ontario (Emily Stowe Public School. n.d.). Her face is included in a sculpture at Western University's medical school honouring eight physicians to have made a significant contribution to medicine. In 1981 Canada Post featured Dr. Stowe on a seventeen-cent stamp as part of a series on Canadian feminists (Canadian Stamp News 2015). York University and the Women's College Hospital Foundation in Toronto both offer scholarships in her name (Women's College Hospital Foundation n.d.; York University n.d.). But none of these memorials, nor the entry about her in the Canadian Medical Hall of Fame (2018), mention her pivotal, problematic role in the history of abortion in Canada. Dr. Stowe was not an activist for abortion and contraception, but she was famously put on trial for being one. Her complicated trial in 1879 foreshadowed the criminalization of abortion in Canada's first Criminal Code, introduced in 1892.

She was undoubtedly a trailblazer. After being denied entry to university in the 1840s and '50s, she became a teacher and rose quickly to become the first woman principal in Canada. She married and had three children. Her husband's experience of tuberculosis is said to have piqued her interest in pursuing medicine. Rejected from medical school in Canada, she went where she could get in: the New York Medical College for Women, which offered a program in homeopathic medicine.

Medicine at the time was subject to a turf war between competing sects, including the "regular" physicians, who were affluent apprentices to licensed physicians and eventually came to dominate the field, and "irregular" practitioners like homeopaths, eclectics and Indigenous healers serving their communities (Backhouse 1991). The irregular practitioner paths were decidedly more welcoming to women. Dr. Stowe left her family behind to complete her homeopathic studies, returning to Ontario after she graduated in 1867. Two years later, regulatory changes in the province required physicians who had trained elsewhere to attend lectures at a Canadian medical school and sit a licensure examination. The University of Toronto Medical School rejected Dr. Stowe's applications several times before relenting and allowing her into classes, where she was mercilessly tormented and harassed by her male classmates. After she graduated from the University of Toronto, she refused to sit the licensure exam because it meant submitting to the evaluation of the very men who had immaturely mistreated her. Dr. Stowe simply continued to practise for a decade without a licence.

Dr. Stowe's story is worth celebrating because of her dogged persistence in seeking inclusion in the male-dominated field of "Western" medicine, and because she lost patience with gender discrimination and flouted the rules, successfully. However, her classist behaviour in the abortion trial did not align with "advocacy in promoting women's rights" (Federation of Medical Women of Canada n.d., 1), unless her feminism is understood through the lens of white feminism: feminism for the lofty few. Despite standing trial for performing abortion, she was not an advocate for it.

The case against Dr. Stowe began in summer of 1879. A nineteen-year-old unmarried woman, Sarah Ann Lowell, was found dead in her home in Toronto on August 12. Her mother, who found her body, was flabbergasted. Sarah had been healthy and out shopping that very morning. Dr. John McConnell, the local coroner, launched an inquest. Two physicians conducted an autopsy and found Sarah's lungs to be congested, which they determined to be the cause of death. No toxins were detected in the contents of her stomach. Sarah was, however, found to be about five months pregnant with a male fetus.

Dr. Stowe testified at McConnell's inquest that Sarah had come to see her in May, teary and complaining of "interrupted menses" (Backhouse 1991), a code for pregnancy. Sarah was so distraught, even expressing suicidality, that Dr. Stowe felt the need to give her something. She prescribed thirty days' worth of a "harmless" tincture containing very small amounts of known abortifacients hellebore (Riddle 1994), cantharides (Moed, Shwayder and Chang 2001) and myrrh, to be taken with sugar water.

Several important shifts were happening at the time with respect to the social and clinical context of abortion in Canada (Backhouse 1991). As a colony, Canada followed English law, and England's 1803 abortion law prohibited the procedure only after "quickening," the point when a pregnant person feels the movement of a fetus, which usually occurs after sixteen weeks. But the Canadian provinces, beginning with New Brunswick, started criminalizing abortion in 1810 (McTavish 2015). People who could get pregnant used everything in their contraceptive toolbox to reverse "interrupted menses" and limit their family size, including "sexual abstinence, prolonged nursing, coitus interruptus, sheaths, pessaries, douches, and abortion where all else had failed" (Backhouse 1991, 168). With these tools at their disposal, the birth rate fell by one-third from 1851 to 1891.

Physicians vocally opposed abortion, as it was prohibited in the original content of the Hippocratic Oath, dating back to the fifth century BCE:

> I will use those dietary regimens which will benefit my patients according to my greatest ability and judgment, and I will do no harm or injustice to them. Neither will I administer a poison to anybody when asked to do so, nor will I suggest such a course. Similarly I will not give to a woman a pessary to cause abortion. (Hippocrates of Cos n.d., 299)

Because of physician opposition, people in need of abortion sought care from nonphysicians. Physicians' withholding of abortion services in nineteenth-century Canada increased the risks associated with the procedure. The elevated risks in turn made abortion even less attractive to physicians.

In the twentieth century this trend was reversed when physicians brought abortion under their purview exclusively. Abortion activists have made use of abortion as the domain of physicians to argue it should not be a matter for state intervention or criminal sanctions: "Abortion is decided between a woman and her doctor" (Norman and Downie 2017, 1). The problem with this framing is there is still an authority standing between pregnant people and abortion, and abortion is ultimately not only a health care decision. It is a political decision made by a pregnant person over their body and life.

For centuries, people have, independently or with the counsel of others, used herbal substances to induce menstruation and terminate pregnancy, with varying efficacy. A missed or interrupted period is the first and principal symptom of pregnancy, and the intention of so-called emmenagogues is to bring menses back. A 2020 study found myrrh, one of the substances Dr. Stowe prescribed to Sarah, to be an effective contemporary treatment for incomplete abortion (Vafaei et al. 2020).

Dr. Stowe undoubtedly had some intention of supporting Sarah in regulating her period, but it is unclear whether she intended to support an abortion. Several male physicians testified at the inquest that the substances Dr. Stowe prescribed could not have had any clinical effect at such low doses. It does raise the question of why she would bother prescribing known abortifacients at all. Perhaps, as some have suggested, she wanted to preserve Sarah's health and worried about the potential impact of the patient ingesting too much of the substances (Backhouse 1991). In 1990 Kok-Choi et al. (1990) published a case study about a patient who died after attempting to procure an abortion by ingesting cantharides (a "herbal" medicine that is made from a beetle), another substance Dr. Stowe prescribed to Sarah. Kok-Choi et al. argued the herbal medicine should be better regulated. Regardless of the optimal or appropriate dosage, Sarah died three months after the substances were prescribed, a full two months after the prescriptions would have been exhausted.

Although Dr. Stowe is heralded as a feminist leader who paved the way for the inclusion of (white) women in the medical profession (McMullen 2003) and for (white) women's right to vote, there is no evidence she was a champion of reproductive freedom. She expressed conservative positions in advocating for abstinence in general (Backhouse 1991). The suffragette movement she was part of was not particularly active in advocacy for access to birth control. In fact, for many in the movement, discussion of contraception was considered undignified and seen as undermining their efforts to gain political acceptability. They believed contraception could encourage more sexual exploitation of women and they instead encouraged married women to refuse sex to control the size of their families (Khazan 2019).

The tincture Dr. Stowe prescribed to Sarah was likely to be ineffective, and perhaps she intended for it not to work because she disapproved of Sarah's situation. The motives will never be clear. What is clear is she could have responded more punitively but did not. For example, in 1869 Dr. Clemence Lozier, who was a close mentor of Dr. Stowe's at her college in New York, called the police when a couple sought her help for pregnancy termination (Backhouse 1991).

Perhaps more disturbing than her failure to provide effective treatment was Dr. Stowe's blatant disrespect for Sarah's privacy and dignity. At the time of her May visit to the doctor, Sarah was employed as a domestic servant at a hotel owned by John Avis. After meeting Sarah, Dr. Stowe sought out Avis's wife and told her about the employee's pregnancy. The doctor even went so far as to advise Mrs. Avis to fire Sarah for her indecent behaviour. This degree of violation and interference is hard to imagine today. Furthermore, Stowe was apparently unconcerned with the outcome of treatment and never saw Sarah again.

Despite the findings from the autopsy, which blamed lung congestion for Sarah's death, and the testimony of Dr. Stowe's medical peers asserting the tinctures would have had no more than a placebo effect, the jury at the inquest determined the patient had died "by means of irritant poison" (Duffin 1992, 883). Dr. Stowe was charged under Ontario law with administering drugs to induce abortion.

She was released on $8,000 bail and pled not guilty (Backhouse 1991). At the ensuing trial, two physician witnesses for the prosecution, Dr. Bull and Dr. Riddell, testified the dose and type of medication she had prescribed would not have been effective as an abortifacient. The defence argued that a prescription is not the same as administration of a medicine and that there was no evidence Dr. Stowe told Sarah the tinctures would work as an abortifacient. The defence implied that by giving Sarah the ineffective tincture, Dr. Stowe had manipulated Sarah into believing she was being treated for interrupted menses and prevented her from seeking abortion care elsewhere. Through this winding logic they argued Dr. Stowe had demonstrated opposition to abortion.

The trial was tumultuous and dramatic. Coroner McConnell had lost key pieces of evidence — namely, the physical prescription and the tincture bottle. Several witnesses, including the coroner and one of the physicians who had participated in the autopsy, Dr. Philbrick, were demonstrably misogynistic in their testimony. Sympathy swayed towards Dr. Stowe, and she was ultimately acquitted.

Dr. Stowe's case had complex layers of conflict. As a forerunner female physician, she resisted the exclusionary, sexist nature of the medical profession but she also sought validation and legitimacy within it. There was a general culture of antiabortion beliefs in the medical profession, struggling against the common (public) desire for birth control. The political emancipation of women was not conceptualized as reliant on autonomy over reproduction, and in fact was seen as incompatible with it. Class loyalty (between Dr. Stowe and hotel owner Mrs. Avis) took precedence over duty to patient privacy and confidentiality. The medical profession was vying for independence and authority outside of legal control (Duffin 1992). There remains a lack of clarity about how Dr. Stowe truly may have acted towards Sarah compared with the self-preserving hostility she projected during the inquiry and trial.

Dr. Stowe's acquittal was unusual for the time (Backhouse 1991). She went on to receive her medical licence eight months later (Duffin 1992). There had been only one white woman licensed to practise medicine before her, Dr. Jennie Trout. Dr. Stowe's daughter, Augusta, became the first white woman to graduate from medical school in Canada in 1883.

In 1892 the federal Parliament of Canada passed the country's first Criminal Code, which included the prohibition of abortion. It also criminalized the sale, advertisement or distribution of contraceptives and sex work (Backhouse 1991). This first Criminal Code baked in gender discrimination just as the Canadian suffragette movement was emerging, with Dr. Stowe in a leadership role.

The trial of Dr. Stowe is a window into the problematic history of white feminism and family planning in Canada. Unlike many of the cases in the twentieth century, with brazen defendants who set out to shift the status quo for abortion and contraception access, Dr. Stowe was focused on accessing the medical profession herself rather than supporting an individual patient or advancing abortion or contraception for people in general. She betrayed the privacy of a patient and failed to give her an effective pharmacological regimen as treatment. She faced improbable charges of facilitating an abortion months after the patient was last in her care. Her trial was steeped, predictably, in the misogyny of the day, but some physicians emerged as her champions. Their objections in the case exposed the unsuitability of criminal law for governing the clinical matter of abortion: Why should the justice system tell a health care provider what to do or what a patient needs when its actors are ignorant on both counts? It would take more than a century for that issue to be resolved through complete decriminalization of abortion in Canada.

Dr. Stowe's trial is an early example of the white supremacist and classist ideology that came to underpin reproductive rights discourse and progress in the twentieth century. White feminism centres the experiences and ambitions of white women, such as achieving success in medical and legal domains. The reproductive freedom of Indigenous, Black and low-income people was and continues to be undermined by colonial, racist and antipoor state policies.

Dorothea Palmer

Dorothea Palmer achieved notoriety as the only person in Canada to ever be charged under Section 207(c) of the Criminal Code, which prohibited the sale, advertisement or distribution of contraception (Deachman 2020). What a trial it was. Lasting from October 1936 to March 1937, it was inordinately costly and reportedly included over 750,000 words of testimony (Stephenson 1957). It was an extraordinary response to Palmer's rather mundane "crime" of giving out boxes of inexpensive, locally produced condoms and contraceptive jelly in the small town of Eastview (now Vanier), Ontario.

Palmer had only come to Canada from Wales a decade earlier. She had trained as a social worker in Sheffield, England, and upon moving to Canada opened a book shop with her husband, Gordon Ferguson, in Ottawa, Ontario. Besides the shopkeeping, Palmer was a Parent Information Bureau field worker, charged with door-to-door home visits in the impoverished town of Eastview to distribute information about how to limit family size.

The Parent Information Bureau was the 1930s brainchild of A.R. Kaufman, owner of Kaufman Rubber Company in Kitchener-Waterloo. Kaufman had noticed that absenteeism at his factory, which caused financial loss, was more common among employees with larger families. The staff who missed the most work could least afford it because they had more mouths to feed, and increased layoffs during the Great Depression were driving workers' families into destitution. In response, Kaufman reoriented part of his rubber factory to produce condoms and diaphragms and started the Parent Information Bureau to oversee contraceptive distribution and family education about their use.

An industrialist, Kaufman was clearly motivated more by profit than altruism, but his impact on family planning in Canada was significant. Starting as what was basically a sexual health clinic at his factory, primarily designated to serve employees and their families, the scope of the Parent Information Bureau grew across Canada. In addition to the clinics, Kaufman felt the Parent Information Bureau could be effective by travelling door to door rather than expecting people with large families to go to them. It would come to employ over fifty people as field workers and served over 200,000 families.

The field workers, sometimes referred to as nurses, were often women from nonclinical backgrounds. Even though they lacked clinical training, Kaufman presumed they would be more familiar with reproductive concerns and more approachable than physicians, who were usually men. Clients could receive referrals for Parent Information Bureau services through friends or physicians. The bureau emphasized the provision of information, including how to order contraceptives for a small fee by mail. Kaufman's organization would also provide them for free. His factory started making contraceptives outright when he determined it would be more economically efficient than buying them from other manufacturers and giving them to clients.

The town Palmer was assigned by the Parent Information Bureau, Eastview, was largely Roman Catholic (she was not) and francophone (she did not speak any French),

and one-quarter of the residents were on social assistance (she was middle class). The incoherence between her religion, language and economic position and those of the Eastview townspeople was stark but ultimately unimportant. They understood what she meant when she came around.

Kaufman's efforts were not solely motivated by concerns about his workers' reliability. He was, like contraceptive innovators Margaret Sanger in the United States and Marie Stopes in Britain, a proponent of eugenics — a discriminatory ideological belief system supposedly seeking to improve humanity by reducing the reproduction of socially undesirable populations. Early in the twentieth century, white Anglo-Saxon people were in a racist panic over their declining birth rates as compared to other groups of people, such as immigrants to Canada, Indigenous people and francophones (Dodd 1985). While early eugenicists opposed birth control, thinking it would be used by and hence decrease births in white families, they soon shifted course to instead encourage birth control among nonwhite, lower-class communities.

Kaufman was a bona fide, card-carrying eugenicist — a member of the Eugenics Society of Canada — and he is thought to be one of the few eugenicist activists who personally arranged sterilization procedures. In addition to contraceptive kits with condoms, spermicide and information, the Parent Information Bureau field workers carried application forms for surgical sterilization procedures for men and women (Revie 2006). Kaufman reportedly funded the surgical sterilization of at least fourteen hundred people. These included a thousand men in a clinic at his factory and four hundred women in various hospitals (Stote 2012).

In September 1936 the police received a complaint from an Eastview resident suggesting Palmer was selling contraceptives, a violation of the 1892 Criminal Code. She was arrested by Eastview police under the assumption she was acting independently to make a bit of money (Stephenson 1957). It became clear she was backed by a large organization and a wealthy businessman when the first telephone call she made from lock-up was to Kaufman.

Kaufman arranged to pay her bail, set at $500, and enthusiastically took on financial responsibility for her legal defence. As would become clear, Palmer's case was an opportunity for Kaufman to challenge the prudish and impractical consequences of the federal ban on family planning. The police offered to drop the charges if Palmer would just leave Eastview, but Kaufman was keen to take the case to trial, hoping an acquittal would facilitate the Parent Information Bureau's work. Kaufman's approach to reproductive rights was, quite frankly, paternalistic and opportunistic. He did not support just principles like living wages and social services to improve the social and economic status of people who worked for him; instead, he urged them to have smaller families. He resisted workers' efforts to unionize. And it was his commercial success that made his venture into the promotion of birth control appear respectable.

Palmer was well read and educated, and unlike Kaufman, she espoused beliefs in rights to reproductive freedom. She is quoted as having said at her arrest, "A woman should be master of her own body. She should be the one to say if she wants to become a mother" (Stephenson 1957, 1).

Her trial was a pageant. Whole rooms were filled with birth control literature from far and wide to inform the defence's arguments. Eastview priests discouraged local congregants from attending the trial, presuming the content of the discussion would be unseemly. The courthouse filled with women's rights advocates who travelled in from Ottawa (Stephenson 1957). Newspapers refused to report on the content of the trial, deeming it "unfit for newspaper publication" (Deachman 2020, 1). In their coverage of Palmer's arrest, they resorted to vague euphemisms for her birth control advocacy, stating she was engaged in "philanthropic activities" and "distributing medicine for an unlawful purpose" (Deachman 2020, 1).

The first trial witnesses in *Rex v. Palmer* were some of the nearly hundred women whom Palmer had visited in her first six months on the job. Some had birthed more than ten children before they met Palmer. All insisted that despite the religious, language and class divides between them and Palmer, they had welcomed her when she came to their homes and appreciated the information she provided. Although the contraceptive kits she carried around did include a product price list, her clients disputed she had ever sold them anything. The prosecution was forced to drop the charge of selling contraception but kept the charge of advertisement.

The Crown called a single expert witness: Dr. J.E. DeHaitre, a religious, Ottawa-based physician who opposed the use of contraception without medical advice. Time and again in the history of reproductive rights in Canada, there is a tension between medicine laying claim to expertise in family planning while simultaneously shaking off ties to stigmatized and prohibited services like contraception and abortion. Despite his opposition Dr. DeHaitre admitted to having seen the consequences of unplanned pregnancy in his practice, including complications from unsafe and illegal abortions, and he even suggested the harm of contraception was secondary to its clear benefits.

Palmer's defence, based on Section 207.2 of the Criminal Code, was that she had acted in the public good. Testifying in her support, Kaufman stated contraceptives were already widely distributed by druggists, and his were simply cheaper. Several men testified they had shopped at local drugstores and found dozens of contraceptive products available for purchase. All of them cost more than Kaufman's (Stephenson 1957). Palmer's lawyer, Franklin Wellington Wegenast, aimed to overwhelm the court with endless, wide-ranging sources of evidence in support of her defence. The trial continued for six months, with over forty witnesses testifying to the clinical, financial, social and religious acceptability of contraception. Every week Palmer dutifully reported for bail. During this time, she faced the disapproval of her husband, family, friends and church, as well as clamorous harassment and even physical abuse from members of the public. She stayed the course. One man reportedly threatened to sexually assault her, and she kneed him in the groin (Buck 2019).

When all was said and done, Kaufman had spent $25,000 on Palmer's legal fees.

We can hold our applause for his generosity, as it should not be lost on anyone that Kaufman had much to gain commercially from the publicity the trial afforded both the Parent Information Bureau's activities and his rubber company. Palmer herself suggested, later in her life, that Kaufman strategically sent her to a Catholic community to stoke conflict and test the "public good" defence (Buck 2019). That a young woman employee, one of fifty doing the same work, was singled out for prosecution and not the organization's very public leader was a telling marker of how social position is more a determinant of criminalization than any subversive act.

The complexity of the trial — the myriad witnesses and exhibits raised for consideration — mirrors some of the complex intersections at the core of reproductive justice: class matters, religion matters and social structures and supports matter in shaping a person's reproductive "choices." When he finally read his ruling, Magistrate Lester Clayton acknowledged it was unfair that the rich and middle classes could control their reproductive lives while the poor were denied the means. He wagered no harm could come from learning how to plan families and Palmer's role as a field worker had served the public good (Stortz and Eaton 1983). The charges against her were dismissed. The Crown took the case to the Court of Appeal, which upheld the acquittal (Deachmann 2020).

Palmer made untold sacrifices during the trial and achieved success not only through her acquittal but also through shifting public attitudes and understanding about birth control across Canada. Despite his exploitative approach and strong eugenicist beliefs, Kaufman was lauded for his role in the advancement of reproductive rights. Eventually, Palmer fell out of Kaufman's favour — or ceased being useful to him — and she was fired. She retreated from public life and moved to Toronto to shield her husband and family from further attention. She became a florist and had a daughter.

Despite the breadth of evidence supporting the value of contraception presented in the Eastview courthouse in the fall of 1936 and winter of 1937, more than thirty years passed before contraception was legalized. In 1969 the federal government enacted an Omnibus Bill to remove contraception from the Criminal Code. In 1978 Palmer emerged from reclusion to speak at the opening of a birth control clinic, affirming that if she had it to do it all over again, she would.

Chantal Daigle

A year after the *Morgentaler* decision in 1988, one of the most sensational and well-publicized cases about reproductive autonomy in the country's history took place. This case determined the fetus does not have rights before the law, and the only person who has the right to decide on an abortion is the person who is pregnant — not their parents, not their family doctor and not their spouse. The courageous hero of this story is Chantal Daigle, a young woman from the small Quebec town of Chibougamau.

In January 1989 Daigle, a secretary, was twenty-one years old and in a new relationship with twenty-five-year-old Jean Guy Tremblay, a former bouncer turned car service technician. She planned to marry him. They moved in together in Montreal and by March she was pregnant. Then the abuse began. Studies have found that up to 21 percent of pregnant women experience intimate partner violence (Taillieu and Brownridge 2010; Daoud et al. 2012). Tremblay came to control all aspects of Daigle's life. The final straw was when he grabbed her by the throat and accused her of being "too social" (Barron 1989, 1; Jenish 1989, 1). Nonfatal strangulation is a key risk factor for domestic violence homicide (Glass et al. 2008). On July 3, when she was about eighteen weeks pregnant, she left, letting him know she had an abortion scheduled for two days later in Sherbrooke (Barron 1989).

Tremblay immediately sought and received an injunction from the Quebec Superior Court to prevent Daigle from procuring an abortion. His lawyer argued the rights to abortion, asserted by the *Morgentaler* decision, have limits, and the fetus should be considered a living person under the Quebec Charter of Rights and Freedoms. The court agreed (Pelletier 2019).

There were a handful of similar attempts by men seeking injunctions to block their partners from having abortions that year. However, in those instances the men were unsuccessful in convincing the courts to rule against their pregnant partners. Those women all legally received abortion care. The cases received extraordinary media attention, particularly Barbara Dodd in Ontario (Rebick 2008).

Daigle took her case to the Quebec Court of Appeal. It is hard to imagine Daigle's incredible courage, being so open and public about her decision despite the persistent stigmatization of abortion. On July 26 the court's five judges upheld the injunction against her in a 3–2 ruling. Justice Yves Bernier is quoted as saying a break-up of a relationship was not adequate grounds for abortion, and the right to abortion asserted by the *Morgentaler* decision could not be exercised "arbitrarily" (Barron 1989, 1). The next day the streets of Montreal flooded with thousands of protesters in one of the most important demonstrations in the province's history.

Daigle was not deterred by her loss at appeal and took the fight to the Supreme Court of Canada. Now over twenty weeks pregnant, she was already beyond the usual gestational age cut-off for most elective abortion providers in Canada, and time was of the essence. For only the second time in the court's history (Radio Canada 2019), the nine judges were recalled from their summer vacations to hear the case on August 8. The speed at which her case was processed through multiple levels of the courts in the summer of 1989 was extraordinary. This swiftness was necessary because pregnancy does not wait, but it added to the uproar surrounding the case. Both pro-choice and antiabortion organizations, including LEAF and the Campaign for Life Coalition, rallied furiously to seek intervenor status in the Supreme Court case. The court granted intervenor status to seven groups, including the federal government, which sought to argue only the federal government could determine the legality of abortion (Van Dusen 1989). Antiabortion protestors reportedly hosted a baby shower for Daigle and collected stuffed animal gifts (Van Dusen 1989), and one even offered Daigle $25,000 to keep her pregnancy (Jenish 1989).

Daigle's lawyer, Daniel Bédard, was on lunch break at the Supreme Court on August 8 when he learned what Daigle had done in the meantime. A week earlier, on August 1, this exceptional person had travelled across the US border with dyed hair and under a fake name to have an abortion in Boston, Massachusetts. Regardless of what the court decided, Daigle had already succeeded in having an abortion. But she had also violated a court-ordered injunction. Contempt of court could be met with a two-year prison sentence or a $42,500 fine. There was no way Daigle could afford this consequence.

It had not been Daigle who called to inform Bédard, but a lawyer for the Quebec provincial government. Police had informed the Quebec minister of justice of Daigle's actions. Montreal Health Centre for Women nurse Lise Gratton and counsellor Marie-Paul Lanthier had arranged care for Daigle in Boston and driven the 400 kilometres to get her there (*Boston Globe* 1989; Wallace, Van Dusen and Allen 1989). An $8,000 fund amassed by Daigle's supporters was used to pay for the abortion. When asked how the police could have been tipped off, Gratton said she had heard clicks on her phone and suspected the line was tapped.

Learning all of this so suddenly, Bédard recognized he needed to persuade the Supreme Court to continue hearing the case (Radio Canada 2019). The court's decision could clarify the rights of other people who were placed in this position, as well as relieve Daigle individually of any potential penalty. The court agreed to move forward. The nine justices unanimously rejected the injunction against Daigle, finding neither civil law in Quebec nor common law in the other provinces recognized rights of the fetus. Fathers' rights to veto abortion are nonexistent in any English, Canadian or American law (McLellan 1990).

But two levels of Quebec court would have allowed the father to veto the abortion. The hostility of these courts put Daigle's life at risk — an abortion at twenty-three weeks pregnant is far more dangerous to the patient than one at eighteen weeks. Daigle faced opposition or at least apathy from the state that should have protected her. The Quebec government did not intervene to support her when the courts put fetal rights before her own (Greschner 1990). Quebec police violated her privacy and exposed her health information. The federal government of Conservative Prime Minister Brian Mulroney even tried to exploit the high-profile, controversial nature of Daigle's case afterwards to introduce new legislation to recriminalize abortion. This attempt failed, and there has not been another since (Rebick 2008).

Daigle's ingenuity, bravery and persistence were widely and wildly celebrated. The public feted her in the streets (Bilodeau 2009). *Chatelaine* magazine named her the 1989 Newsmaker of the Year. Overwhelmed by press attention, she granted just two exclusive interviews, one to the British newspaper the *Mail on Sunday* and the other to Radio-Canada in Quebec. On her monumental role in reproductive rights in Canada, Daigle was straightforward and self-confident, saying, "Est-ce qu'il y a vraiment quelqu'un qui va oser mettre une femme en prison parce qu'elle a voulu faire valoir ses droits?" (Radio Canada 2019, 1; Is there actually someone who would dare put a woman in jail for wanting to assert her rights?).

Daigle proved prescient about the danger posed by Tremblay. The man who received injunctions from two courts to control the uterus of his ex-girlfriend was eventually sentenced fifteen times for domestic violence and criminal harassment (Blatchford 2008). Daigle testified against him in 2000 (CBC *News* 2000).

Clinic 554

In 2022 New Brunswick is the only province or territory that still, more than three decades after the *Morgentaler* decision, manages to uphold unconstitutional restrictions to abortion. These restrictions caused the closure (due to financial insolvency) of Clinic 554, the long-standing, and for the past twenty years the only free-standing, abortion clinic in the Maritimes. Although the current Liberal opposition claims it would do away with the lingering restrictions, New Brunswick's anomalous situation has persisted through many changes in the province's political leadership.

It is possible that by the time this book is published the winds will have finally changed. On January 7, 2021, the Canadian Civil Liberties Association filed a lawsuit against the New Brunswick Conservative government led by Blaine Higgs, challenging Section 2.a.1 of Regulation 84-20 of the province's 1984 Medical Services Payment Act (Poitras 2021). The Act states abortion is "deemed not to be entitled services" under the list of publicly insured services unless the procedure occurs in an approved hospital facility. "Abortion" in this case refers only to aspiration abortion, as medication abortion was not on the consciousness of regulators in the 1980s.

The specification that abortion only take place in hospitals, and not in free-standing clinics, has been in place since Conservative Premier Richard Hatfield passed Bill 92 in 1985 to prohibit abortion clinics in the province. Dr. Henry Morgentaler had sought permission to open a clinic in New Brunswick that year, and in so doing "ironically compelled the government to pass anti-abortion legislation" (Ackerman 2012, 77). Morgentaler undoubtedly inspired more than one province to make restrictive laws just to keep him at bay. In 1989 Nova Scotia similarly passed the Medical Services Act to prohibit abortion clinics in the province. Manitoba did the same in 1993. In 1995, after thirteen years without abortion services, PEI began paying for islanders to have procedures in Nova Scotia to undermine a lawsuit Morgentaler was poised to bring against it.

New Brunswick, like PEI, developed a provincial identity around a cultish adherence to antiabortionism (McTavish 2015). Borrowing the tenets of the law in England, New Brunswick was the first province in Canada to criminalize abortion provision, in 1810, eighty-two years before a federal law was legislated. In 1842 the province amended its law to remove a distinction permitting abortion before "quickening," the point around sixteen weeks when fetal movement is felt, making all abortion illegal. New Brunswick's law criminalized not only the people who performed the abortion but also the patient who sought care.

New Brunswick's Bill 92 butted up against the new federal Canada Health Act of 1985. Under the Canada Health Act, universality, comprehensiveness, accessibility, portability, and public payment became the five-chamber beating heart of the lauded Canadian health care system. Restricting services based on the type of building that care is provided in arguably violates all five principles. There are many reasons why a clinic may be a preferable environment for abortion care. Compared to a hospital, it is approachable and small, it can guarantee a pro-choice politic, clinical and counselling staff can focus on abortion care, and there are fewer logistical hurdles to get bloodwork, ultrasounds, and counselling. More than that, a clinic abortion entails less than half the costs of a hospital-based procedure. Excluding clinic services from public payment did not make any sense.

Despite the province's ambitions, Bill 92 did not keep Morgentaler out of New Brunswick. He announced plans for a clinic in 1991 and in June 1994 finally opened its doors on Brunswick Street in downtown Fredericton, next to a graveyard and a junior high school. The clinic had a waiting room, counselling services, a procedure room, a recovery room, and office spaces. In an effort to shut Morgentaler down, the province invoked the Medical Services Payment Act, arguing that abortion outside of hospital was impermissible, and the provincial College of Physicians and Surgeons restricted his medical licence for violating the Act. In September the New Brunswick Court of Queen's Bench ruled the province could not prohibit abortion clinics. The province appealed. Further, despite the Supreme Court of Canada having struck down the 1969 requirement for a Therapeutic Abortion Committee to approve publicly funded procedures in the 1988 *Morgentaler* decision, New Brunswick continued to require that patients seek approval from a committee of doctors prior to receiving hospital-based care. By choosing the private Morgentaler Clinic, patients avoided the bureaucracy of referral and the humiliation of seeking permission from a physician panel. However, this was not without cost: the clinic charged patients privately, about $700 to $850. Dr. Morgentaler subsidized patients who were unable to pay.

While this conflict about the application of the Medical Services Act was playing out, an important and convoluted case about fetal rights was also underway in the province. In March 1993 Cynthia Dobson, seven months pregnant, lost control of her car on the highway while en route to Moncton. She survived but required an emergency C-section to give birth to her son, Ryan. He was born with cerebral palsy, a set of permanent movement disorders, attributed to injuries he received while in the womb during the car accident. His grandfather, acting on Ryan's behalf, launched a civil lawsuit against the mother, seeking an award for damages to Ryan resulting from her "negligent driving." In 1997 the New Brunswick Court of Queen's Bench concluded such a lawsuit was allowed. The New Brunswick Court of Appeal agreed. Dobson's lawyer stated, "A mother is inseparable from the fetus during the nine months of pregnancy. To equate her risk and her duty of care to that of a third party discriminates against her: she is always at greater risk of liability" (Janigan 1998, 1). When the case arrived at the Supreme Court of Canada in 1998, most of the judges ruled in Cynthia Dobson's favour. Among their many reasons was concern that if a pregnant woman could be held liable for damages to her fetus, it would be up to the court to decide what constituted appropriate behaviour in pregnancy, something it simply could not and should not do. Despite the persistent antiabortion rhetoric in New Brunswick, which played out as an emphasis on fetal rights in the Dobson case, the Supreme Court of Canada favoured the autonomy of the pregnant person.

In 2002 Dr. Morgentaler announced he would take the province to court over its failure to fund procedures at his clinic. He issued a statement of claim the next year. The New Brunswick government's defence was that funding clinic abortions would be too expensive and furthermore it was unnecessary given the availability of procedures in several hospitals across the province. This rang false, as hospitals in Moncton and Fredericton announced cessation of abortion services at various points from 2000 to 2010. For several years during this period, antiabortion organizational leaders gummed up the courts with petitions for intervenor status in the lawsuit, although they were consistently denied. Access to abortion became exceedingly difficult: very few physicians were performing procedures in hospital, and those that were tended to limit procedures to a gestational age of twelve weeks or less. As mentioned earlier, gestational age caps for abortion are not an issue of law in Canada and instead are related to the individual health care practitioner's skills, comfort, equipment and resources. Larger centres such as Vancouver and Toronto have more patients requiring care at a later gestational age, and more practitioners who are competent at providing such care. However, New Brunswick also refused to fund procedures for patients who sought abortion care out of province.

Dr. Morgentaler's lawsuit rested on the court's determination he had standing in the case. In other words, was it right for him, a cisgender man not personally in need of abortion, to bring forward the case, as a matter of public interest? After protracted opposition by the province, he was granted standing in 2009 (CBC News 2009). There was not a conceivable alternative plaintiff: the acrimonious public attitude to abortion in the province, not to mention the enormous cost of legal action, barred an individual patient from taking on the burden of litigation. But Dr. Morgentaler died in 2013 before his court case could be decided (CBC News 2013).

After his death, things began to change. Without his personal subsidization, the clinic was not financially viable. It was usually only open on Tuesdays, a predictable routine that unfortunately attracted a reliable cache of antiabortion protestors and required a volunteer team of escorts to manage. Although Morgentaler himself had not performed the procedures for many years, he had always held responsibility for the practice, and no one wanted to pick it up. For a year, the clinic went unused. Then a collective of reproductive rights advocates, under the banner of Reproductive Justice New Brunswick, decided to fundraise to purchase the clinic from Morgentaler's estate and determine a future course from there. Reproductive Justice New Brunswick raised well over $150,000 through an online fundraiser, at a time when such campaigns were novel and rare. The funds were turned over to Dr. Adrian Edgar, a young family physician in Vancouver who had trained in abortion care as well as prison and street health and harm reduction (Leeder 2021). The future looked progressive and bright.

Dr. Edgar, once he finally had a New Brunswick medical licence and other logistics arranged, opened a full family practice in the Morgentaler building. He renamed it

Clinic 554, a reference to the Brunswick Street address, and painted all the railings in a rainbow as a proud marker of queer health services (Ibrahim 2020). One day a week (but not always Tuesdays) he would provide abortions, and all the other days of the week he could bill the province for his family practice appointments, including his specialization in care to support trans patients. Abortion patients continued to have to pay privately, despite Dr. Edgar continuing Morgentaler's vocal advocacy for public funding.

Buoyed by the success of the fundraiser, Reproductive Justice New Brunswick continued to advocate for changes to the province's unique abortion laws. The restrictions became a critical issue in the 2014 provincial election. When the Liberals gained power on a pro-choice platform, they removed the Therapeutic Abortion Committee requirement, established permanent abortion services in three hospitals and introduced a self-referral process. But they did not address Regulation 84-20's restriction on public payment to clinics. This lingering issue put Clinic 554 in a deeper bind. Effectively, the permanent, public hospital services reduced demand for abortion care at Clinic 554 and threatened the clinic's viability. Regardless, the clinic still served an important role — not only are clinic services often more convenient and more comfortable for patients, but Clinic 554 was the only provider of aspiration abortion in Fredericton, the provincial capital. Because of Dr. Edgar's skills and preferences, Clinic 554 provided abortions up to sixteen weeks, whereas the hospital services in New Brunswick usually stopped at fourteen. Stigma, cuts to intercity bus service and a family doctor crisis in the province mean two weeks of extra time to seek services could be necessary for some patients.

Reproductive Justice New Brunswick expanded its advocacy from a focus on abortion to petition New Brunswick to cover the cost of gender-affirming surgery, which the province agreed to fund in 2016 (McHardie 2016). A similar shift in policy to cover clinic-based abortions never came. Without public coverage for its abortion procedures, Clinic 554 struggled to stay afloat. Although operation of a full-time family practice made upkeep of the clinic more viable, and private payment was occasionally secured from abortion patients, this was not enough to compensate for the significant costs of running clinic operations, which included a counsellor and nurse, procedure and recovery rooms and specialized equipment and sterile instruments. In fall 2020 Dr. Edgar closed his family practice. Hundreds if not thousands of patients lost access to primary care. Dr. Edgar had focused care provision on oppressed and marginalized populations, especially trans and nonbinary people. The closure of Clinic 554 was a severe blow to the LGBTQ+ community.

In 2020 the federal health minister Patty Hadju held back $140,000 in federal transfer payments for New Brunswick as a penalty for violating the Canada Health Act by failing to fund essential care. The province had been warned before of such a course of action by many Liberal health ministers, including Allan Rock, Anne McLellan and Ujjal Dosanjh. The penalty did not cause New Brunswick to change course. The province spends over $2 billion on health care annually; a $140,000 fine simply does not go far enough.

The Canadian Civil Liberties Association lawsuit might work, but whether it happens in time to reverse the course for Clinic 554, already closed for over a year as of this writing, is very hard to imagine. New Brunswick has a long history of protracted disputes going nowhere. Out of what seems like a lingering grudge against Morgentaler, the province has worked hard to box the current formulation of the clinic into a corner. With medication abortion theoretically available in any primary care office, three hospitals providing abortion services in both official languages and coverage for out-of-province services for New Brunswick residents under provincial health insurance, the province paints Regulation 84-20's Section 2.a.1 as a minor nuisance. It would take nothing radical at all to upend it, just a stroke of the premier's pen (Save Clinic 554 2021).

iamkarats

It was the winter of 2016, and the guerilla image was popping up everywhere: a screen print of "Anne with an E" in her trademark orange braids, with a black bandana across her face and the hashtags #AccessNow #HeyWade #SupportIslandWomen. An anonymous pop artist, iamkarats, was papering the province with her revamp of the PEI's icon: a feminist Anne Shirley, ready for war.

In Lucy Maud Montgomery's eponymous 1908 novel *Anne of Green Gables*, the red-haired heroine is bullied on her first day of school by a boy named Gilbert Blythe, who calls her "Carrots." Enraged, Anne smashes a schoolhouse writing slate over his head and refuses to forgive him for many years. The name "iamkarats" was instantly understood as a cunning made-in-PEI response to the province's blatantly sexist and decidedly old-fashioned ban on abortion care, which by 2016 was thirty-four years running. The "Wade" in question in iamkarat's posters was then premier Wade MacLauchlan, sworn in to lead the province a year earlier. MacLauchlan was a professor of law, having held positions at the University of New Brunswick, University of PEI and Dalhousie University. His research concentrated on constitutional law issues, and he had clerked for the Supreme Court of Canada. Thus, he would have been deeply familiar with the province's Charter rights violations in failing to provide on-island abortion services. He was also entangled in the legacy of Anne of Green Gables as a partner and director of Anne China Inc. (Trudeau Foundation n.d.), a subsidiary of the Sunrise Group and the sole authorized distributor of Anne publishing and merchandise in China. The kerchiefed Anne that iamkarats created was a shrewd mascot for calling out MacLauchlan's failure to address the abortion ban he had inherited when he took office. Upending the wholesomeness of Anne's image, iamkarats also deeply offended the powerful antichoice movement on the island (Stewart 2016).

That same winter a lawsuit was underway to reverse the ban. The plaintiffs were an anonymized group called AANPEI, a clever Anne-themed acronym for Abortion Access Now PEI. The unincorporated group comprised frontline activists, students and professors at the University of Prince Edward Island, as well as long-standing feminist advocates in the community, including co-chairs Dr. Colleen MacQuarrie and Ann Wheatly. The national organization LEAF supported the suit under the leadership of pro bono lawyers Nasha Nijhawan and Kelly McMillan and their brand-new feminist firm in Halifax. Once the paperwork went in at the beginning of January in 2016, MacLauchlan had three months to figure out what to do. All winter long, protestors garbed up in homemade yarn wigs and kerchiefs and put the costume on statues around town — iamkarats quickly became legendary.

How PEI had made it to 2016 without a major legal challenge over abortion is a riveting drama; it was not without effort. Kate McKenna chronicles over three decades of struggle in *No Choice: The 30-Year Fight for Abortion on Prince Edward Island*. The antichoice lobby was incredibly strong on the island and especially effective in the 1980s in shifting public policy. Just under half of the island's 166,000 people identify as Roman Catholic and only 3 percent as non-Christian. Religious organizations provided financial resources, and clergy, nuns, nurses, doctors and teachers "provided the movement with authority when lobbying governments and hospital corporations" (Ackerman 2015, 15).

After partial decriminalization by the federal government in 1969, abortion was available to islanders, but it was uncommon, requiring a patient to plead their case to a Therapeutic Abortion Committee made up of at least three physicians. This bureaucratic requirement secured a path for legal access to abortion, but not without stripping patients of their decision-making autonomy. Having to seek physician agreement that an abortion was required for health reasons was shame-inducing, stigmatizing and sometimes unsuccessful for those who tried (Ackerman 2015; Mombourquette 2018).

Things got worse long before they got better. In 1982, just before the Charter of Rights and Freedoms became law, the secular Prince Edward Island Hospital and the Catholic Charlottetown Hospital merged to become the Queen Elizabeth Hospital in Charlottetown. The island's Right to Life Association inundated the election for the new hospital's Board of Directors with its own candidates, effectively making one of the conditions of the hospital merger that abortions would no longer be obtainable (Mombourquette 2018). In fact, the first decision of the newly elected board "was that there would be no abortions in that hospital" (Mombourquette 2018). The effectiveness of this strategy further empowered antichoice activists. In 1986 they flooded a meeting about the Therapeutic Abortion Committee at the Prince County Hospital in Summerside and won a vote to have it abolished, meaning that no abortions could be provided there.

Incredibly, the *Morgentaler* decision in 1988 cemented PEI's ban on abortion. In response to islanders' overwhelming disapproval of complete decriminalization, the provincial government under Liberal premier Joe Ghiz defiantly introduced Resolution 17:

> WHEREAS the Parliament of Canada must now legislate a new law concerning abortion;
>
> AND WHEREAS the great majority of the people of PEI believe that life begins at conception and any policy that permits abortion is unacceptable;
>
> AND WHEREAS the great majority of Islanders demand that their elected officials show leadership on the very important issue and demonstrate the political will to protect the unborn fetus;
>
> THEREFORE BE IT RESOLVED that the Legislative Assembly of PEI oppose the performing of abortions;
>
> AND BE IT FURTHER RESOLVED that this Resolution be forwarded to the Leaders of all three Federal political parties requesting the passage of legislation consistent with the intent of this Resolution. (PEI 1988, 90–91)

In essence, the island adopted an antichoice identity.

For the next three decades, patients managed without local access by taking the ferry, and later the Confederation Bridge, to Morgentaler's Fredericton or Halifax clinics, hospital-based services in New Brunswick or Nova Scotia or facilities even further afield. Throughout his lifetime Morgentaler was a constant antagonist to abortion restrictions. In reaction to a lawsuit he brought against PEI, the government quietly arranged in 1995 to pay for the costs of hospital-based abortion procedures for islanders at the Victoria General Hospital in Halifax. Patients required a referral from an on-island physician as well as an ultrasound, and the procedure had to be completed by sixteen weeks gestational age. The agreement with Nova Scotia got PEI off the hook for the constitutional violation the government incurred by banning procedures on the island, as it created a route for access, albeit a circuitous one that was poorly understood. Only due to extraordinary advocacy efforts by activists did the provincial government finally put information about this process on the website for Health PEI, the provincial health authority, in 2011 (Lewis 2014).

Until recently, a small but consistent number of the two thousand or so procedures happening every year in Victoria General Hospital's Termination of Pregnancy Unit were for patients from the island (Statistics Canada 2005). The PEI government claimed the island simply did not have the resources and willing providers to support an abortion service, and therefore it had to send patients elsewhere, as was the case for many specialized procedures. Except, of course, abortion is not a specialized procedure, nor were all physicians on the island unwilling to provide it. An aspiration abortion is a ten-minute procedure that can even be performed without anaesthesia if a patient consents to this. Family physicians routinely provide aspiration abortion care.

In 2013 Health PEI convened a working group to consider the business case for a twice-monthly, half-day abortion clinic at the Queen Elizabeth Hospital with care provided by three physicians, one local and two from off island. The group estimated the clinic would save the province tens of thousands of dollars every year compared to having to pay for out-of-province procedures, not to mention the personal travel costs patients absorbed privately. Dr. Rosemary Henderson, medical director of the Queen Elizabeth Hospital, and Richard Wedge, CEO of Health PEI, supported the proposal, presuming such a reasonable and cost-saving pitch would be acted on. Premier Robert Ghiz (son of Joe Ghiz) and Minister of Health Doug Currie reminded the health authority and the working group of the province's policy against on-island abortion procedures and shut the project down (CBC News 2014). But the justifiability of the ban, based on the argument that abortion care could only be provided off-island given the province's small population, was losing ground.

In the summer of 2014, the University of Prince Edward Island hosted an international conference on abortion access called the Unfinished Revolution. Organized by activist academics Shannon Stettner, Colleen MacQuarrie and Tracy Penny Light, the event was the first of its kind on the island and indeed in the country. It brought together activists, academics, clinicians and world-renowned experts to cover seventy topics in two days.

Dr. MacQuarrie presented research she and colleagues conducted to understand how islanders sought abortion care. They interviewed twenty-two participants who described a web of entangled barriers related to information, access, resources and travel. What these participants endured was indescribably cruel (MacQuarrie, Macdonald and Chambers 2014). Alicia Lewis (2014) analyzed International Classification of Diseases (ICD) codes — diagnostic and procedural codes that physicians also use for billing — for pregnancies with abortive outcomes from 1996, when PEI began paying for procedures, to 2013. She found illegal or self-induced abortions (ICD code 636) occurred in 1996, 2000, 2003, 2004, 2006, 2007, 2009, 2011, 2012 and 2013, with and without varying types of complications. Her research proved the ban on abortion was not actually stopping on-island abortion from happening.

After the decades of abortion exclusion, the province's position was becoming fragile. The conference, a brazen act in such an antichoice place, went off without a hitch, without violence or intimidation. And it may have lit a spark for the changes that were to come.

In 2015 a patient went public with her experience seeking abortion care from the emergency department at Queen Elizabeth Hospital. She had taken prescribed medication for an abortion but the results were not in line with what her doctor told her to expect. Medication abortion causes quite significant bleeding, and is not just "a heavy period" as some health care providers describe it. The patient called the province's health line and a nurse recommended that she get emergency medical attention. At the hospital she waited five hours to be seen and then was told by a doctor to go to the abortion clinic in Halifax (CBC News 2015b). The story was picked up across the country as an example not only of PEI's failure to provide adequate services but also of individual physicians perceiving they had a licence to deny care. The physician in question, Dr. Chris Lantz, wrote to the patient to apologize, which the patient posted to Facebook (CBC News 2015a). Social media was making it harder to hide what was happening on the island.

Activists in PEI, Nova Scotia and across the country gathered to strategize. Mobilizing a human rights complaint was difficult because the time limit ran out too quickly — once a person had recovered from the humiliation, shock or pain of navigating access barriers and mustered the courage to come forward, the one-year deadline to file with the PEI Human Rights Commission always seemed to have come and gone. A complaint to the PEI College of Physicians and Surgeons against clinicians who failed to refer patients properly would not work either, as people were terrified of losing access to primary care. The only option was a lawsuit.

On January 5, 2016, AANPEI filed a lawsuit against the province. Lawyers Nasha Nijhawan and Kelly McMillan had worked thousands of pro bono hours preparing the case. They argued the PEI government's position was unconstitutional as a violation of the Charter of Rights and Freedoms, including Section 7, the right to life, liberty and security of the person; Section 15, the right to freedom from discrimination based on sex and gender; and even Section 12, the right not to be subjected to cruel and unusual punishment. Premier MacLauchlan had three months to plan a response. He knew the law. Meanwhile, iamkarats was covering public spaces with positive propaganda. Before the April deadline came, the PEI government determined there was no argument to counter the evidence AANPEI's legal team had compiled. The province agreed to open an abortion clinic within the year.

The Women's Wellness Program opened in January 2017. Between then and August 2021, nine hundred abortion procedures were completed through the program. Aspiration procedures take place at a brand-new clinic space in the Prince County Hospital in Summerside. Additional services, such as medication abortion, pap tests and treatment for postpartum depression, are available in Charlottetown. Most services, including abortion, do not require a referral. The province went from having no abortion services on the island to providing some of the most accessible care in the country (Cadloff 2019; Paynter 2021). This success fuels inspiration for the reproductive justice fights ahead.

Chapter 3

HAVING CHILDREN

While the struggle for abortion access and the right not to have children is dominant in the history of white feminism, protecting the right to have children is disproportionately a Black and Indigenous struggle. Black and Indigenous families face elevated state threats against their rights to get pregnant and parent the children they choose to have in safe and sustainable communities. As described in the introduction, reproductive justice is a framework for examining how social justice, reproductive health and law intersect to support — or hinder — the right to determine how many children you will have, if you choose to have them, and how those children will live. Strategic state interference in some groups' rights to have children prevents those groups of people from thriving. Reproductive justice leader Loretta Ross (2017) describes state restraint of reproduction among a particular group of racialized people as *reprocide*: genocide through reproductive oppression.

Canada has pursued the reprocide of Indigenous people since its inception. The Indian Act of 1876 cemented policies that have caused generations of reproductive injustice. As Indigenous feminist scholar Sherry Pictou (2017, 17) describes,

> Most severely impacted were and still are the lifeways of Indigenous women, children, and Two-Spirited Indigenous people … as these legislative polices became institutionalized with Eurocentric heteropatriarchy coupled with racism. For example, Indigenous women were not allowed to vote in community elections, and women and their children would lose status if they married a non-Indigenous man. Even if an Indigenous woman did marry a status-Indian from another community (reserve), she was required to move to her husband's community.

That controlling women's decision-making and family arrangements was central to foundational Canadian law speaks to the grounding of state creation in reprocidal strategies.

Reprocide can manifest through many types of legal mechanisms, but the most obvious and egregious is state policy to remove reproductive organs and directly cause infertility. Permanent, surgical sterilization of state-determined "defective" individuals was the law in parts of Canada from 1928 to 1973 (Grekul, Krahn and Odynak 2004). Just as there was overlap between regimes of confinement of intellectually disabled people and the Indian Residential School system, so too are there parallels between sterilization programs focusing on intellectually disabled people and those targeting Indigenous people (Chapman, Carey and Ben-Moshe 2014; Chapman and Withers 2019). In the colonial project of Canada, eugenics policies disproportionately affected Indigenous families.

The invention of British statistician and scientist Francis Galton, eugenics manipulated the emerging understanding of genetics to argue for selective breeding of people of "good stock," defined through a distinctly racist, ableist and classist ideology. Galton unreservedly sought to bring about the "extinction of an inferior race" (Gunderman 2021). As philosopher Robert Wilson (2019, 69) has written, the "best-known part of the history of eugenics … was not about producing people with traits that enable them to thrive" but "instead about eliminating people with undesirable traits or preventing their birth." The "science" of eugenics merged with the politics of reprocide, to be exercised through the practice of medicine.

The first section of this chapter tells the story of an abused and unwanted child who was cruelly diagnosed as a "moron," institutionalized at age ten and sterilized at age fourteen (Muir 2014). *Leilani Muir* sued the province of Alberta in 1995 for reparations for the salpingectomy (removal of the fallopian tubes) she was unknowingly subjected to in 1959. She received a settlement of $740,000. A National Film Board documentary chronicled her experience, as did a 2012 play by David Cherios. She wrote a gripping memoir about her experience, *A Whisper Past: Childless after Eugenic Sterilization in Alberta*, in which she stated, "When I was born, God made me a whole person. When they sterilized me, they made me half a person. You never get over that hurt…. My philosophy is that history repeats, but as long as I keep talking about it, it will not happen again" (Muir 2014, 186).

The repeal of sterilization laws in the 1970s did not end the practice because racist ideology remains ingrained in clinical service delivery. In recent years, about a hundred Indigenous women have come forward with accounts of coerced sterilization surgery, one as recently as 2019 (Baig 2021). In most cases they were subjected to tubal ligation immediately following operative births, when they were exhausted, in pain, medicated and overwhelmed. The plaintiffs have launched class-action lawsuits, including a large action led by Mi'kmaw lawyer Alisa Lombard (Rao 2019).

The violence of forced sterilization is repeated in the violence of forced removal from community and family, which the Indian Residential Schools required and incarceration continues to require. Those of us who are horrified by forced sterilization cannot ignore the parallels. Residential schools and contemporary prisons have prevented Indigenous people from building their families by removing them from their communities, language and support systems; restricting contact with partners and children; and denying them traditional medicine, teachings and spiritual care (Battiste 2013).

During the spring and summer of 2021, while I was writing this book, thousands of un-marked graves were discovered at the sites of former Indian Residential Schools across Canada and the United States. There could be no more vivid example of reproductive oppression than state-authorized removal of children from families and placement into institutions in which they were abused and killed. Although the discovery of bodies shocked most people in Canada, it simply confirmed what Indigenous communities had long known. In her text *Out of the Depths*, survivor Isabelle Knockwood (2015) exposed the code of silence that children held in residential schools were forced to adopt. In 2015 the Truth and Reconciliation Commission, a public inquiry into the abusive operations of the residential schools, issued six calls to action related to missing children and burial information. The violent legacy of the residential school regime and other sequelae of the Indian Act continue to have a widespread impact. Mi'kmaw lawyer and Ryerson (X) University professor Dr. Pam Palmater describes contemporary Canada as "in a human rights crisis" (Somos 2021, 1). Reparations for state violence and prevention of further harm to Indigenous communities must be central to work for reproductive justice in Canada.

Other prominent restrictions on the rights to have children in Canada relate to access to fertility support and state recognition of LGBTQ+ family formations. Infertility affects at least one in six families in Canada (Canada, Public Health Agency 2019), resulting in enormous stress and expense. Although economic barriers to fertility treatment were publicly debated in the early 1990s through the Royal Commission on New Reproductive Technologies, treatment for infertility is, with a few small exceptions, not included in the definition of medically necessary care funded by the provinces and territories. Infertility can be caused by physical factors like age or blockages in reproductive anatomy, environmental factors like pollution or unknown reasons. Single people and LGBTQ+ families may require fertility clinic support to become pregnant. People facing intersecting oppressions of racism, homophobia, transphobia and poverty experience the physical and emotional strain of fertility treatment and the economic risks very differently than do white heteronormative couples with the economic means to pursue round after round of in vitro fertilization (IVF).

Crucially, inadequate regulation of reproductive technologies in Canada has also created space for exploitation of egg and sperm donors and surrogate gestational carriers. The second section of this chapter describes the history of federal legislation governing assisted reproductive services, and how *Leia Picard* saw a business opportunity in the gaps in regulation. The only person ever prosecuted for violating the Assisted Human Reproduction Act, her conviction led to the creation of clear guidelines for reimbursement of surrogates' expenses in 2019. The impact of their rollout remains to be seen, but equity issues in the field of fertility treatment are almost entirely unresolved.

Canada is considered a world leader in legal protections for LGBTQ+ people. Sexual orientation, gender identity and gender expression are protected grounds against discrimination under the Canada Human Rights Act. Since 1996 same-sex couples in BC have been allowed to adopt children, and Ontario was the first province to legalize same-sex marriage in 2003. Over time these provisions were adopted nation-wide. But labelling couples "same sex" and "opposite sex" fails to capture the realities of LGBTQ+ parenting. Laws in Canada are not keeping up with the dynamic forms of LGBTQ+ families. The third section of this chapter describes how *Kirsti Mathers McHenry*, who was legally married and legally permitted to adopt children, still had to fight for the right to be on her child's birth certificate. Ontario now allows up to four parents to be registered on a birth certificate, recognizing LGBTQ+ families may share responsibilities for parenting in many ways.

Upholding the right to have children clearly requires the state, and public servants like health care providers, to respect the reproductive autonomy of all people and resist entrenched stereotypes and discriminatory norms. Given that demand for reproductive technologies will only grow, developing regulations that support ethical, equitable access to and use of reproductive technologies should be a paramount priority for governments in Canada. Lawmakers must abandon anachronistic definitions of the family to embrace new models; it is in the best interests of children to be parented by all the people who love them.

It could be argued that no area of reproductive health and justice is shifting more rapidly than the right to have children, and these three stories are a small window into what has happened and what is possible.

Leilani Muir

Leilani Muir was eleven years old when her mother dropped her off at the Provincial Training School for Mental Defectives in Red Deer, Alberta, in 1955. As a condition of admission to the school, her mother signed a form stating, "I am agreeable that sterilization be performed on my child Leilani Marie Scorah if this is deemed advisable by the Provincial Eugenics Board" (Muir v. Alberta 1996).

Eugenics gained momentum in Canada in the early twentieth century, as eugenicists promoted the reproduction of upper- and middle-class white women and reproductive control of poor, disabled and nonwhite women (Dyck 2013a; de la Cour 2017). In the Depression era in particular, marginalized women were blamed for the costs their families imposed on state services such as public health and social assistance. Although the eugenic ideology first developed in Britain, the only place in the British Commonwealth in which it was "vigorously implemented" through law was Alberta (Wahlsten 1997, 185; see also Grekul, Krahn and Odynak 2004; Odynak 2004; Grekul 2008).

In 1928 Alberta passed the Sexual Sterilization Act with the objective of preventing "the transmission of any mental disability or deficiency." The Act called for the creation of a four-person Eugenics Board, represented by two physicians nominated by the University of Alberta and the province's College of Physicians and two nonmedical appointees nominated by the lieutenant governor. Candidates for sterilization were described as "inmates" of institutions nearing their release date into the community. The Act required consent from the patient or their parent or guardian and also protected surgeons performing the sterilizations from being held liable for their actions. But in 1937, through the Act to Amend the Sexual Sterilization Act, the requirement for consent from people deemed "mentally defective" was removed. The Sexual Sterilization Act was amended again in 1942 to add neurosyphilis, epilepsy and Huntington's chorea to the list of conditions making a person eligible for sterilization. However, the Eugenics Board only loosely adhered to legislated requirements (Muir v. Alberta 1996) and certainly sterilized more people than allowed by the law.

No one tested Muir's learning abilities or cognition before she was admitted to the Provincial Training School. When she was seven, her school at the time had referred her to a guidance clinic because she routinely stole lunches from other children, but there were no other references to unusual behaviour, and it is apparent she stole food because she was desperately hungry. Her mother starved, abused and humiliated her (Muir 2014). She arrived at the Provincial Training School covered in scratches but without evidence of any "mental defect." When her IQ was finally tested in 1957, two years after she had been institutionalized, she was thirteen years old. She received a score at the borderline of what was constituted mentally defective. Despite this borderline score, she was labelled "defective" and considered eligible for sterilization under the law (Muir v. Alberta 1996).

Muir was fed and clothed and had toys and company at the Provincial Training School, and she characterized it as an improvement over her abusive home life (Muir 2014). However, the experience was effectively detention. The monitoring she was subjected to was gendered and sinister. Her menstrual cycles were tracked and documented. Her letters were preread, her visitors few (Muir 2014). She slept in a cement room and ate from a tin bowl. Most egregiously, she was routinely subjected to unwarranted pharmacological treatment with antipsychotic drugs: "At breakfast they gave us medications. I remember the little cups they put the pills in, but we weren't told what it was for. Sometimes the medications were given by needle. Only much later in life, during preparation for the trial in 1995, did I learn that I and many other kids in the PTS [Provincial Training School] had been used as guinea pigs with powerful drugs" (Muir 2014, 40).

Muir was surgically sterilized in 1959, when she was fourteen years old. She was not about to be discharged from the facility, a requirement for eligibility for sterilization under the Sexual Sterilization Act. Indeed, she did not leave the Provincial Training School until seven years later. At fourteen she was a normal teenager with a developing sexuality, and the school administration evidently felt it had to be suppressed. A demonstration of "interest in the opposite sex" was noted in the application for sterilization (Muir v. Alberta 1996). Eugenics boards like those in Alberta and BC specifically targeted female sexuality, and promiscuous behaviour was a commonly cited reason for sterilization of institutionalized women and girls in BC (Stote 2012).

When the nurse took Muir in for surgery, which was performed at the Provincial Training School and not in hospital, she was told her appendix required removal. To justify this lie, an unnecessary appendectomy was performed as well as a bilateral salpingectomy, or removal of the fallopian tubes, which carry the ova from the ovaries to the uterus. When people talk about getting their "tubes tied," they are referring to tubal ligation, where the fallopian tubes are blocked off with a sterile clamp or tie, or perhaps cut, but not removed. The entire length of both of Muir's fallopian tubes were removed, rendering the procedure irreversible. After her first marriage ended, she sought medical advice to understand why she and her husband had not been able to conceive a child. Only then did she learn what had been done to her, and why.

Alberta sterilized over 2,800 people from 1928 to 1972, when the Sexual Sterilization Act was finally overturned (CBC News 2010a). About half of all applications to the Eugenics Board were approved. The number of people subjected to sterilization in Alberta is well above the number of people sterilized in BC, whose Act Respecting Sexual Sterilization was in effect from 1933 to 1973. The practice also occurred in other provinces and territories, even in the absence of legislation. People living in poverty, like Muir, were targeted and labelled "feeble-minded," as were immigrant women and Indigenous families.

Karen Stote (2012) has extensively studied how Indigenous women were targets for sterilization as part of the genocidal colonial project of Canada. She characterizes the federal government as complicit in Alberta's sterilization program, explaining that the federal government paid the surgeons who operated on Indigenous women through Indian Health Services. The federal government failed to object to the practice of sterilization even when it violated the terms of provincial legislation, such as those cases where there was inadequate consent and where the patient did not clearly meet the clinical eligibility criteria. Furthermore, the federal government created legislation deepening the oppression of Indigenous people generally, fuelling anti-Indigenous racism and increasing the likelihood they would be sterilized. A parliamentary inquiry into sterilization in Northern Canada in 1976 found shocking results: 12 to 21 percent of women of child-bearing age in six surveyed communities had experienced surgical sterilization (Stote 2012, 129). Of course, in all critical discussion of sterilization, it must be acknowledged that sterilization is not always coercively imposed. Many people choose it as a method of birth control, and in this period of history there were few contraceptive options available, particularly in rural and remote places (Dyck 2013b). Assuming all these procedures were performed coercively denies individual autonomy.

With decision-making power in the hands of a committee, Alberta's sterilization program was definitely coercive, and it targeted Indigenous people aggressively. As Stote (2012) recounts, a disproportionate number of Indigenous women were put before the province's Eugenics Board, and the number increased steadily over time until approximately 25 percent of sterilizations were being performed on Indigenous women. Over three-quarters of Indigenous people undergoing state sterilization in Alberta were labelled mentally defective and thus their consent was not legally required.

What happened to Muir did not meet any of the requirements in the Sexual Sterilization Act. She was not mentally defective. She was not about to be discharged. She had been in an institution designated for the mentally defective for two years before she was even assessed, which biased the mindset of those who eventually evaluated her IQ. Further, IQ tests are highly problematic, developed from and used to justify racist and xenophobic ideologies.

Muir did not consent to the bilateral salpingectomy. She was informed about the appendectomy, but the word "appendix" meant nothing to her (Muir 2014). Michelle Goodwin (2020, 156), a leading legal scholar of reproductive injustice in the United States, points out that "in the South, when Black girls were forcibly sterilized, doctors referred to the practice as 'Mississippi appendectomies.'" Muir was lied to by two levels of care providers, those in the Provincial Training School and those in the health system, and she was physically harmed in two ways, through sterilization without her consent, and through an unnecessary appendectomy performed for the purpose of covering up the sterilization procedure. These were unquestionably violations of the most basic bioethical principle of not doing harm.

When Muir was twenty-one, her mother took her out the school, and she again suffered abuse in her home. "I did not leave the PTS [Provincial Training School] because I was formally discharged. My mother more or less kidnapped me," wrote Muir (2014, 64–65). "I was her captive." She escaped and married an abusive man. She divorced and married again, hoping to adopt children, but her application was rejected on the grounds of her historic institutionalization for mental defectiveness. Her choice to have a family was doubly erased by the experience of state care: she would never experience pregnancy, and she was disqualified from adopting.

Learning she was not actually "mentally defective," Muir sued Alberta in 1996 for the harms of the surgeries and the impact of a life spent mislabelled. She had her IQ tested by BC clinical psychologist George Nicholas Kurbatoff and scored 87. At trial, Kurbatoff said, "I was surprised — based on her history, I was — I was quite surprised that she had the score that she did. I can't — and I can't account for why she scored as high as she did" (Muir 2014, 130–31). Her childhood score was, of course, manufactured as part of a classist, abusive eugenics scheme.

The success of her lawsuit is remarkable not only because she was the first in Canada to sue for damages from state sterilization policies, but also because of damning language used by the judge: "Because the government's own standards for sterilization were ignored in Ms. Muir's case, the conduct of the government was more than negligent, it was intentional. The sterilization became an assault and battery.… The defendant's actions were unlawful, offensive and outrageous" (Muir v. Alberta 1996, 18). The judge made clear that Muir's sterilization was not an unfortunate accident but deliberate violence, something for which the state must accept responsibility.

Muir received close to one million dollars for damages and legal costs. Her extraordinary memoir details her childhood abuse, her struggles in adulthood, the legal case and its aftermath. She toured the country to speak out about forced sterilization and its immeasurable impact on her physical and emotional life.

Just before her death in 2016, news stories began emerging about forced and coerced tubal ligations and sterilizations of Indigenous patients after they had given birth by C-section at Saskatoon Health Region hospitals in Saskatchewan. The health region enlisted Dr. Yvonne Boyer, a nurse, lawyer, professor and member of the Métis Nation of Ontario, and Dr. Judith Bartlett, a Métis family physician and professor of medicine, to conduct an external review. With the help of an Elder and a First Nations woman hired as a review assistant, Boyer and Bartlett began the work in 2017. As the reviewers wrote,

> The loss of identity through colonizing actions such as the Indian Act, residential school policies, mental health laws, forced removal of children and the Sixties Scoop are some of the determinants that have contributed to erosion of women's roles in Aboriginal cultures. Eroding the position of Aboriginal woman as caregivers, nurturers and equal members of the community inflamed the false colonial perception that Aboriginal women were somehow worthless and free to be exploited. (Boyer and Bartlett 2017, 6).

In other words, these colonial systems are the root of the extreme harm Indigenous people experience in the present day, including pervasive poverty, intimate partner violence and incarceration.

The team conducted interviews with seven Indigenous patients who reported forced tubal ligation procedures following childbirth in Saskatoon. The overarching theme in these interviews was "feeling invisible, profiled, and powerless" (Boyer and Bartlett 2017, 2). Patients described being spoken to by nurses and physicians as if the decision for sterilization was already made or as if it was a negligible procedure. Some said when they told the health professionals they did not want the procedure, they were ignored. They could not stop what was happening because they were in need of health care. "It feels like, if you go to the doctor to have a broken finger fixed and they cut off your hand to fix the finger problem," said one participant. "I went to have a baby, not a tubal ligation" (Boyer and Bartlett 2017, 19) The impacts of coerced sterilization included emotional distress and mental health disorders, relationship breakdown and disengagement from the health care system.

Addressing the violence of sterilization requires health systems and providers to acknowledge the systemic racism in operation, and the Boyer and Bartlett review found many providers simply did not understand the incredible power differential between the Indigenous patients in their care and their position as care providers. This occurred despite the reckoning about anti-Indigenous racism in health services demanded by the inquiry into the death of Brian Sinclair, which released its report in 2017. Sinclair, an Indigenous man, was ignored in the waiting room of a Winnipeg emergency department for thirty-four hours in 2008 while nurses and physicians assumed he was drunk. He died of sepsis (Brian Sinclair Working Group 2017). Meaningful action remains wanting.

In response to the 2015 news stories about forced sterilization, Saskatoon hospitals rushed to implement a policy against making tubal ligation decisions during pregnancy. But this approach creates new barriers for people who want the procedure but do not have a family practitioner to help them after they give birth as well as those who come for care from the northern part of the province and would have to travel a second time for the sterilization procedure. It impedes autonomy.

The Boyer and Bartlett review called for changes to training and education for care providers, restructuring of the health region to include Indigenous governance of care and development of a reproductive care centre providing wraparound support. The latter now exists in the form of Sanctum 1.5, a ten-bed home in Saskatoon with 24/7 nursing care for pregnant and postpartum mothers at risk of child protection involvement. The review authors also argued reparations were needed for those harmed by discriminatory clinical practices (Boyer and Bartlett 2017). In 2018 a class-action lawsuit was launched in Alberta on behalf of Indigenous patients who experienced forced sterilization in the province (Koskie Minsky 2018). Similar lawsuits have been filed in Manitoba (Cohen 2020) and Saskatchewan (Zingel 2019). In summer 2021 the state of California approved a plan to compensate victims of its forced sterilization regime (Foster 2021). The generations of harm caused by forced sterilization cannot be remedied, but reparations are a minimal requirement to signal state responsibility for the harm caused.

Leia Picard (Swanberg)

In 2013 Leia Picard was convicted in the first and thus far only prosecution in Canada under the Assisted Human Reproduction Act for purchasing ova, paying surrogates and taking payment for arranging surrogacy agreements (Motluk 2014). Picard ran a company called Canadian Fertility Consultants in Brighton, Ontario, 150 kilometres outside of Toronto. For years she had advertised for egg donors through online classifieds sites like Craigslist and paid them $5,000 per donation. Surrogates were remunerated approximately $2,000 per month of pregnancy. Clients paid up to $150,000 for Picard to match them with surrogates. All of this was entirely against the law, but what was permitted under the law was less than clear.

The first fertility clinic in Canada was established in 1980 in Laval, Quebec, under the direction of Dr. Jacques Rioux and a researcher named Raymond Lambert. Two years later Dr. Victor Gomel launched an IVF program at University of British Columbia, and in 1983 the country's first successful delivery of an IVF pregnancy, where the egg and sperm are combined in a laboratory setting and then transferred into a uterus, was registered in Vancouver (Yuzpe 2019). The industry grew rapidly, without any regulation.

To inform the development of a regulatory regime for the industry, in 1989 the Conservative federal government appointed the Royal Commission on New Reproductive Technologies, a ten-member expert panel led by Dr. Patricia Baird, a geneticist based at University of British Columbia. The commission held hearings in seventeen sites during fall 1990 to gather information from members of the public about their hopes and concerns regarding assisted reproduction technologies including IVF, artificial insemination and surrogacy (Royal Commission on New Reproductive Technologies 1991). Over 550 people presented. Feminist organizations at the time spoke about how the technologies had the potential to "erode rather than enhance women's reproductive choices" (Cox 1993, 87) because the new options could place patients in physical danger or put pressure on families to accept more interventions.

The commission published a summary of the public hearings in 1991. Major themes included concern about the power of reproductive technologies, with vast potential consequences, and the breadth of consideration required in providing services with these technologies. The public felt that they lacked adequate information about risks and effectiveness and that the medical profession was not adequately involving them, especially women, in decision-making. Access was a critical interest: Would the technologies be universally available? On what grounds would access be determined? Would LGBTQ+ families be included? How would infertility and need for service be defined — is infertility a clinical or social issue? Furthermore, what were the equality implications of these technologies? Would they increase discrimination against people with disabilities? Would racialized women be exploited in surrogacy or coerced into sterilization? Ongoing regulatory mechanisms were needed, and presenters at the hearings "said that the participation of women was particularly vital, as it is ultimately women who are most affected by these decisions" (Royal Commission on New Reproductive Technologies 1991).

The Royal Commission on New Reproductive Technologies released its final report in 1993 with two sets of recommendations to the federal government. The first was to introduce Criminal Code prohibitions on the sale of ova, sperm, zygotes and fetal tissue, on the use of embryos in cloning research and on interference in the autonomy of pregnant people. The second was to create a National Reproductive Technologies Commission to license and monitor reproductive technologies and practices. It took eleven years for federal law to catch up: in March 2004 Bill C-6, the Assisted Human Reproduction Act, received royal assent. The Act criminalized cloning, paying for surrogacy, arranging for surrogacy and paying for sperm, ova or embryos — "except in accordance with the regulations" (Canada, Department of Justice 2004, s.12). There was broad public agreement that reproduction ought not be for sale. However, altruistic donors and surrogates would have expenses that should be reimbursed. To do otherwise would be exploitative, with the most marginalized people in society likely to face the greatest risk of exploitation. Where, exactly, were these regulations?

The demand for assisted reproductive care boomed. By 2019 there were at least thirty-three fertility clinics in Canada, up from two in 1982 (Yuzpe 2019), though none were located in New Brunswick, Newfoundland and Labrador or the territories. Statistics Canada found that infertility in heterosexual couples, defined as the inability to conceive after twelve months of trying, also grew during this period, from 4 percent in 1984 to 12–16 percent by 2010 (Bushnik et al. 2012). The proportion of babies born in Canada through IVF increased from 0.7 percent in 2001 to 1.8 percent in 2012 (White 2016). Almost all the costs of this care are borne privately. Ecofeminist Greta Gaard (2010, 105) argues new reproductive technologies "medicalize and thus depoliticize the contemporary phenomenon of decreased fertility in first-world industrialized societies, personalizing and privatizing both the problem and the solution when the root of this phenomenon may be more usefully addressed as a problem of PCBs, POPs, and other toxic by-products of industrialized culture that are degrading our personal and environmental health." Excluding fertility services from the basket of medicare not only skews access towards the white, wealthy and heteronormative, it also obscures public responsibility for preventing and addressing ecological causes of rising infertility.

People seek fertility services for a number of reasons. Clinical infertility can be caused by physiological issues, like blocked fallopian tubes or ejaculatory ducts, inflammation caused by endometriosis, hormonal imbalances or abnormal sperm. Assisted reproduction patients also include cancer survivors, because of the impact of chemotherapy, radiation and transplants on fertility, and people with sexually transmitted and blood-borne infections like HIV. Single people and LGBTQ+ families may seek fertility support for social reasons. The World Health Organization (2020) recognizes access to fertility treatment as a human right. In Canada this is largely discussed as a right to affordable treatment, not the right to personal and environmental health described by Gaard (2010).

By paying egg donors and hiring surrogates, Leia Picard unquestionably broke the rules of the Assisted Human Reproduction Act, but it was unclear at the time how exactly she could reimburse the donors and surrogates she worked with. Intended parents did not object to her requests for payment. Picard asked donors and surrogates to provide receipts for their expenses, but she did not specify what expenses qualified, and her payments to donors did not necessarily correspond to their receipts. The RCMP investigated Picard only after being tipped off by US law enforcement, who found Picard had collaborated with an American fertility lawyer, Hilary Neiman. Neiman falsified documents and was imprisoned for defrauding the US government (Stickney 2011).

Bioethics scholars including Dr. Françoise Baylis, Dr. Jocelyn Downie and Dr. Alana Cattapan had long warned of the consequences of the federal government failing to provide clear direction on the matter of reimbursement. Without clarity or enforcement of the law, commercialization of the body becomes very likely. When she first faced the charges, Picard said she would challenge the constitutionality of Canada's law, which she described as "abusive to those trying desperately to become parents" (Blackwell 2013, 1). She obviously wanted to help families: she was a surrogate herself, three times (Picard n.d.). She admitted, however, that her business practices "crossed the line" (Motluk 2014). It was obvious she was accepting fees from clients far above what could be considered reimbursable costs for donors and surrogates. Picard pled guilty and received a $60,000 fine. The lawsuit provided her with publicity that more than made up for the cost. She continues to work in the field under the name Leia Swanberg, running a surrogacy agency called Egg Helpers with locations in Ontario and BC. Since her conviction, she reports demand for her services has quadrupled (Motluk 2016).

After Picard's conviction, the federal government invited a private organization to draft standards on the specific issue of surrogate reimbursement. A series of public consultations followed. In this midst of this, Liberal member of Parliament Anthony Housefather introduced a private member's bill in 2018 to reverse the major tenet of the Assisted Human Reproduction Act and allow commercialization of assisted reproduction (Harris 2018). The bill failed to move forward, but it highlighted the urgency of clarifying surrogate reimbursement. In 2019 the federal government finally put the regulations in place — a full fifteen years after they were required by law. The regulations permit reimbursement for travel, dependent care, doula services and prenatal classes, counselling, legal services, food, insurance, telecommunications and birth-related expenses (Canada, Department of Justice 2019).

These regulations mark significant progress in creating a just context for assisted reproduction in Canada. However, a major issue first considered by the royal commission goes unaddressed: equity in access. Financial coverage for infertility treatment varies widely across the country. So does physical proximity to a clinic, which has consequences for travel expenditures. Ontario is the only province with a funded IVF program and seventeen clinic locations (Stasiuk 2020). Quebec used to fund three rounds of IVF but stopped in 2015 because of the cost, and now provides a tax credit for receiving services at one of the province's seven clinics. Manitoba also offers a tax credit, and New Brunswick provides a one-time $5,000 grant. Outside of Ontario and Quebec, twelve other clinics are spread out across the country.

The economic pressure has physical consequences. A single round of IVF costs $10,000 to $20,000 (Lee 2018). The industry-described success rate for IVF is 23 percent (Canadian Fertility and Andrology Society 2016). To improve the odds, multiple embryos are often implanted per cycle. Carrying multiples increases the health risks to the pregnant person, the risk of preterm delivery and the likelihood of associated complications. Research found surrogates are more likely to experience multiple implantations, raising questions about the extent to which they are fully informed about and genuinely consenting to treatment (White 2016).

Without public funding, access to assisted reproduction is highly unequal. In 2010 Statistics Canada found women in the highest income quintile were the most likely to seek assistance with fertility issues (Bushnik et al. 2012). This a question of income inequality, but it is also one of ageism, ableism and discrimination based on sexual orientation and family status. How is it some provinces, including Ontario, Quebec, New Brunswick and Manitoba, offer support for fertility treatment costs, while the others provinces and territories do not (Scala 2019)? There are also differences in coverage depending on the cause of the infertility: a myomectomy procedure to remove fibroids in the uterus that may be interfering with implantation would be covered, but medications to support egg retrieval would not. Unsurprisingly, fertility businesses are keen advocates for expanding public funding.

The demand for assisted reproduction technologies will only continue to grow. With one hurdle now overcome, there is a need to develop cross-country coherence in financial coverage and eligibility to reduce unequal access to the right to have a family. The people most affected by these issues — people experiencing clinical and social infertility, and the donors altruistically willing to support them — must be central to decisions about how this rolls out.

Kirsti Mathers McHenry

Until 2016, if a lesbian couple had a baby using anonymous donor sperm in Ontario, only the mother who physically gave birth to the baby could be registered on the child's birth certificate. The other mother had to go through the legal processing of adopting her own baby, at a cost of about $5,000. In contrast, if a heterosexual couple used donor sperm, both parents could be listed on the birth certificate.

Lawyer Kirsti Mathers McHenry faced the terrifying prospect of not only becoming her child's sole living parent but also not being legally recognized as the child's parent when her wife, Jennifer Mathers McHenry, had heart trouble while in labour with their first child, Ruby, in 2009. Although Jennifer survived, Kirsti was scarred by the fear and anger she had felt. Later, going through the process of seeking legal approval to adopt her own child, she felt anxious and demoralized. She said when the adoption authorization was granted, "the judge suggested we take a picture and, in shock, I posed for the camera. We took a picture and celebrated the most direct discrimination at the hands of the law that I have ever experienced" (Mathers McHenry n.d.).

The Ontario Superior Court had already ruled on this issue several years prior. Four sets of parents, all lesbian couples, launched a Charter challenge over provisions in the Vital Statistics Act that excluded nonbirth parents from being immediately named as legal parents to their children. One set of parents, BV and BA, were a married couple who used known donor sperm to conceive a pregnancy. When their baby was born in 2005, they refused to go through the required adoption process, "stating it felt immoral and dishonest to them to do so" and they saw "no difference between their situation and that of a heterosexual couple who have used donor sperm to conceive" (MDR v. Ontario 2006, 2). But then BA, the birth mother, developed breast cancer, leaving the couple with ambiguity about what their child's legal parentage would be if BA died.

The other families all used anonymous donor sperm to conceive. The deputy registrar of Vital Statistics refused to register both LE and RF, a lesbian couple, on their child's birth certificate, and also would not allow the child to take a hyphenated surname using both parents' names. When the couple separated, the status of the nonbirth parent was unclear. The third lesbian couple, MDR and MPS, used MDR's ova for IVF, and two embryos were then implanted in MPS. MDR was denied parental status, but as the birth mother, MPS was registered on the birth certificates, although the twin babies had none of her genetic material. The fourth lesbian couple, RNG and VD, felt they were devalued and their child was stigmatized by the state when rather than include VD, the nonbirth parent, on the birth certificate, the registrar advised they leave the spot for the second parent "completely blank" (MDR v. Ontario 2006, 3).

Represented by prominent feminist lawyers Martha McCarthy and Joanna Radbord, the applicants in MDR v. Ontario argued that to be required to go to court to ask permission to adopt their own children was an affront to their dignity, made lesbian motherhood invisible and failed to recognize their humanity. As the Lesbian Parents Project

Group stated in a submission to the Court, "Equal familial status sends a powerfully positive message to all social institutions that have an influence on our children's lives. It obliges them to acknowledge and respect the families our children live in" (MDR v. Ontario 2006, 54). You should have the right for your child to be your child. Judge Paul Rivard ruled that the purpose of the birth certificate is to provide a "foundational document," and if it fails to accurately document a child's parents, it fails in its purpose. He declared the birth registry provisions of the Vital Statistics Act violated Section 15 of the Charter and were therefore invalid. In January 2007 amendments to the Act allowed an "other parent" to be added in addition to the biological mother, but only if the biological father or sperm donor was unknown. If known, his name would be listed, even if he had no intention of parenting (Manitoba Law Reform Commission 2014).

When Kirsti and Jennifer's second child, Cy, was born in 2014, Service Canada rejected Kirsti's application for parental benefits. Canada is revered internationally for offering widely accessible parental benefits through the federal Employment Insurance program. Kirsti had paid into the insurance program every year of her working life. To Service Canada though, because she was not a parent under the eyes of the law of Ontario, she was ineligible for parental benefits. The definition of parents in Ontario remained one mother and one father/other parent.

Both lawyers with graduate degrees in constitutional law, Kirsti and Jennifer took on the fight (Fulford 2017). To change the law, they joined forces with Peter Taubuns, their member of provincial parliament, and Reverend Cheri DiNovo, arguably the foremost member of provincial parliament when it came to the advancement of LGBTQ+ rights. DiNovo was the minister who officiated the first official same-sex marriage in Ontario and had succeeded in passing a bill to add gender expression and gender identity to the Ontario Human Rights Act in 2012 (Ontario 2012). In 2015 she presented private member's bill 137, An Act to amend the Children's Law Reform Act, the Vital Statistics Act and other Acts with respect to parental recognition. Nicknamed the Cy and Ruby Act, Bill 137 would remove "mother" and "father" from the birth certificate and replace them with "parent" and "parent." Kirsti and Jennifer Mathers McHenry's team had modelled the proposed legislation on what was already in place in BC, and it passed with support from all parties.

In 2016 Ontario's All Families Are Equal Act clarified that the people who donate sperm or ova for use in assisted reproduction are not considered the parents of the child conceived as a result. A person who gives birth to a child is the child's parent, as is a person whose sperm, through sexual intercourse, results in the conception of a child. A spouse of someone who gives birth to children conceived through assisted reproduction is also a parent of the child. Preconception agreements about parentage will be honoured. A child may have up to four intended parents, and the parents do not need to be married, living together or romantically involved.

While the Ontario approach has yet to be emulated elsewhere in Canada, in 2018 Justice Robert Fowler of the Newfoundland and Labrador Supreme Court family division ruled that three unmarried adults, a polyamorous family, could be listed on the birth certificate of their child (MacDonald 2018). "I have no reason to believe that this relationship detracts from the best interests of the child," he said, observing that polyamorous families had not been considered when the Children's Law Act was passed (MacDonald 2018, 1). Similarly, in 2021 BC Supreme Court Justice Sandra Wilkinson ruled a triad could be named on the birth certificate of their son (Proctor 2021).

Family law in all provinces and territories will have to continue to adapt, and quickly, to all the forms families can take, while upholding the inherent dignity of people who intend to parent and recognizing it is in the best interest of children to be parented by those who choose the role.

Chapter 4

PARENTING IN SAFETY

The right to parent in safe and sustainable communities involves layers of social, political, economic and environmental protections. In the absence of these protections, it is individual parents — and disproportionately Black, Indigenous, low-income, queer and disabled parents — who experience punishment and child removal. Black feminist scholar Dr. Beth Ritchie (2012, 56) explains, "A key dimension of the hostile social world created for Black women is the stringent regulation by public policies that constrain the opportunity to lead health, safe, full, and self-determined lives." She gives the example of "child welfare policies that apply harsh sanctions against women who have difficulty performing tasks associated with their duties as mothers" (Ritchie 2012, 56). Similarly, Indigenous activists and survivors in Canada have dubbed the ongoing removal of children from Indigenous families the Millennium Scoop, echoing the Sixties Scoop and, of course, Indian Residential Schools (Cardinal 2018; CBC News 2018). To be able to parent in safety demands human rights protections across all aspects of life: it pushes consideration of reproductive rights far outside of sexual and reproductive health care into social, political and environmental domains. But because these all circle back to impact the well-being of parents and children, they are connected to the work of health care providers and reproductive rights activists. Reproductive justice exposes how racism and colonialism shape who is protected and who is not, whose children are protected and whose are not.

This chapter covers just some of the key issues this aspect of reproductive justice unearths. Parents need to start out with access to high-quality, unbiased information about safe pregnancies. Pregnant people need to govern what happens to their bodies during pregnancy, not only in terms of safety from obstetric violence in labour and birth but also from state control of their bodies throughout the whole nine months of pregnancy. Instead of being stigmatized and punished for poverty and discrimination, parents need relief from these social harms and supports to parent. As they grow, children need protection from violence and neglect, including and especially violence and neglect inflicted by agents of the state such as police and social workers. Children also need to grow in environments that are sanitary and adequately resourced. Asking for these things should not be too much; these basics should inform the organization of all public services.

The first section of this chapter puts together two critical incidents in the history of how Canada has failed to protect the right to parent. In the early 1960s, inadequate drug safety regulation resulted in serious birth defects among the children of people who were prescribed thalidomide. The government needed to be more cautious about drug approval, and people needed more information about the impact of drugs in pregnancy. From 1985 to 2019, *Motherisk* operated a national toll-free helpline to provide information about the safety of substances for pregnant and lactating people. Motherisk also opened a laboratory to test for the presence of drugs in hair samples. The laboratory's work ended up supporting a neoliberal provincial agenda in Ontario to exclude families from social assistance by requiring recipients submit to mandatory drug testing. Positive test results were used in child custody decisions and even criminal cases. However, the testing was faulty, and it had catastrophic results.

The next section explains the 1996 fight of *Donna George* to have control over her own body during pregnancy, after the province of Manitoba took her to court to force her into rehabilitative treatment. The war on drugs in the United States and Canada was and remains a state tool to criminalize trauma and retraumatize families through carceral health, foster care and prison systems. George fought Manitoba's Department of Child and Family Services all the way to the Supreme Court of Canada. Her success prevented serious escalation of state interference in the rights of pregnant people. It is unthinkable what surveillance and forced treatment pregnant people might have had to endure had she not been so determined and well supported by feminist and Indigenous organizations.

In the immediate postpartum period, people in Canada can be subject to a gross infringement on their rights to parent through a blunt state instrument known as "birth alerts." This describes the practice of a hospital alerting child protection services when a person on their radar gives birth. Child protection services then removes the newborn from their parent's care, usually while the parent is still recuperating in hospital, based on information obtained during pregnancy and the perceived potential for harm to the child. These perceptions, of course, rely on systemic racism and stereotypes circulating in the health and social welfare systems (Smylie and Phillips-Beck 2019).

The third section of this chapter recounts how *Baby H* was removed from her mother's care while the mother was still in hospital, convalescing from an operative delivery, and in no way demonstrating active neglect or abuse. Baby H's family, like most who are subjected to birth alerts, is Indigenous. Most children in foster care in Canada are Indigenous, although only about 8 percent of children under 14 years old in the country are Indigenous (Indigenous Services Canada 2021). The first of the Truth and Reconciliation Commission calls to action was that all levels of government work to reduce the number of Indigenous children in state care (Truth and Reconciliation Commission 2015). The National Inquiry into Murdered and Missing Indigenous Women and Girls (2019) identified birth alerts as a contemporary manifestation of colonial policies like the residential school regime, the Sixties Scoop and forced sterilization, and called for their end as a necessary step in addressing cultural genocide in Canada. Although most of the provinces and territories in the country have banned them, birth alerts continue.

Reproductive justice scholar Dr. Dorothy Roberts (2020, 1) calls the foster care system the "family policing system," rejecting the language of care or protection to emphasize the violence and control that child protection agencies enact. For many children, state care is a site of routine sexual, physical and emotional abuse — of willful neglect and disenfranchisement. As described in this fourth section, Somali refugees *Fatuma Alyaan* and her brother, Abdoul Abdi, endured unspeakable violence as children in foster care in Halifax, Nova Scotia. Fatuma was trafficked and had her children taken from her as a teenager. Abdoul was traumatized, criminalized and federally imprisoned at age eighteen. The Children's Aid Society never bothered to apply for citizenship for either of them. Fatuma's bravery and tenacity rescued her brother from deportation. Now she is suing the state for damages.

State agencies can inflict vast harm, but another crucial thread to the right to parent is the safety of the physical environment for child-rearing. The complex interaction between climate catastrophe, ecological collapse, environmental destruction and reproduction is deserving of many books devoted to this issue alone and is furthest from my area of expertise as a nurse and health services researcher. This fifth section focuses on the impact of poisoned water on reproductive health in Canada, describing just some of the critical activist efforts of *water protectors* for community survival. Poisoned water will poison families for generations. It is a state responsibility to regulate water safety, to oversee wastewater management, to fund responsible public infrastructure and programs that protect water sources and the people who use them.

Climate change indisputably puts every family in Canada at risk, but racism and colonialism are so deeply ingrained in public works policies that Black and Indigenous communities face disproportionate burdens from poor environmental and infrastructural planning. Environmental racism describes the systemic practices that download pollution and ecological harms onto Black and Indigenous people. Reproductive justice demands antiracist action for environmental justice. As Mohawk midwife Katsi Cook (2007, 32) describes, "Environmental justice and reproductive justice intersect at the very center of woman's role in the processes and patterns of continuous creation … we as women are earth." There must be an acknowledgement of and action to address how environmental catastrophe is gendered and threatens both fertility — as described in Chapter 3 — and the right to parent in safety.

This chapter is a condemnation of colonial, xenophobic and racist state practices in relation to their impact on the right to parent. It is also a celebration of extraordinary people resisting these practices with all their might.

Motherisk

Healthy pregnancy depends on having the knowledge and resources to keep both the pregnant person and the fetus safe. Inadequate information or misinformation can cause significant harm and spur generations of fear. Canada has a tarnished history of drug safety for pregnant people with a cascade of harmful effects.

In 1961 thalidomide officially entered the Canadian market under the brand name of Kevadon (Thalidomide Victims Association of Canada n.d.). Physicians prescribed the drug, a sedative that at the time was believed to be harmless and effective, for the treatment of nausea in pregnancy. By December 1961 several European countries had pulled thalidomide from pharmacy shelves. There were enough concerns the drug might have been responsible for a wave of severe birth defects — that it might be a dangerous teratogen — to merit caution. A teratogen is any substance or infection that, when administered to or experienced by a pregnant person, can cause fetal abnormalities. Alcohol is one of the most known teratogens; the teratogenicity of measles is why vaccination is encouraged for all pregnant people. Canada, however, did not ask the manufacturer to withdraw the drug from the market until March of 1962. Sample packets remained in the hands of medical professionals across the country for months after that.

Thalidomide is believed to have affected 24,000 babies worldwide, including a hundred in Canada (Lexchin 2018). Much of the tragedy could have been prevented through a more rigorous drug approval process. Canadian pharmacist Dr. Frances Kelsey, working for the Food and Drug Administration in the United States, was lauded for her precautionary approach to thalidomide: she insisted on reviewing evidence from the manufacturer demonstrating the drug was safe in pregnancy, and when they failed to provide it, she refused to approve it. Canadian families were doubly failed when the Canadian Food and Drug Directorate did not respond immediately to concerns about the teratogenicity of the drug.

To prevent a repeat of the thalidomide tragedy, in December 1962 the Canadian government amended the Food and Drug Act to limit distribution of samples and to prohibit the sale of certain drugs, including thalidomide (Herder et al. 2014). However, the federal government could not require manufacturers to provide safety information, could not issue recalls on unsafe products and could not impose tough penalties for noncompliance until 2014 when the Protecting Canadians from Unsafe Drugs Act received royal assent.

In the 1970s people across North America learned of the teratogenic effects of diethylstilbestrol, a synthetic estrogen that physicians had prescribed for the prevention of miscarriage since 1938. Although studies as early as 1953 demonstrated the drug was not effective in miscarriage prevention, it continued to be prescribed during pregnancy until research showed a connection between in utero exposure to the drug and vaginal and cervical cancers. In the 1980s evidence emerged that in utero exposure to diethylstilbestrol also caused developmental issues related to the penis, urethra and testes, including microphallus, urinary problems and sterility (McQuaig 1980). In Canada, although the federal Ministry of Health and Welfare advised physicians to contact exposed patients, few did, resulting in alarm and confusion among people who wondered if they (or their parents) had taken it (McQuaig 1980).

With these tragedies in the background, in 1985 the Motherisk program opened at SickKids pediatric hospital in Toronto with the express purpose of educating pregnant and lactating people about "potential risks to a developing fetus or infant from exposure to drugs, chemicals, diseases, radiation, and environmental agents" (Lang 2015, p. 68). Motherisk was the tonic to the fear the thalidomide and diethylstilbestrol scandals had caused. Pregnant patients or their care providers could call Motherisk for information both about the potential impact of prescribed medications and of nonprescribed drugs and alcohol. The program was attached to a research laboratory that conducted hair analyses to understand drug exposures in pregnancy.

In 1995 Progressive Conservative Mike Harris was elected premier of Ontario on an austerity platform the party called the Common Sense Revolution. Its key feature was slashing public funding for education, health care and welfare (Hennessy 2015). It was a war on the poor. Harris made it illegal to receive both welfare benefits and student loans in 1996. This measure notoriously led to the death of Kimberly Rogers, a student in her thirties who was convicted of "fraud" for continuing to claim both student loans and social assistance. She wrote in a court affidavit, "I do not know whether or not I will receive the help I need, and currently live one day at a time. Emotionally, I am doing worse, and I worry all the time about how I am going to care for this child inside of me" (MacKinnon and Lacey 2001). Destitute, alone, and unable to pay for medications for her depression, Rogers died by suicide on August 9, 2001. She was eight months pregnant. Her death is a stark symbol of the reproductive injustice characterizing the era: punishing poverty so harshly it resulted in generations of death.

In 2000, during Harris's second term, the Ontario government introduced mandatory drug abstinence for welfare recipients and a testing regimen to enforce it. Those found to use drugs had their welfare eligibility rescinded. Drug policy scholar Susan Boyd (2019, 111) describes how "it [was] against this environment that the MDTL [Motherisk Drug Testing Laboratory] began to move away from studying drugs in hair to more aggressively promoting drug testing services to child protection agencies throughout Ontario." Ultimately, welfare agencies in five provinces paid for tests.

Making money off a program that cut people off welfare proved lucrative; the Motherisk laboratory's hair analysis business brought in millions of dollars for SickKids. Reciprocally, SickKids, an internationally lauded centre for pediatric care and science, lent credibility to the laboratory's practices. SickKids did not, however, oversee the laboratory's practices or scrutinize the capabilities of lab staff to see if they could do what they claimed to be doing. From 2005 to 2015, Motherisk analyzed hair samples from sixteen thousand people under investigation by child welfare agencies. It also occasionally produced evidence for criminal cases.

One of those cases was against Tamara Broomfield, a Black woman and mother to a two-year-old boy named Malique. In 2009, based partially on testimony provided by Dr. Gideon Koren, the founding director of the Motherisk program, Broomfield was convicted of administering cocaine to her toddler over the course of more than a year. On appeal in 2014, Dr. Craig Chatterton, the deputy chief toxicologist in the Office of the Chief Medical Examiner of Alberta, called Motherisk's methods into question (Lang 2015). Broomfield's conviction was thrown out, but she had already served a forty-nine-month sentence and permanently lost custody of her son.

The Ontario government appointed Susan Lang to conduct an independent review of Motherisk's work. In her report, tabled in December 2015, Lang found the lab's methods were inadequate, unreliable and not in keeping with international forensic standards. Black feminist scholar Robyn Maynard notes the Motherisk hair testing suffered not only from social bias but also from physiological bias: "Persons with black hair may demonstrate concentrations of drugs up to ten times higher than other hair colours" (Maynard 2017, 202). Lang rebuked SickKids for failing to provide oversight of the laboratory under its roof, and she called for a review of child protection and criminal cases that had made use of Motherisk test results.

A month later Ontario appointed Judith Beaman to lead the Motherisk Commission and legally review affected cases. Beaman titled her 2018 report *Harmful Impacts*. Beyond the cruel impact on fifty-six families who lost custody of their children in part due to Motherisk's fraudulent findings, Beaman recognized that systemic use of faulty tests in twenty years' worth of cases had led to deep public distrust of the child protection and legal systems. The harm was disproportionately felt by Indigenous communities: of the twelve hundred cases the commission reviewed, 15 percent of the families were Indigenous, despite being only 3 percent of Ontario's population (Mendleson 2018). Lack of race-disaggregated data prevents analysis of how racism and colonialism affected other groups, but one can surmise given the disproportionately racialized populations in prisons and state care. The impact on affected families was permanent: generally speaking, adoptions cannot be undone and children returned to their original parents.

The consequences of this series of oversight failures — the approval and distribution of thalidomide and diethylstilbestrol and the workings of the Motherisk laboratory — are long-lasting. In 2014, at age 52, thalidomide survivor Mercédes Benegbi led a national campaign for the federal government to demonstrate accountability for the thalidomide tragedy through meaningful financial reparations. In 2015 Canada introduced the Thalidomide Survivors Contribution Program to provide each survivor a lump-sum support payment of $125,000 as well as access to a medical assistance fund for those facing extraordinary circumstances. Bruce Wenham, also a survivor, launched a class action, alleging the program was excessively difficult to qualify for and provided inadequate financial compensation. Four years later, it was replaced with the Canadian Thalidomide Survivors Support Program, which is "intended to contribute to meeting the needs of Thalidomide Survivors for the remainder of their lives so that they may age with dignity" (Canadian Thalidomide Survivors Support Program n.d.). Under the new program, survivors can receive $250,000, or a top-up of $125,000 if they were already paid under the previous program (Canada 2019).

Meanwhile, the discredited Motherisk laboratory closed in 2015. The Motherisk helpline and website, which were a go-to information source for pregnant and lactating people and their care providers, closed in 2019 (SickKids 2019). There is no central service in Canada providing evidence-based information on the safety of drugs in pregnancy and lactation; individuals are advised to contact their care providers. Research has found that people are generally reluctant to use medication in pregnancy and overestimate the teratogenic risks (Ceulemans et al. 2019). While careless approval and prescription of potential teratogens is a serious reproductive justice issue, so is restricting needed medications for pregnant people.

Forgoing necessary medications in pregnancy can have a host of negative consequences for the person who gives birth. As but one example, depression is one of the most common complications of pregnancy, and untreated depression is associated with preeclampsia and other health problems before, during and after birth (Dubovicky et al. 2017). Understanding the safety of medications in pregnancy and lactation is necessary for reproductive health but is so often dismissed as too challenging to do. Most recently, despite evidence COVID-19 was more severely experienced by pregnant people, they were excluded from vaccine trials and faced conflicting recommendations about whether to vaccinate (Rubin 2021).

For people to safely parent the children they choose to have, those children must be protected from teratogenic harm. The impacts of drugs and alcohol should be well researched through transparent and ethical processes, and findings should be made easily available to keep the public informed. The dangers must not be inflated.

To parent in safety, families also need state support for income equality. Requiring drug and alcohol abstinence from individuals on social assistance is discriminatory, invasive and ineffective at reducing the incidence of substance use disorders and improving child well-being. The use of drug tests as a marker for parenting ability is unconscionable, a relic of racism, colonialism and misogynistic stereotypes of what is acceptable parenting. Parents use drugs and alcohol: this is a fact, not a disqualification for parenting. The following section describes some innovations in Canada to support parents who use substances.

Donna George

Donna George was twenty-three years old and pregnant with her fourth child in 1996 when Manitoba's Department of Child and Family Services took her to court to force her into rehab (CBC News 2010a). George, an Indigenous woman, was the youngest child in her family and had seven siblings. Her mother died when she was very young, leaving her in the care of her father. He relinquished custody of the children to Manitoba Child and Family Services in the early 1980s. George moved to Winnipeg at the age of thirteen. She was forced to live on the street and sold sex to survive. By taking her to court, Child and Family Services pitted the future rights of her fetus against her current rights to govern her body, even though, as was already established in cases like Chantal Daigle's, the fetus does not have rights in Canadian law.

George's substance use included the inhalation of glue vapours, which produces short bursts of euphoria and is associated with damage to the nervous system, heart, liver and lungs. Two of George's children has been born with disabilities attributed to substance use during her pregnancies. Identified in the case as Ms. G., George was characterized by Child and Family Services as "unwilling to stop sniffing glue" despite the harm it could cause the fetus. Then and now, substance use disorder is misunderstood as a choice, not as a response to trauma, pain and suffering (Hirsh 2020). Rather than address the root causes of trauma and offer therapeutic and social support and safer substances, people who use substances are criminalized, marginalized, isolated and re-traumatized (Tyndall and Dodd 2020).

The Manitoba Supreme Court judge ruled George could be forced into treatment for substance use. George appealed the ruling against her, and the Manitoba Court of Appeal judges overturned it. Child and Family Services then brought the case to the Supreme Court of Canada, insisting George and all pregnant people owed a "duty of care" to the fetus. But this duty falls inequitably and only on those people who can get pregnant, and should be protected by the Charter right to freedom from discrimination based on sex and gender.

This case presented a conflict not just between the rights of pregnant people and fetal rights but also between health care providers' ethics and court decisions. Forcing treatment is a direct and clear violation of patient autonomy (Ubel, Scherrkmath and Fagerlin 2017). Health care providers cannot ethically provide treatment unless a patient has provided full and informed consent; this requirement is clear in professional codes of ethics and practice guidelines (Beauchamp and Childress 2001; Canadian Nurses Association 2017). But health care providers regularly find themselves caught between justice systems and patient autonomy. They may be asked by police officers to draw blood for forensic toxicology (Warner, Walker and Friedmann 2003) or expected to treat an incarcerated patient in shackles (Clarke and Simon 2013). Expert clinical opinions are routinely sought to support (or defend against) criminal charges (Iacobucci and Hamilton 2010). Health care is itself hierarchical and authoritarian

(Green et al. 2017), and providers are as likely as anyone to absorb norms of obedience to structures of power, including the justice system. Health care providers may fall into the paternalistic line of thinking that forced treatment is "for the patient's own good," despite codes of ethics requiring them to centre patients in clinical decision-making.

Further, the value of substance use treatment is up for debate. Many of the available treatment programs for substance use disorder require physiologically painful experiences of withdrawal, complete social detachment from support systems and subservience to religious authority. Treatment programs can also be sites of gendered violence and sexual assault (Brown 2017). Even with full and informed patient consent, treatment programs are not all the same, and they are not all clinically effective.

A coalition of provincial and national health care providers and advocates came together to intervene in George's case to prevent what could have become an overarching and gendered threat to patient autonomy. The Women's Health Rights Coalition was led by the Winnipeg Women's Health Clinic, an abortion clinic with a long history of leadership for reproductive justice. Other members included the Métis Women of Manitoba, Native Women's Transition Centre, Manitoba Association for Rights and Liberties, LEAF, Canadian Abortion Rights Action League and Canadian Civil Liberties Association (Tait 2002). The coalition sought and received intervenor status to appear before the Supreme Court of Canada, where it put forward five positions in support of Ms. G. and patient autonomy (Canadian Women's Health Network 1997):

(1) Forced treatment simply does not work.

(2) Forced treatment will result in less health care seeking. If Child and Family Services is allowed to force treatment, people who use substances in pregnancy would rationally expect the agency to also remove their children from their custody once they are born. They would avoid care.

(3) The requirement of treatment is more likely to be forced on marginalized women, such as Indigenous women like George.

(4) Forcing treatment does nothing to address the underlying causes of substance use, such as colonialism, racism, violence and trauma.

(5) Ruling the fetus has a right to care places all women (people) who could theoretically get pregnant at risk of state control over their actions and bodies.

As the case was making its way to the Supreme Court of Canada, George took matters into her own hands, just as Chantal Daigle had done, and sought treatment of her choice, voluntarily. Despite this, Child and Family Services persisted with the case, seeking a ruling that would empower the department to force other pregnant people into treatment. In June of 1996, seven of the nine Supreme Court justices ruled against Child and Family Services. George's resistance has protected untold numbers of people from forced treatment in pregnancy.

This type of state control evolved differently in Canada than in the United States. In the 1980s Shirley Brown, a white nurse from South Carolina, launched a campaign to criminalize prenatal drug use and force pregnant people into treatment regimes. Her campaign targeted Black women (Roberts 1997). Brown's efforts seeded laws across half of the United States that classified substance use in pregnancy as child abuse, subject to duty to report. These laws remain on the books today.

When nurses, social workers and other health care providers approach issues of health such as substance use or food insecurity with a lens of punishment instead of one of compassion, the result is a perversion of care. George, like all parents in her position, deserved support. The contemporary phenomenon of removing children from families because of classist and racist assumptions about an inability to parent is a reincarnation of historic oppressive systems including sterilization programs and institutionalization.

The need for compassionate support is increasing. Canada is experiencing an overdose crisis based largely on a poisoned supply of opioids (Tyndall 2020). The crisis worsened with the emergence of COVID-19 and remains underappreciated as a major threat to public health. The impact of the crisis is gendered. Not only are mothers more likely to face social consequences for opioid use, such as the removal of their children by the state, but research has also found that women experience sociodemographic and clinical differences in risk factors associated with overdosing.

There is so much to consider, starting with pregnancy. Birth is the most common reason for hospitalization in Canada (Canadian Institute for Health Information 2019) and one-third of births are operative, meaning delivery via C-section (Redden 2017). Patients usually receive an opioid prescription for postpartum pain management, and women are more likely than men to develop opioid use disorder after being prescribed opioids. Women are also more likely than men to use opioids to cope with pain and emotional distress and more likely to have a diagnosis of depression or posttraumatic stress disorder (McHugh et al. 2013). In fact, women are twice as likely as men to develop posttraumatic stress disorder (Olff 2017). Broadly speaking, women develop substance use disorder more quickly than men (Becker, McClellan and Glover Reed 2017) and present for substance use disorder treatment with more severe clinical problems associated with substance use (Greenfield et al. 2010). Women experience worse physiological symptoms of withdrawal than do men (Becker and Chartoff 2019). For those under the age of seventeen, girls are more likely than boys to experience nonfatal overdose (Bagley et al. 2020).

Opioid agonist therapy refers to when a patient receives a lower risk opioid, such as suboxone or methadone, in place of a higher risk opioid. These substitutes have a longer half-life, meaning they have a longer effect on the body before a person experiences withdrawal symptoms. Opioid agonist therapy does not work for everyone, and there is increasing support in Canada for access to safe supplies of shorter half-life substances, including heroin, to decrease the risk of using poisoned products. Improved access to safer supplies of substances such as heroin and of equipment for substance use reduces the risk of overdose, withdrawal symptoms and blood-borne infection. It is particularly important to prevent withdrawal in pregnancy because withdrawal symptoms can cause miscarriage.

Canada now has several evidence-based support programs for pregnant people who use substances in cities across the country. One of the first, Sheway, was established in 1993 in Vancouver's Downtown Eastside. This community-based service for pregnant people and parents in the neighbourhood is based on a philosophy of flexibility and nurturing, meeting people where they are at. It aims to increase access to perinatal care, improve maternal and infant nutrition, reduce the risk of substance use and support parenting goals, and it recognizes that the threat of child removal will impede all these things. Sheway is paired with YWCA Crabtree Corner, an early learning and childcare centre, and has a clinical floor for exams and treatment as well as a community-centre space for meals, sharing circles and resources including pregnancy wear and infant clothes.

When pregnant people are nearing their due date, they may be admitted to Fir Square, a dedicated unit at BC Women's Hospital in Vancouver for parents experiencing substance use disorder in the perinatal period and their babies. Fir Square, which opened in 2003 and was renovated recently, now has a kitchen, laundry facilities, program rooms, a smoking patio and a centralized nursery. The program aims to support emotional and physiological health and to discharge parent and baby to safe housing together in the community, usually several months postpartum.

A newer program launched in 2018 in Saskatoon. Sanctum 1.5 is a ten-room home in the downtown area with 24/7 nursing coverage, where pregnant people at risk of Child and Family Services involvement, who have substance use disorders or who are living with HIV, reside during pregnancy and for a few months after their babies are born. Saskatchewan has the highest rate of HIV in Canada, at twice the Canadian average, which has been described as a localized epidemic (CATIE 2018). Strains of HIV are adapting to the immune defences of people in the province, causing more virulent disease. Across Canada, Indigenous mothers with HIV and injection drug users with HIV are more likely than other pregnant people to receive suboptimal perinatal care, increasing the risk of HIV transmission to the baby (Singer et al. 2020). A person is less likely to seek treatment if they fear their baby will be taken from them because of their drug use. Indeed, a large study in Manitoba found women who have had one child taken from them by Child and Family Services avoid seeking prenatal care in future pregnancies (Wall-Wieler 2019). Sanctum 1.5 was created to address these risks. Recently, it received a large grant to support prenatal care (Vescera 2021). To achieve clinical goals like reducing vertical transmission of HIV, the program had to satisfy the social goal of preventing removal of children from their families. Sanctum 1.5 prioritizes this goal and is achieving success.

Several perinatal hospitals across the country have instituted what is known as rooming-in therapy for parents with substance use disorders and babies who show signs of prenatal exposure to substances and are experiencing symptoms of withdrawal. Instead of stigmatizing parents who use drugs and separating them from their babies, rooming-in therapy allows the parent to stay in the same room as the baby 24/7, hold the baby for skin-to-skin contact as much as possible and breastfeed or chestfeed. These methods reduce the need to treat the baby with medication and reduce the length of stay for babies in hospital.

In different ways, Sheway, Fir Square, Sanctum 1.5 and rooming-in all use harm reduction approaches. Potential harms associated with opioid use and injection drug use include acute (sepsis) and chronic infection (HIV, hepatitis C) and overdose, as well as miscarriage, preterm delivery, neonatal complications and infant withdrawal in the perinatal context. These health harms are directly preventable by providing pregnant people access to safe equipment, safe spaces to use and safer substances (Kolla et al. 2019). Harm reduction includes human rights–oriented policies and practices that are nonjudgmental and noncoercive with respect to what people choose to do with their bodies (Vasilakopoulos 2020). "When applied to substance abuse, harm reduction accepts that a continuing level of drug use (both licit and illicit) in society is inevitable and defines objectives as reducing adverse consequences. It emphasizes the measurement of health, social and economic outcomes, as opposed to the measurement of drug consumption" (Canadian Paediatric Society 2008). Simply put, harm reduction aims to reduce suffering and maximize well-being.

Refusing to report parents who may use drugs to child protection services is an essential element of harm reduction for reproductive justice because it breaks the cycle of traumatic family separation. Reproductive justice and harm reduction also include decriminalization of all drugs, so people who use drugs are protected from the racist and colonial violence of policing. Harm reduction is not only about safer use of substances — it's about addressing the social causes of substance use. Problematic substance use is often a consequence of the harms of childhood abuse and trauma (Werb et al. 2018), so these latter threats to well-being must be addressed to substantively reduce risks associated with substance use. Safe consumption sites, needle exchange and even safer supplies are not enough when the trauma of racist, colonial and gendered violence persists.

Despite the progress made in Canada over the last three decades, George's case should not be construed as a clear victory. Enormous government resources that could have been directed to support for truly helpful interventions — housing, health care and nutritious food — were instead used against her to fight a losing legal battle. Public health ministries and substance use treatment programs continue to inadequately address the unique needs of women, trans people and nonbinary people. Drug use, clearly a health issue, remains criminalized. George's victory has not prevented the postpartum involvement of child protection services in the lives of marginalized families, or the removal of children from their parents' arms as soon as or immediately after they are born.

Baby H

The case of Ms. G. confirmed that child protection services cannot put the rights of a future child before its parent's and interfere in a pregnant person's life. In Canada the fetus and the pregnant person are one and the same. Only after a baby is born do they become a person under the law. The state can then immediately take the newborn from the family through a process known as birth alerts.

If representatives of child protection services are concerned a pregnant person is likely to place a child at risk after birth, they communicate the concerns to the hospital where the birth is likely to occur so the patient is red-flagged. When the patient is admitted in labour or for a planned operative delivery, the hospital staff are obligated to inform child protection services. Everyone in Canada, whether they are a physician, nurse or person walking down the street, has a duty to report potential or actual child abuse or neglect to child protection services. A birth alert prompts a duty to report. Once the child is born, representatives from child protection services come to physically remove the baby from the parent's custody, usually while parent and baby are still hospitalized. The baby might be cared for in one room under the observation of a child protection services representative, such as a foster parent or a staff person. Meanwhile, the postpartum parent will be cared for in another room, and may not be permitted to see, hold or feed their baby.

For optimal infant and maternal health, skin-to-skin contact, breastfeeding and rooming-in are clinically recommended in the early postpartum period. It has been commonly known for over half a century that interfering with a child's attachment to the primary parent in the first two years of life has long-term consequences for the child's emotional, cognitive and social development (Bowlby and World Health Organization 1952). Physical contact between a newborn and their mother improves infant physiological outcomes like heart and lung function (Moore et al. 2016) and reduces the risk of postpartum hemorrhage for the birth parent. Early physical separation of the birth parent and child places the breastfeeding relationship in jeopardy. The potential harms of not breastfeeding include increased risk of infant infection and of childhood and maternal chronic diseases, including cancer (Dieterich et al. 2013; Victora et al. 2016; Bartick et al. 2018).

It is in the best interest of a child to be with their parents. The Convention on the Rights of the Child stipulates that a child has a right "to know and be cared for by his or her parents" (United Nations General Assembly 1989, Article 7). If the state requires an infant and parent to forgo the beneficial experience of being together, it should account for the harm caused. The benefit of removing a child while still under the care and surveillance of 24/7 clinical staff should be highly compelling. The risk of not doing so should be clear if clinical staff are to allow child protection services into the private space of a postpartum parent's earliest hours with a newborn.

In June 2019 Baby H was born to two first-time Indigenous parents in their thirties at the Kamloops Royal Inland Hospital. Within ninety minutes of her birth by C-section, representatives of the BC Ministry of Child and Family Development showed up to re-

move her, citing reports of neglect. The C-section is a large abdominal incision through multiple layers of tissue and involves the physical removal of the baby from the incised uterus. C-section births require significant medication for the birth parent, such as local anesthesia like bupivacaine and pain medication like fentanyl. After the procedure it may take two or more hours for the patient to regain feeling in their legs, and vomiting, dizziness and exhaustion are common. All postoperative obstetric patients require close monitoring and treatment from experienced nursing staff. They cannot be expected to independently care for their newborns.

On her daughter's behalf, Baby H's grandmother negotiated with the Child and Family Services staff members, but they returned two days later and took the newborn away while the mother was medicated and sleeping. Baby H was taken to a non-Indigenous foster home. No reason was given for why the child was removed.

There are forty-three hundred Indigenous preschool-age children in foster care in Canada (Barrera 2018). Fifty-two percent of all children in care across the country are Indigenous. In some provinces, the proportion rises to 70 percent (Hampshire 2016). The Truth and Reconciliation Commission (2015, 5) called for the federal, provincial, territorial and Indigenous governments to reduce the number of children in state care and to provide "adequate resources to enable Aboriginal communities and child-welfare organizations to keep Aboriginal families together where it is safe to do so, and to keep children in culturally appropriate environments, regardless of where they reside." What happened to Baby H is a clear repetition of colonial practices recognized to have genocidal impacts: Indigenous children taken from their families and communities lose language, culture and the security of being home, belonging and feeling loved.

Two weeks after Baby H was apprehended, her parents had their first opportunity to appear in court to regain custody. The judge ruled if the parents were to care for her, either the maternal or paternal grandmother would have to live with them in their apartment and supervise their parenting around the clock. This caused conflict — who would they live with? Neither Baby H's mother nor father knew the other's parents well. The paternal grandfather disputed the need for grandparent supervision, arguing the family had yet to hear the reason for the apprehension in the first place (Ridgen 2019). Almost immediately after getting her home, the couple got into an argument with the paternal grandmother, who called the police, who called Child and Family Services. Baby H was removed again.

A year later, in 2020, her baby brother was born preterm, and Child and Family Services apprehended him directly from his incubator (Ridgen 2019). COVID-19 restrictions have resulted in layers of barriers for parents to visit children who have been taken. At the time of writing, Baby H and her brother had not been returned to their parents' custody. No reason for the birth alert had been provided to the family. This lack of transparency about child protection investigations impedes families from righting whatever wrong they are suspected of.

Mi'kmaw lawyer Pam Palmater describes what happened to Baby H as "race-based genocide" (Martens 2019, 1). Building on the Sixties Scoop pattern of removing Indigenous children from their families for placement in white households, John Beaucage coined the term "Millennium Scoop" to describe the current disproportionate numbers of Indigenous children in foster care (Canadian Press 2011). The Truth and Reconciliation Commission (2015) called on governments to reduce the number of Indigenous children in state care. The National Inquiry into Murdered and Missing Women and Girls (2019, 24) specifically called on governments to "end the practice of targeting and apprehending infants from Indigenous mothers right after they give birth." Though construed as intended to prevent harm, the removal of children from Indigenous families and communities is clearly harmful and a structural determinant of negative health outcomes (Ritland et al. 2021).

The very possibility of birth alerts causes terror for some families. Indigenous parents are less likely than non-Indigenous parents to seek health services because they fear child protection services will become involved with their families (Denison, Varcoe and Browne 2014). A study in Manitoba showed that mothers whose first child was apprehended were less likely to seek prenatal care in their next pregnancy when compared to mothers who did not experience child apprehension (Wall-Wieler et al. 2019). The removal of a child is also linked to parents' deteriorating mental health and social status (Kenny et al. 2021) and an increase in the likelihood of developing substance use problems (Wall-Wieler et al. 2017). Young Indigenous mothers whose children are removed are twice as likely to attempt suicide than those young Indigenous mothers who do not experience child removal (Ritland et al. 2021).

The harms of child removal all disproportionately affect Indigenous families. Manitoba, which has the most children in care per capita in the country, studied the impact of birth alerts and concluded they did not improve child safety (CBC News 2020). In PEI, Kelly Peck, the province's director of child protection, said, "There have been many indications that some expectant parents will avoid seeking prenatal treatment and connecting with community services in order to avoid that alert being placed with the hospital" (Desjardins 2021, 1). Parents living in fear of child removal cannot be expected to seek out or even accept support from the same agency that has the power to take their children away.

A birth alert may be put in place for a long list of potential risks to a child: If the mother was previously incarcerated, even if she is now in community. If the father was abusive, even if the parents are not living together anymore. If one of their previous children was in foster care, even if the context of their lives has changed significantly since. If the parent themselves was placed in foster care as a child. Potential risk is interpreted by child protection workers through a colonial lens.

BC announced a ban on birth alerts in September 2019 (McKenzie 2021). The Yukon and Alberta banned the practice that same year. In 2020 Manitoba and Ontario announced bans of their own. PEI, Saskatchewan, Newfoundland and Labrador, New Brunswick and Nova Scotia joined them in 2021 (Chandler 2021; Cooke 2021; CTV News 2021; Whiffen 2021). The Northwest Territories said birth alerts have not been in effect in the territory for a decade. The practice continues in Quebec (Ambroise 2021; Vikander and Marelj 2021).

To get a picture of the scope of the issue, consider Nova Scotia, where there are about eight thousand births per year, and where a hundred birth alerts were reported in 2019 (Smith 2021). The province has about a thousand children in foster care (Nova Scotia 2019), 23 percent of whom are Indigenous (Aboriginal Children in Care Working Group 2015), although only 6 percent of children in the province are identified as Indigenous. Ontario does not track birth alerts, but 442 children were removed from their families within the first month of their lives in 2019 (Howells 2020). Recognition that birth alerts disproportionately affect Black and Indigenous families prompted the Ontario Ministry of Children and Women's Issues to discontinue the practice. Systemic racism in social and health services has resulted in disproportionate child protection investigations of Indigenous families and disproportionate representation of Indigenous children in foster care across every province and territory. Most child welfare workers in Canada are non-Indigenous (Aboriginal Children in Care Working Group 2015), and these non-Indigenous state representatives are deciding what is best for Indigenous children.

Research has found the dominant reason Indigenous children are taken into state care is not child abuse but neglect (Aboriginal Children in Care Working Group 2015). Neglect is largely a product of poverty, which among Indigenous communities is rooted in long-standing colonial policies and practices. Jurisdictional conflicts about the remedies persist, as provinces and territories fight with the federal government about which is responsible for supporting Indigenous families. There are gaps in terms of what each level of government offers, and it is confusing to navigate between them. This continues despite the 2007 federal adoption of Jordan's Principle (Union of Nova Scotia Mi'kmaq n.d.), which holds that Indigenous children should be prioritized over jurisdictional disputes. Educational, health and child welfare needs should be addressed by whichever level of government a family encounters first — a determination of who is ultimately responsible for covering the costs can occur later.

A ban on birth alerts is symbolically important, but it has yet to be seen if they make a difference in people's lives or the numbers of Indigenous children in state care. Baby H's brother was taken in the spring of 2020, a full six months after birth alerts were supposed to end in BC. To reverse the harms of birth alerts, provinces and territories will need to make family preservation and harm prevention the overarching goal of state services. Addressing systemic anti-Indigenous racism is necessary to shift the over-representation of Indigenous children in state care: "stopping cycles of apprehension and respecting Indigenous self-determination over child welfare is critical to the future health of Indigenous children, families and communities" (Ritland et al. 2021, 13). The best interests of Indigenous children are prioritized when Indigenous people are centred in the development and governance of services (Aboriginal Children in Care Working Group 2015; Ritland et al. 2021).

Fatuma Alyaan

In January 2018 Fatuma Alyaan attended a town hall in Halifax organized by the office of Prime Minister Justin Trudeau. She asked the prime minister, a father of three, if he would deport his own children (Jones 2019). She was trying to save her younger brother from that fate. "Why aren't you helping my brother? If it was your son, would you do anything to stop this?" she asked.

Fatuma moved to Canada in 2000 with her brother, Abdoul, and two aunts. Born to a Somali family, she spent her earliest years living in a United Nations refugee camp in the East African country of Djibouti. Her mother died in the camp (Jones 2020). Abdoul later recounted, "I was very young, but I saw a lot of my family members die, like my grandparents, my sister, my aunts and uncles and my mum" (Saltwire Network 2017). Shortly after their arrival in Halifax when they were about ten and eight years old, respectively, Fatuma and Abdoul were removed from their aunts' custody and placed in the care of what was then called the Children's Aid Society. Fatuma's hijab was confiscated and they were prohibited from engaging in Somali cultural practices and speaking Somali to each other, among many other abuses they experienced in group homes.

In 2003 they were placed in the permanent care of a Somali family in Halifax. This did not make things better — quite the opposite, in fact, as the family was from a rival tribe (Jones 2020). Fatuma reported being sexually, mentally and physically assaulted by this family. The Children's Aid Society admonished her for making what it said were false accusations (Jones 2020). Essentially, she was mistreated for complaining of mistreatment. Only when schoolteachers noticed signs of abuse and reported them was Fatuma taken seriously. The Children's Aid Society removed her from the home but left Abdoul there for three more years, resulting in their early separation. Throughout their childhoods, Fatuma and Abdoul's aunts tried unsuccessfully to regain custody of them.

Fatuma was sent to the Wood Street Centre, a secure treatment facility in Truro, Nova Scotia, in 2006, when she was fourteen years old. She was in and out of the facility many times. Children who are sent to the facility for "behavioural disorders" have described it as "more traumatizing than helpful" (Toth 2018, 1). The twenty-bed facility holds approximately 120 children per year, keeping them in barren rooms and barring them from having private discussions with each other. Minimal, if any, professional psychological therapy is provided. Though a carceral environment, Wood Street is operated under community services, not corrections. A youth held there cannot be found "not guilty" and released. Fatuma alleges that during the periods she was detained at Wood Street she was subjected to sexual and physical abuse (Jones 2020). As recently as 2019, a youth worker at Wood Street was charged with sexual exploitation of a youth in care (Prentiss 2019).

Fatuma gave birth for the first time in 2007, when she was fifteen, and again the next year (Jones 2020). Despite all the maturity she demonstrated, and all she had already endured, both babies were removed from her care immediately. She then had twin boys in 2010. One was placed in the care of his paternal grandparents, and Fatuma cared for the other, who had special needs. Then in 2014, that child was also removed from her custody and placed in foster care. He died soon afterwards.

After his removal from his aunt's home in 2001 until his late teenage years, Abdoul was cycled through thirty-one foster homes in Nova Scotia. He spent five months in the notorious Home for Coloured Children in 2008, and has described experiencing repeated sexual abuse there (Grant 2020). The facility opened in 1921, when white orphanages refused to accept Black children, part of Nova Scotia's long history of racial segregation and racism. Allegations of sexual and physical abuse at the Home for Coloured Children surfaced in 1998, resulting in a class-action lawsuit by survivors of the home, a public inquiry (Nova Scotia Home for Colored Children Restorative Inquiry 2019) and an apology from the province in 2014 for the systemic racism that nurtured the facility's culture of abuse.

State care is described by many as a pipeline to incarceration (Matheson and Stratford 2018). When conflict occurred at Abdoul's group homes, youth did not lose privileges or get grounded; instead, the police were called. Abdoul regularly interacted with police officers, and criminalization became normalized in his life. When he aged out of the foster care system, he struggled as a young man with deep psychological scars from so much loss and trauma. He frequently got into trouble with the law. At age eighteen, he was sent to the federal Dorchester Penitentiary in New Brunswick to serve five and a half years for aggravated assault.

In Canada, permanent residents and even refugees can be deported for "serious criminality." Receiving a prison sentence of more than six months constitutes serious criminality. There is no consideration made for a person having completed a sentence and expressed remorse for the offence. It does not matter if no family remains in their "home" country, if they have not been there since they were a child or if they have never been there because they were born in a refugee camp. The only protection is Canadian citizenship, which provides immunity from the risk of deportation. But no one ever applied for citizenship for Fatuma and Abdoul.

When the state removes a child from their family, it assumes responsibility to parent and care for the child. If a child is removed from a home because of perceived or potential abuse or neglect, it seems impossible to believe the consequence for the child would be more extreme abuse and neglect. Yet the Province of Nova Scotia ignored Fatuma and Abdoul's experiences of emotional harm, sexual assault and physical violence and failed in its basic obligations to the children to fill out paperwork to apply for Canadian citizenship. It is hard to imagine how these children could have been treated worse. After an early childhood spent in a refugee camp and marked by the deaths of his parents, followed by relocation to Canada where he was stripped of his culture and language in state care, moved through dozens of foster homes and incarcerated for over five years in a federal prison, Abdoul faced deportation by the Canadian Border Services Agency.

Fatuma stepped in. Only twenty-five, she cold-called abolitionist activists, including Dr. El Jones, Desmond Cole and Dr. Idil Abdillahi, and human rights lawyer Benjamin Perryman, creating a national team of support to demand mercy for her brother (Cole 2020). She went to a town hall in Halifax and stood up to the prime minister there. There were petitions, press releases, protests, letter campaigns and direct actions. The Canadian Civil Liberties Association took on the case. Finally, in spring 2018, Minister of Public Safety Ralph Goodale issued a stay of deportation for Abdoul. That part, at least, was over.

Because of Fatuma's activism, Nova Scotia now requires child protection social workers to note the citizenship status of children on their caseload and reassess this status every ninety days. If a child is in permanent care, workers can apply for citizenship on their behalf (Luck 2019). Although it was far too late to help her or Abdoul, Fatuma said, "I was happy because that means no other child will have to experience what me and my brother and other kids that were in the same situation as us have to go through" (Luck 2019, 1).

In 2020 Fatuma launched a lawsuit against Nova Scotia for the abuse she, her brother and her children experienced in state care. The ongoing case argues the province violated their Charter right to security of the person. But it is only the tip of the iceberg of Fatuma's work for reproductive justice. She is pushing not only for children to be safe from harms in state care but also for children to never have to face the violent threat of deportation.

Black children are overrepresented in foster care in Canada. An Ontario study found Black children are 2.2 times more likely than white children to be removed from their homes (Ontario Human Rights Commission 2018). Increasingly, newcomers to Canada are vulnerable to removal by child protection services. The fruits of Fatuma's persistence will help protect them. But Fatuma and Abdoul are still seeking citizenship in adulthood, and Canada has not changed its position on deporting people for serious criminality even if they came to the country as children (Schwartz 2021).

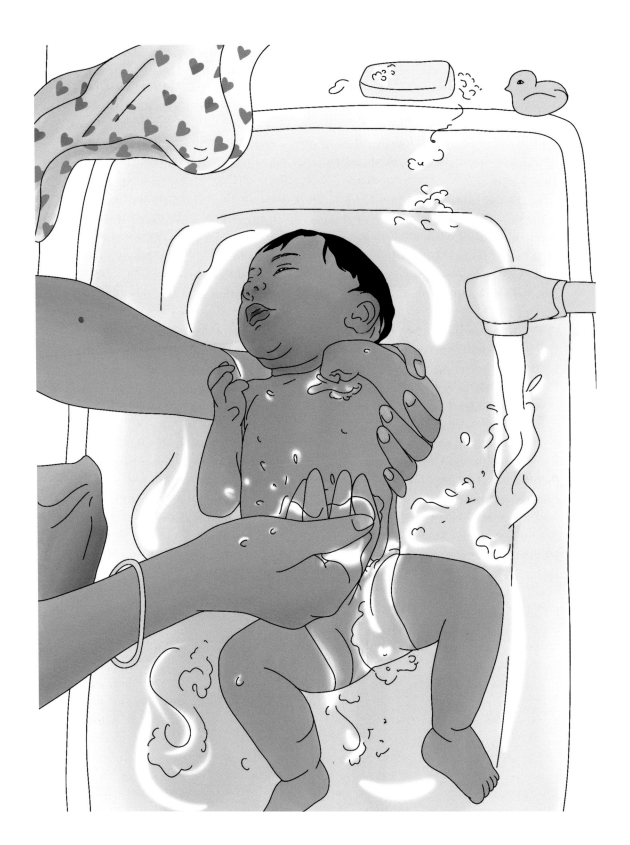

Water Protectors

Reproductive justice requires people have the resources to make their own decisions about reproduction and to raise children in safe, sustainable environments (Ross 2017; Ross and Solinger 2017). As a result, reproductive justice and environmental justice are closely connected (Liddell and Kington 2021). To exercise bodily autonomy requires protection from state-orchestrated or state-permitted environmental harm. Contamination of the environment directly affects fertility and pregnancy (Carson 1962; Richardson 2006). Pollutants and contamination are also responsible for childhood illness and premature death. Like reproductive justice and prison abolition, environmental justice centres racism in analyzing the unequal burden of environmental destruction and the unequal experience of healthy environments. The colonial project of Canada has resulted in environmental racism: poisoned spaces are disproportionately the burden of Indigenous and Black communities (Hoover et al. 2012; Waldron 2018).

The impact of environmental harm on reproductive health is complex and includes everything from the immediate consequences of industrial pollution on physical health, to the long-term impact of climate change on community survival, to gendered differences in occupational exposures to chemicals and sexual violence associated with natural resource extraction in so-called "man camps" (Morin 2020). This section focuses on water and a few of the activists working to secure and maintain access to clean water in Canada.

Water is an integral aspect of human health, and yet it requires fierce protection. Reproductive health is the canary in the coal mine when water is contaminated. The infamous 2014 crisis of lead contamination of the water supply in Flint, Michigan — a majority-Black city with high rates of poverty — was especially dangerous for pregnant people and children (Kennedy 2016). In utero and early childhood lead exposure affects the brain and central nervous system, resulting in intellectual disabilities, behavioural problems and even coma, convulsions and death if lead levels are high (World Health Organization 2021). Infant life revolves around water. Outside of sleeping, babies' only activities are being held in washed hands, being changed and bathed and being fed with either formula milk or human milk — ideally all based on clean, healthy water. The Flint water crisis prompted extensive research and recommendations to address the risks of breastfeeding amid lead exposure versus not breastfeeding, which itself has a host of negative consequences (Schrek and Lothamer 2016). The long-term fallout from the Flint water crisis on child health remains to be seen.

The "most serious case of water contamination in Canadian history" (*CBC News* 2010b) happened in the small town of Walkerton, Ontario, in May 2000. Several days of heavy rain caused manure from a farm in the area to seep into one of the wells that fed the town's water supply, contaminating it with E. coli bacteria (O'Connor 2002a). This coincided with the Public Utilities Commission manager, Stan Koebel, being out of town. He failed to ensure the replacement of a necessary chlorinator (O'Connor 2002a). On May 17, back at work, Koebel learned of the contamination from a lab result. He did not report it.

On May 18 two Walkerton children were admitted to hospital for diarrhea, and twenty were reportedly missing from school. Koebel continued to conceal the lab results, and the health department did not issue a boil water advisory until May 21. It was too late then. In total, the water contamination made twenty-three hundred people sick and killed seven, including a two-year-old girl, Mary Rose Raymond (Cox 2000). The town was devastated by loss, anger and fear: how could tap water in Canada turn deadly?

A 2002 inquiry led by Associate Chief Justice of Ontario Dennis O'Connor (2002a) found that the disaster was caused by long-standing improper operational practices by the Public Utilities Commission, including a failure to use continuous chlorine residual and turbidity monitors, and inadequate inspections by the Ministry of Environment. Stan Koebel and his brother Frank, the foreman for the Public Utilities Commission, were convicted on criminal charges for their roles in the disaster.

O'Connor released a second part of his inquiry report with recommendations to reduce future risks to the drinking water supply. By putting in place barriers to contamination, adopting a cautious approach, requiring quality monitoring and management and enforcing strict government regulations, water quality could be protected (O'Connor 2002b). The province, in turn, passed the Safe Drinking Water Act in 2002, recognizing "the people of Ontario are entitled to expect their drinking water to be safe" (Ontario 2002) and stipulating stricter controls and testing of drinking water systems, and the Clean Water Act in 2006, to protect existing and future sources of drinking water. To the horror of survivors and frontline activists from Walkerton, in 2019 the Conservative Ford government passed the Restoring Ontario's Competitiveness Act, aiming to reduce red tape and regulation in the province. While drinking water does not appear in the contents of the Act, conservationists fear it deliberately increases vulnerability and ignores the lessons learned from the Walkerton tragedy (Dhanraj 2019). Access to clean water is fundamental to reproductive health and well-being. Parents cannot parent in safety if their children can become sick and die from a drinking water supply that public servants have failed to protect.

Canada has less than 0.5 percent of the global population but 7 percent of the world's renewable freshwater resources (Canada 2018) and the most lakes in the world (Canada 2013). In short, Canada has more than its fair share of fresh water (Human Rights Watch 2016) and a great responsibility to preserve this gift. Despite the lessons of Walkerton, and the country's heightened position of responsibility for water safety and vast economic wealth, thousands of people in Canada are without access to clean water. Most of these people are Indigenous.

Of the 633 First Nations in Canada, one-third have water systems at risk (McClearn 2017). In 1977 Prime Minister Pierre Elliott Trudeau promised First Nations access to quality drinking water — through a memo, not legislation (Cheung 2019). Nearly forty years later, in 2015, his son Justin Trudeau was elected prime minister on a platform that included a pledge to remedy the existing 106 boil water advisories in Indigenous communities within his first five years in office. As of April 2021, more than half of these advisories remained — and even if some are resolved, more continue to pop up (*Globe and Mail* 2021). Boil water advisories require all water be boiled for at least one minute before use for drinking, cooking or bathing infants and older adults (Gerster and Hessey 2019). Some of the boil water advisories in Indigenous communities have persisted for decades.

Boil water advisories are not just bad for health because they signal people are at risk of water-borne diseases like infection by E. coli. It is also extremely emotionally taxing to manage a boil water advisory — to have to boil water to take a sip of water, brush teeth or wash a toddler's hands. The labour of dealing with a boil water advisory is gendered because managing household responsibilities is gendered. And indirect costs must also be considered: heavily chemically treated water can destroy clothes, and the disinfectants themselves can cause health problems like skin and eye irritation. Water chlorination can also create trihalomethanes, chemicals that can be carcinogenic (World Health Organization 2005).

A boil water advisory will not solve the problem if the problem is heavy metal contamination. One of the worst environmental disasters in Canada — and a clear example of environmental racism — is the mercury poisoning of Grassy Narrows First Nation. In the 1960s a pulp and paper mill in the predominantly white town of Dryden, Ontario (Statistics Canada 2016), used mercury in its processes. Tens of thousands of tonnes of mercury waste were dumped in the river and flowed downstream to Grassy Narrows, an Indigenous community of approximately one thousand people (Resolute FP Canada Inc. v. Ontario). Grassy Narrows sued the company in 1977, but the province, wanting the mill to stay open "for the local economy," granted new owners of the mill an "indemnity" — financial protection from legal claims over pollution (Resolute FP Canada Inc. v. Ontario, 1). Meanwhile, the commercial fishery in Grassy Narrows collapsed (Scharper 2016).

In public health, the upstream–downstream parable speaks to the limited value of treating people found poisoned at the end of the stream if upstream nothing changes and the poison keeps flowing (National Collaborating Centre for Determinants of Health n.d.). And the poison did keep flowing in Grassy Narrows — at least three generations have dealt with the consequences, and approximately 90 percent of residents now have symptoms of neurological damage caused by mercury poisoning (CBC Radio 2017).

Food insecurity — having inadequate income for and access to nutritious food — is endemic among Indigenous communities (Chan et al. 2019). Fish is a high-protein, traditional, healthy food and was a staple of the local Grassy Narrows diet. When fish are contaminated with mercury and people consume them, the toxin builds up in the human body. It can also pass through the placenta to a fetus: the effect is environmental racism, bioaccumulated. Examining hair samples from 650 Grassy Narrows residents who died from 1970 to 1997, researchers found that increased exposure to mercury was associated with premature death (Philibert, Fillion and Mergler 2020).

The physical consequences are one thing. The emotional anguish of the community stemming from the poisoning of their water, food and people is quite another. In a survey of the health of Grassy Narrows residents, researchers found higher rates of suicidal ideation and suicide, not only compared to the general public in Canada but also to other First Nations in Ontario (Mergler et al. 2019). Despite over fifty years of evidence, the community lacks monitoring and adequate health services, and the river has yet to be cleaned up (Scharper 2016). Grassy Narrows is a straightforward story of how environmental racism operates to prioritize white economic interests over Indigenous health and lives.

Although "water does not respect boundaries" (Walkem 2004, 1), water resources in Canada are mainly under provincial jurisdiction. Provinces issue licences for use and are responsible for quality monitoring — for better or, as was the case in Walkerton and Grassy Narrows, for worse. Provincial legislation fails to protect Indigenous water rights (Phare 2009). The Constitution Act of 1867 placed Indigenous people and land under the power of the federal government, and the Indian Act of 1876 established the colonial concept of reserves, forcing many Indigenous communities onto small parcels of federally "owned" land. The federal government is responsible for financing public infrastructure, including water management, for Indigenous communities. Water infrastructure for Indigenous communities is clearly underfunded, and researchers have found that only 67 percent of the already inadequate funding provided by Ottawa makes it to community. The rest is absorbed by the costs of the federal bureaucracy (Phare 2009).

The United Nations (2015) has recognized access to clean water and sanitation as a human right and a prerequisite to realizing other human rights. Water protection is at the core of Indigenous livelihoods, not only for physical and spiritual health but also political autonomy and economic prosperity. As described by legal scholar Ardith Walkem (2004, 1–2), a member of the Nlaka'pamux Nation who became a BC Supreme Court judge in 2020,

> Water calls forth all other life and is required to sustain all other life. Knowledge of this simple truth forms the foundation of Indigenous laws and responsibility to care take water. Our decisions are measured against their possibility to impact upon present and future generations of other Peoples and life who depend upon water. The survival of Indigenous Peoples as unique and distinct members of the world community requires recognition of our relationship with and reliance upon the waters of our territories.

Indigenous women, girls and Two Spirit people are protectors of water across the country. Deborah McGregor, Anishinaabe from Whitefish River First Nation, Birch Island, Ontario, is a Canada Research Chair in Indigenous Environmental Justice. She has written about the Mother Earth Water Walks, a practice of walking the perimeters of the Great Lakes, "to raise awareness of the sacred connection between people, especially women, and the waters" (McGregor 2015, 74). The movement was initiated and led by Anishinaabe grandmother Josephine Mandamin, who walked 25,000 kilometres before her death in 2019. She was the great aunt of Autumn Peltier, one of the youngest and most well-known water protectors in Canada. Peltier was born in 2004 in Wiikwemkoong First Nation on Lake Huron, the second largest of the five great lakes of North America and the fifth-largest lake in the world. Her work began at age eight, when she and her family visited Serpent River First Nation, which has been subject to boil water advisories on and off for over thirty years.

A 2017 *Globe and Mail* exposé found water was still being shipped in to Serpent River and a boil water advisory was in effect a year after a new treatment plant was installed in 2015 (McClearn 2017). In the early 2000s, the federal government spent almost $2 billion to build water infrastructure for Indigenous communities, but it was simply not enough for proper installations and had barely any impact. Through Indigenous and Northern Affairs Canada, the Liberal Trudeau government in 2016 directed another nearly $2 billion to water treatment, which again experts assessed as deficient.

That year, twelve-year-old Peltier faced Prime Minister Trudeau and directly called out his inadequate response to the water crisis. Frankly speaking truth to power earned her respect around the world. She was called to present to the United Nations year after year and has received countless nominations and awards for her efforts. She has spoken publicly over two hundred times, including at the United Nations and the Assembly of First Nations. In 2019 she was named the Anishanabek Nation Chief Water Commissioner. She identifies the incomparable importance of water: "We can't live in our mother's womb without water. As a fetus, we need that sacred water for development" (Erskine 2019). To Peltier, poisoned water is a gender equity issue.

On the west coast, Indigenous water protectors have been steadfast in their opposition to the Trans Mountain expansion of an oil pipeline running from Alberta to BC. The pipeline traverses Indigenous land, crosses over fifteen hundred waterways and jeopardizes the safety of community water sources. The risks posed by pipelines are high. In 2016 a Husky Energy oil pipeline leaked 225,000 litres of oil into the Saskatchewan River, the "most significant environmental incident that's ever happened in the province" (*CBC News* 2019, 1). While pollution at this level affects everyone, impacts are disproportionately borne by Indigenous people. In Saskatchewan 16 percent of people identify as Indigenous (Statistics Canada 2016).

Despite the clear threats to human health that pipeline projects involve, opposition is criminalized. It is so often Indigenous women, girls and Two-Spirit people who face police actions for defending the water and land. In March 2018 Crystal Smith, a young Indigenous mother and protestor against Trans Mountain in BC, was violently arrested in front of her children (Brake 2018). Dr. Sherry Pictou asserts, "There is something fundamentally wrong when corporate rights and law supersede human and Indigenous rights, and the rights of Indigenous women in particular. Instead, law works to criminalize land and water defenders, while the acceleration of unsustainable natural resource commodification is facilitated by law" (Puentes 2021). Water protection connects the reproductive justice issues of police racism and violence against women.

In Minnesota police have arrested over six hundred water protectors for protesting the Enbridge Line 3 tar sands pipeline, including Winona LaDuke, a global leader in water protection and author of *To Be a Water Protector* (2020). Enbridge is a Canadian company, and as LaDuke says, "it's a civil crisis when a Canadian multinational controls your police force" (*Democracy Now* 2021, 1). In addition, the Enbridge project received an allocation from Minnesota's Department of Natural Resources of five billion gallons of water — in the middle of a drought. Water protectors consistently point out where water safety, and the health of the public, is subjugated to corporate interests through government manoeuvres.

On the east coast, on the ancestral and unceded territory of the Mi'kmaq, Indigenous people were on the front lines in Nova Scotia to protect water resources from the harm presented by the Alton Gas project. The project, launched in 2004, aimed to create engineered underground caves for the storage of up to ten billion cubic feet of natural gas. To do so would require drawing ten thousand cubic metres of fresh water from the Shubenacadie River and using it to flush out underground salt, releasing brine back into the river (Campbell 2020). The brine would be toxic to fish and other life, and the plan lacked consultation with Indigenous Peoples and violated Treaty rights (Poulette and Greenland-Smith 2019). Nevertheless, the AltaGas company received provincial approval for the project in 2016, which the Sipekne'katik First Nation, located near the community of Alton, appealed in court three times.

While the legal dispute made its way through the courts, grandmother water protectors began occupying the company gates to prevent entry to the project site. They built a treaty truckhouse to make their opposition known — the Peace and Friendship Treaty of 1752 established the right of the Mi'kmaq to construct and gather at truckhouses, a type of trading post (Lewis n.d.). Yet AltaGas succeeded in having an injunction put in place requiring the grandmothers relocate to a small nearby site, which they refused to do (Rutgers 2019). In April 2019 grandmothers Madonna Bernard, Darlene Gilbert and Paula Isaac were arrested by the RCMP. Bernard said, "We decided that we were going to be civilly arrested under the so-called Canadian laws we do not recognize" (Googoo 2019).

The grandmothers' opposition and the Sipekne'katik First Nation lawsuit continued, with widening public support from non-Indigenous Nova Scotians. In spring 2020 a judge finally ruled in favour of Sipekne'katik First Nation, granting a temporary reprieve (Grant 2020). Then in October 2021, AltaGas cancelled the project (AltaGas 2021). The water protectors had won.

As Cheryl Maloney, a Mikm'aw leader, explained, "This was for the seven generations of everyone. You know, protecting the river isn't just seven generations of Mi'kmaq — it's seven generations of Nova Scotia that this work has been done for" (Ryan 2021). Reproductive justice and the right to parent in safe and sustainable communities relies on water safety. Protected by a brave few — disproportionately Indigenous women — clean water must be recognized as a public responsibility and receive greater consideration as a requirement for reproductive health and survival.

Chapter 5

PARENTING IN PRISON

The prison system violates reproductive justice in every possible way (Sufrin, Kolby-Molinas and Roth 2015; Roth 2017; Shlafer et al. 2019; Hayes et al. 2020). Bodily autonomy is under constant threat: what you do, how you move, who you touch and when you eat, urinate and sleep are all observed and policed. People in prison are systematically withheld health care, including family planning services and assisted reproductive technologies, denying them the right to choose to have or not have children. Prison is a two-sided violation of the right to parent: parents are separated from their children when those children, as youth or young adults, experience incarceration (Gilmore 2005), and when parents are incarcerated, they are separated from their children, partners and communities, impeding their ability to parent their children. These reproductive injustices are disproportionately borne by Black and Indigenous people.

Rife with violence and disease, prisons are inherently incompatible with parenting safely. The fight for the rights of parents in prison is not just about the right to parent while incarcerated. It is about the fundamental human rights violations of prison, and how prison dehumanizes, invalidating family, love and parenthood. Reproductive justice includes the right to parent because being able to parent your own children is essential to your health. You cannot be healthy if you are terrified about what is happening to your baby in foster care. You cannot be healthy if how your baby is fed is determined by someone else while your breasts swell and ache. You cannot be healthy if you are constantly worried about demonstrating imperfect parenting under the watch of prison guards. You will be anxious, angry and unwell.

In Canada the health of incarcerated people is protected by provincial and federal corrections legislation. The state has a duty to provide health care to incarcerated people beyond its obligation to nonincarcerated people because prisoners are under state custody: they have lost the autonomy to make their own appointments, choose their own food, decide when and how to exercise and so on. Federal legislation stipulates incarcerated individuals have the right to the same health services as are available outside. Section 77 of the Corrections and Conditional Release Act (Canada, Department of Justice 1992) instructs CSC to provide programs specific to women's needs. Section 86 stipulates that federally sentenced people must receive essential health care and reasonable access to nonessential health care and that health care must conform to professionally accepted norms. Section 87 requires consideration of a prisoner's health in all decisions affecting them. Despite these directives, health care is the most common issue in complaints by federally sentenced people (Public Safety Canada 2019).

The Charter of Rights and Freedoms (Canada, Department of Justice 1982) covers human rights protections for all persons in Canada, including prisoners. Section 7 protects the right to life, liberty and security of the person, and separation of mother and baby violates their security. Section 12 protects people from cruel and unusual treatment by the state, which should preclude putting pregnant prisoners in solitary confinement or shackling them in labour. Section 15, also called the equality provision, guarantees everyone equal protection under the law regardless of sex or gender. Pregnancy and the possibility of becoming pregnant are experiences that can only happen to people who have a uterus, and failure to account for them in carceral systems is discriminatory.

Those are just federal-level requirements in Canada. The United Nations Rules for the Treatment of Women Prisoners and Non-custodial Measures for Women Offenders (United Nations Office on Drugs and Crime 2011) outline international responsibilities for the treatment of people incarcerated in facilities designated for women. Rule 10.1 specifies prisoners are to receive gender-specific health care, including accommodation of pregnancy. Rule 22 prohibits the solitary confinement of any prisoner who is pregnant, has infants or is breastfeeding. Rule 24 prohibits the use of restraints during labour and birth.

Wherever children are concerned in policy domains, the Convention on the Rights of the Child (United Nations General Assembly 1989) applies. Article 3 introduces the principle that all government decisions affecting children be made in that child's best interests. This should include decisions to separate a child from their parent. Article 7 asserts a child's right "to know and be cared for by his or her parents." Article 24 states children have a right to "enjoyment of the highest attainable standard of health and to facilities for the treatment of illness and rehabilitation of health." Parental incarceration is well understood as an adverse childhood event associated with increased risk of disease and premature death (Felitti et al. 1998). Yet children are almost never considered in sentencing decisions (Canadian Friends Service Committee 2018; Minson 2020).

The dehumanization of prisoners results in the dehumanization of their children. This chapter begins with the story of *Emily Boyle,* who went to federal prison twice, in the 1920s and 1930s. Each time she was pregnant and advocated to keep her baby with her when it was born. The first time she was successful; the second time she was not. She was not the first woman to have a baby stay with her in a prison in Canada, but she is possibly the first for whom there is a strong record, thanks to the historical research of Dr. Ted McCoy. In her story a core conflict is at play: although the state understood babies need their mothers, particularly in an era before the popularization of infant formula, and motherhood was patronizingly perceived as potentially rehabilitative for criminalized women, no prison's mandate was served by accommodating babies. Babies were assessed as a means to an end but not considered humans with rights of their own, and certainly not as humans whose rights the carceral system had to uphold.

Just after Boyle's second incarceration, the central Prison for Women opened in Kingston, Ontario. The pain and dire conditions experienced by prisoners there, and the increasing incarceration of Indigenous women, prompted the formation of the Task Force on Federally Sentenced Women in the late 1980s. The task force published *Creating Choices*, a blueprint for reforming the system, in 1990. Major upsets occurred in the following years, including the 1994 strip-search of shackled women at the Prison for Women, a commission of inquiry report on the incident (Arbour 1996) and then the closure of the federal prison in 2000. A regional system was designed to replace it, and each facility was supposed to house parents and children together through the Institutional Mother-Child Program, starting in the late 1990s. At the provincial level, BC first opened a mother-baby program in the 1970s, and it remains the only province with an operational program.

The next three stories in this chapter, centring the experiences of Indigenous women *Renee Acoby, Lisa Whitford* and *Amanda Inglis,* explain and critique the federal and provincial programs. The egregious and incessant violations of the reproductive rights of Indigenous people in Canada — to access health care, to live in safety from violence, to parent their children and to have their children be parented — are at their most extreme in the prison system. The incarceration of parents denies their children the right to be parented and renews the trauma that fuels criminalization. As of 2021, Indigenous women make up almost 50 percent of the women behind bars (Office of the Correctional Investigator 2021). The Truth and Reconciliation Commission (2015) called for an end to the disproportionate incarceration of Indigenous people, yet the numbers have climbed every year since and remain completely unaddressed, despite report after report calling for action.

The final story is about *Julie Bilotta,* who experienced the unimaginable. Ignored, insulted and isolated in labour, she gave birth in a filthy jail cell — not a hundred years ago in a medieval lockup, but in Ottawa in 2012. She required emergency treatment for massive blood loss, and the baby, Gionni, required intensive care. The two faced a year of torment by the justice system and the child protection system, all in the full glare of the media. When Gionni was just thirteen months old, he died in his sleep.

There is no righting the wrongs of incarcerating pregnant people, parents and caregivers. Mother-baby programs will not solve the systemic social problems facing criminalized families: colonialism, racism, poverty and trauma. These programs are a stopgap at best, and at worst a manifestation of further racism, inequality, surveillance and punishment. The women in this chapter worked incredibly hard to stop prisons from trampling their rights to health and to parent, and in so doing have exposed just how incompatible incarceration is with both. Prison abolition is a necessary part of reproductive justice work

Emily Boyle

The incarceration of people in prisons designated for women in Canada has steadily increased over time, with a web of consequences for reproductive health and justice. Most women, trans people and nonbinary people who experience criminalization have themselves experienced violence and harm. Prisons are unhealthy environments and retraumatize those who are incarcerated. Rates of suicide, homicide, death, injury, infection and illness are all higher in prison than outside it (Kouyoumdjian et al. 2016). Restraints, use of force, isolation and surveillance trigger people who have experienced abuse, creating a cycle of distress, reaction and discipline. The trauma of incarceration itself is cyclical: most incarcerated people have children (Bertram and Sawyer 2021), who are inevitably left behind, traumatized.

Prisoner rights advocates have long supported so-called prison nurseries or mother-baby programs in jails. The programs are not new or novel, and in fact some form of maternal-child co-incarceration is a global norm (Paynter, Jefferies, McKibbon et al. 2020). The impact of these programs on child and parent health, including attachment, is poorly studied. It is not clear if the programs provide better outcomes for participants. Some studies have found participants in these programs may experience higher rates of breastfeeding, and others have found lower rates of vaccination and high rates of illness among children in such programs (Paynter, Jefferies, McKibbon et al. 2020). It cannot even be assumed the programs preserve families, as some studies have found higher rates of removal to foster care among children who participated in a prison nursery (Blanchard et al. 2018).

There is evidence of infants in Canadian prisons designated for women as early as the 1850s (McCoy 2017, 2019). The twentieth-century story of Emily Boyle paints a vivid picture of the incompatibility between the objective of incarceration and the experience of parenthood. Born Emily Lindholm, she was twenty-six years old and working as an accountant when she was charged and sentenced for committing arson and theft at her place of employment in southern Saskatchewan. In 1926 she was sent to the Saskatchewan Penitentiary, then on to the federal Kingston Penitentiary in Ontario. When she arrived in Kingston, she was pregnant and unmarried.

Although Boyle had been sentenced to two years, once her pregnancy was discovered by the prison physician, arrangements were made for her to receive parole. She was sent to live with her sister in Edmonton. In 1931 she was convicted again for charges related to her employment at a bank and returned to Kingston Penitentiary. She had married James Boyle in the interim, and eventually it became clear she was pregnant again.

This time, Boyle was refused any opportunity of early parole, and so she set to work on securing the right to parent the baby from inside the prison. Both her husband and the prison superintendent supported her wish to keep the child with her after birth, especially while they were breastfeeding. Initially, they believed their agreement with the plan was sufficient to ensure the baby would be permitted to stay at Kingston

Penitentiary. However, the warden, Gilbert Smith, argued that infants disrupted prison routines and undermined carceral discipline.

Boyle pled her case to the federal Department of Justice. "It is my desire to give my baby every right to its life. It has had a bad beginning because during my pregnancy I have suffered untold mental torture," she said. "If my baby is taken from me during its birth, I fear for its life and for my mental stability" (McCoy 2017). Boyle clearly understood what vast amounts of clinical research have gone on to show: stress in pregnancy is harmful to the developing fetus, and taking children from their mothers not only negatively impacts the children but can cause emotional and physical harm to their mothers (Kenny et al. 2021; Thumath et al. 2021). Research about the negative impacts on children of early separation from their primary parent — usually, especially in that era, the mother — has a long history, beginning in the1940s, when British psychologist John Bowlby and Canadian–American psychologist Mary Salter Ainsworth developed attachment theory. They theorized that children who are denied the opportunity or fail to develop strong bonds with their primary caregiver experience behavioural and emotional hardship in adulthood. Bowlby's report about attachment theory was first published in 1951 by the World Health Organization (Bowlby and World Health Organization 1952).

Late in her second pregnancy, Boyle began to refuse clinical examinations. She did not disclose to staff when she went into labour and locked herself in a bathroom for the birth. Prison matrons broke through the door to get to her. Boyle's actions are very much in keeping with findings from contemporary research. Pregnant people who experience the removal of a child are less likely to seek perinatal care, anticipating contact with health services will result in removal of the infant (Wall-Wieler et al. 2019). People in prison cannot govern when and how they receive perinatal support.

After the birth Boyle and her baby girl were taken to hospital by ambulance. The baby was then sent to the Kingston Home for Infants, and Boyle returned to the prison alone. Both she and her husband wrote regularly to the Department of Justice, asking for the baby to be permitted to live inside the penitentiary with her mother. Their petitions were unsuccessful, though the baby was allowed to visit. The warden believed that the purpose of incarceration was to provide labour useful to the state, not to care for children, and that family separation was simply the reality for incarcerated people (McCoy 2017).

Boyle was punished for complaining, an outcome incarcerated people continue to face today when they oppose the conditions of their confinement. Prisoner hunger or labour strikes are met with lockdown or loss of "privileges," which are usually basic rights (Washington 2016). The theme of ill treatment for opposing ill treatment recurs again and again in this chapter as institutions and institutional actors pathologize the intentions of incarcerated people. Boyle's efforts to preserve her private health information were interpreted by the prison administration as deception. Her autonomy was criminalized. Her maternal devotion and persistent attempts to be with her baby were perceived as oppositional and obstructionist in a power struggle with prison authority. Eventually, she secured early parole.

Incarceration is only meant to be a denial of liberty; it is not meant to involve other forms of punishment, and certainly not the denial of health to a child. The Convention on the Rights of the Child (United Nations General Assembly 1989), which Canada signed onto in 1991, insists states must protect children from discrimination or punishment based on the status or activities of their parents. How could a parent be incarcerated without punishing their child? The canonical study on adverse childhood events by Felitti et al. (1998) found incarceration of a household member is one of twelve childhood events associated with chronic disease in adulthood and premature death. The gendered nature of caregiving and childrearing, true in Boyle's time but still very much true today, means the incarceration of women, trans people and nonbinary people has different consequences on children than does the incarceration of cisgender men. Boyle's story, juxtaposed with the four others in this chapter set in the twenty-first century, demonstrates how little has changed in ninety years. There is a fundamental incongruity between prisons and parenting.

Renee Acoby

In 2000, when she was twenty years old, Renee Acoby, an Ojibwa woman, received a federal sentence for assault and drug trafficking and was incarcerated in the women's unit of Saskatchewan Penitentiary. She had been raised by her grandmother after her father killed her mother —one of at least 1,017 Indigenous women killed in Canada from 1980 to 2012 (RCMP 2014).

When Acoby arrived at Saskatchewan Penitentiary, she was pregnant. There are no reliable statistics on pregnancy in prison in Canada, but US studies have found about 5 percent of incarcerated women are pregnant (Sufrin et al. 2019). Recent studies in Canada have found that pregnant prisoners are less likely to receive adequate prenatal care and more likely to give birth prematurely or have babies that are small for their gestational age (Carter Ramirez, Liauw, Cavanagh et al. 2020; Carter Ramirez, Liauw, Costescu et al. 2020).

Soon after her prison admission, Acoby joined in a collective action to protest inhumane conditions in the facility. Prisoners there could not access mental health care or even sanitary napkins (Fraser 2010). Although women are the fastest growing population in prisons, and the population of incarcerated Indigenous women is growing faster still, the prison system remains dominated by cisgender men, and the concerns and needs of women, trans people and nonbinary people are secondary, if ever considered. For example, in 2017 the Senate Committee on Human Rights decried inadequate access to menstrual products in prisons (Senate of Canada 2017). As a result of her role in the protest, Acoby was charged with hostage taking. She pled guilty and received three additional years on her sentence. This was the beginning of a string of institutional charges, which are charges related to actions and experiences inside the institution. These types of charges are harder to dispute than those brought forward in the community and can significantly impact the experience of incarceration not only through more prison time but through elevation in security level and placement in solitary confinement as punishment.

Ten years before Acoby was incarcerated, the Task Force on Federally Sentenced Women — a partnership between CSC and nonprofit organizations including CAEFS and the Native Women's Association of Canada — released the 1990 report *Creating Choices* on the future of federal corrections. At the time, the only federal facility designated for women was the Prison for Women in Kingston, Ontario. Having a single central federal facility meant the people incarcerated there could be "2000 miles from home" (Task Force on Federally Sentenced Women 1990, 7) and their children. *Creating Choices* recommended closing the Prison for Women and replacing it with a system of "cottages" considered more appropriate for women's needs and lives, such as their roles as mothers. It acknowledged that women's experiences of criminalization differed from those of men and called for empowerment, meaningful choices, dignity, respect and support. Emphatically "women-centred" in its approach, *Creating Choices* recommended the implementation of a regional system so families could visit more often, and the creation of an institutional mother-child program. The report recommended that if children had to be removed by child protection services could not reside at the regional facilities, they should be placed in foster homes close by.

As criminologist Kelly Hannah-Moffatt (2001, 175) has critiqued, this focus on empowerment "is used to justify and rationalize a variety of disciplinary techniques through a parallel discourse of responsibility." Like the inadequate discourse of "choice," the discourse of empowerment implies people have full agency and control, and negates the heavy impact of racism, colonialism, sexism, classism, homophobia, transphobia and ableism on individual lives. Social work professor Shoshana Pollack describes the *Creating Choices* characterization of federally incarcerated women as dependent and in need of empowerment from the state as a discourse of social control. In her research with federally sentenced women, she found them to be seeking independence from "both the state and other people" (Pollack 2000, 77).

In April 1994, four years after *Creating Choices* was published but before any action was taken to close the Prison for Women, a chilling "incident" occurred there. A six-man riot squad shackled and strip-searched eight women who had been placed in segregation for participation in what was described as a riot. The strip searches were videotaped and portions of the footage were shown on CBC's *Fifth Estate*, sparking national outcry. Madame Justice Louise Arbour was tasked to lead a commission of inquiry. Among her many recommendations, she called for the creation of a deputy commissioner for women within CSC to take over implementation of the new facilities called for in *Creating Choices*. She recommended the deputy prioritize the release of women from custody and support community reintegration.

The Prison for Women did close, and regional facilities replaced it: Nova Institution for Women in Truro, Nova Scotia; Joliette Institution for Women in Joliette, Quebec; Grand Valley Institution for Women in Kitchener-Waterloo, Ontario; Okimaw Ohci Healing Lodge in Maple Creek, Saskatchewan; Edmonton Institution for Women in Edmonton, Alberta; and Fraser Valley Institution of Women in Abbottsford, BC. There is also a small CSC-affiliated healing lodge called Buffalo Sage Wellness House in Edmonton. The introduction of regional centres did not decrease the number of incarcerated women; the opposite occurred. In 1995 there were 322 federally sentenced women (142 of those at the Prison for Women), of whom 19 percent were Indigenous (Arbour 1996). Twenty-five years later, in 2019, there were almost 700 federally incarcerated women (Public Safety Canada 2020), of whom 42 percent were Indigenous (Office of the Correctional Investigator 2020). In 2021 that figure rose to nearly 50 percent (Office of the Correctional Investigator 2021). Evidently, the healing promise of *Creating Choices* was never realized (Hayman 2006). Instead, there are more prison facilities, more prisoners, more racism and tighter restrictions.

Acoby's baby, Anika, was born in October 2000. The pair were sent to Okimaw Ohci Healing Lodge, a minimum to medium security federal prison that opened in 1995 and prioritizes admissions of Indigenous women. Like all five of the other federal prisons designated for women in Canada, Okimaw Ochi has an Institutional Mother-Child Program. Children under the age of five can live full-time with their mothers; under the age of six they can participate part-time. Participating mothers must be classed as medium or minimum security and must agree to surveillance by provincial child protection services. Although 700 women are incarcerated in the federal system on a given day (Public Safety Canada 2020), only about 133 mother-child pairs have participated in the program from 2001 to 2018 (Paynter et al. 2022). Research has found that Indigenous women, despite experiencing disproportionately high rates of incarceration, are less likely than non-Indigenous women to participate in the Institutional Mother-Child Program (Miller 2017; Paynter et al. 2022).

Just before Anika turned one, while she was still breastfeeding, Acoby was caught using marijuana and diazepam with some other women at Okimaw Ohci (Fraser 2010). In response to this infraction, child protection services immediately removed baby Anika from Acoby's care. Heartbroken, Acoby escaped from Okimaw Ochi, hoping to reunite with her daughter. When she was caught, she held a correctional officer hostage, demanding to see Anika. At her sentencing for the hostage taking, she told the judge, "Because they took her away from me, that's why I did it" (Fraser 2010, 1).

The criminal justice system is not designed with gender sensitivity. There is no understanding of the "mama bear" reaction when threats are made to a parent's children or to the parent in front of their children. The risk of losing a child can make a parent terrified, enraged, impulsive and violent. Films glorify these reactions as brave and pure. But prisons do not see it that way; it is oppositional behaviour to be punished. Additionally, in the correctional system, gendered histories of trauma such as childhood sexual abuse and domestic violence are associated with volatility and interpreted as risks to security. In effect, those who need the most support to recover from trauma are classified at the highest levels of security and face the greatest restrictions on access to programming for rehabilitation and a chance at parole. Not only is this risk classification scale unfair to women, trans people and nonbinary people, but it is also especially unfair to Indigenous people, who have endured colonialism and racist violence and as a consequence are more likely to have experienced trauma.

In 2003 the Canadian Human Rights Commission called for action to address continued discrimination against federally incarcerated women. Two years later the United Nations Human Rights Commission reported on Canada's failure to implement these recommendations (Balfour 2018). In 2007 Ashley Smith, a teenage girl imprisoned at the Grand Valley Institution, died in a segregation unit while under active suicide watch by multiple guards. In 2013 the coroner's inquest into her death ruled it a homicide (csc 2013). Increased public scrutiny following these kinds of events and the ongoing efforts of feminist advocates have resulted in minimal meaningful systemic change. Indeed, solitary confinement, use of force and strip searches have remained carceral practice norms despite the optimism generated by *Creating Choices*.

During the years she remained separated from her daughter, Acoby accumulated several charges for further incidents of violence while incarcerated. Although there is a belief that prisons keep people safe, prisons are dangerous spaces and the risk of injury, suicide and homicide is far higher in a prison than in community. Acoby received an additional ten years on her sentence because of internal charges. Despite the possibilities presented in *Creating Choices* through the regional "cottage" system, Acoby only saw her daughter one more time during her incarceration, when Anika was eight. In 2011 Acoby was classified as a dangerous offender, the first woman in Canada to ever receive the designation.

The second woman designated a dangerous offender, Lisa Neve, is also Indigenous (Omstead 2018). She was adopted into a white family in Saskatchewan as a baby. The accelerated process of her criminalization began when she was picked up by police at age twelve for drinking and was forcibly strip-searched. During her adolescence she experienced state care, detention and sexual exploitation. As a young adult she pressed charges against her pimp for assault and was cross-examined on the witness stand (Renke 1995). Traumatized by how she was treated, she checked herself into a psychiatric hospital and made threats against the defence counsel. In 1991 she participated in a robbery. A conviction for this offence served as grounds for the dangerous offender hearing. Neve's private diaries and fantasies were used as evidence against her.

Acoby's and Neve's experiences show clearly how racism and colonial attitudes persist and generate further trauma through the criminal justice system. A 2020 study found Indigenous women were 64 percent more likely than white women to be classified as maximum security (Cardoso 2020). There is simply a double standard against Indigenous women, and Indigenous people broadly, intensifying the experience and consequences of criminalization.

Seventeen years after cannabis use was used to justify removing Acoby's baby, the government of Canada legalized cannabis and began selling it directly, generating approximately $186 million in tax and general revenue in the first five months (Statistics Canada 2019c). An estimated ten thousand people hold criminal records for simple cannabis possession (Harris 2020), and research has found Black and Indigenous people are overrepresented in cannabis arrests (Owusu-Bempah and Luscombe 2021). After legalizing cannabis, the federal government introduced a cumbersome but free process to apply for a pardon; only a few hundred people have been successful in attaining one. Today diazepam and other antianxiolytics are routinely prescribed to manage postpartum depression and anxiety, which is one of the most common complications of pregnancy (CAMH n.d.), affecting approximately one in seven pregnant people (American Psychological Association 2008). But when Acoby was caught using it in 2000, she was punished by having her baby taken from her, an unimaginable loss after losing her own mother.

Acoby was punished for decades for her protective reaction to the threat and realization of her child's removal by the state. Not paroled until 2018, she lost the opportunity to have other children. Like forced sterilization, the Indian Residential Schools and the Sixties Scoop, prison represents an arm of colonial reprocide in Canada, one that is ongoing and a fundamental threat to reproductive justice (Ross 2017; Ross and Solinger 2017).

Lisa Whitford

Lisa Whitford's experience as a mother in prison straddled two carceral systems and two ideologies about permitting babies inside. Her early life was typical of women who experience incarceration. She was born in 1972 in northern BC, and her childhood was rife with abuse (Culbert and Bellett 2008). Her mother was an alcoholic and her mother's boyfriend routinely sexually assaulted her (Miller 2017). By age eleven she was using alcohol and drugs to cope. As a teenager she was strangled, raped and left for dead by a "friend."

In adulthood Whitford continued to be victimized. She lost three children to the BC Ministry of Children and Family Development, the provincial child protection service. She was hospitalized at least forty-one times in her early thirties, including five times for a broken jaw. Then in July 2006, at age thirty-three, she shot and killed her common-law husband, Anthony Cartledge, in Prince George, BC. Although he had never been convicted of violence against Whitford, her recent injuries were telling. She was sent to the provincial Alouette Correctional Centre for Women in Maple Ridge to await trial. Whitford was in the first month of pregnancy, and because Alouette had an active Mother-Baby Program at the time, she could participate while on remand during pregnancy and the first year of her daughter's life.

Instead of enduring a trial, Whitford decided to plead guilty to manslaughter and be sent to the federal Fraser Valley Institution for Women, in the hopes she would be accepted into its Institutional Mother-Child Program (CSC 2020). Even in the absence of such a program, mothers facing charges often plead guilty in order to more quickly make plans for the care and custody of their children. Whitford was supported by Professor Michael Jackson, a legal expert on prisoner rights; Sarah Rauch, director of the First Nations Law Clinic at the University of British Columbia; and defence lawyer Bruce Kaun.

Fraser Valley Institution for Women opened in 2004 in Abbottsford, BC, replacing the Burnaby Correctional Centre for Women, which had held both provincial and federal prisoners. Fraser Valley had space for 112 people and separate maximum-, medium- and minimum-security areas, with mothers and babies expected to live in the minimum-security unit outside the main gates. In 2007 Whitford was the first person to participate in Fraser Valley's Mother-Child Program, and much was made of the fact (Woodward 2008) even though provincial institutions in BC, including Burnaby and Twin Maples, had such programs long before that. Further, six additional women were participating in the federal Mother-Child Program across the country that same year (Paynter et al. 2022). Whitford was not the last to join the program at Fraser Valley: nine women participated in it from 2007 to 2019 (Paynter et al. 2022). Unlike the provincial program, which stopped when a child reached two years of age, the federal program at the time allowed full-time participation until the child reached elementary school age.

Justice Glen Parrett, who presided over Whitford's sentencing, was required to con-

sider her experiences as an Indigenous woman in determining her penalty (Johnson 2008). Recognizing the enduring impact of colonialism and racism in Canada, and disproportionate rates of incarceration of Indigenous people, Section 718.2.e of the Criminal Code reads "all available sanctions other than imprisonment that are reasonable in the circumstances should be considered for all offenders, with particular attention to the circumstances of aboriginal offenders." Although Parrett expressed doubt Whitford could change her "destructive lifestyle," indicating a shallow understanding of how colonialism, racism and misogyny had shaped her life, he did collaborate with the many players working to keep Whitford and her child, Jordyn, together. He assigned a sentence of six years, two of which she had already served at Alouette. This allowed her daughter to live full-time at the prison with Whitford until she was released.

Justice Parrett, the Fraser Valley prison warden, CSC and the BC Ministry for Children and Families all supported Whitford's participation in the Mother-Child Program. Given what Whitford had survived, she should have garnered profound understanding and sympathy. But inflammatory media coverage of the case, headlines like "Killer Mom to Raise Baby in Prison" (*Times Colonist* 2008) and "Newborn Goes to Prison in BC First" (Woodward 2008) incited public and political disapproval.

Stockwell Day, minister of public safety for the Conservative federal government, demanded a review of the program, and in June 2008 he issued a series of major changes (Stone 2011). From then on, the program would exclude anyone convicted of crimes against children or violent offences. Women are usually charged for nonviolent crimes, but in the federal prison system, where people with sentences of two years or more are sent, 66 percent of the women at the time had convictions related to violence (Miller 2017). Day also dramatically cut the eligibility of children for part-time participation in the program, changing the maximum age from twelve to six. All the mothers who joined the program had to agree to surveillance by the respective provincial ministry in charge of child protection services. Perhaps most jarringly, mothers had to allow correctional officers to search their children's bodies for contraband. Day framed the changes as "in the best interests of the child," in reference to the 1989 United Nations Convention on the Rights of the Child. But health care providers of broad stripes knew it was in a child's best interest to stay with the mother — psychologist John Bowlby's work on the science of attachment theory had been first published in 1951.

After Day's changes took effect, participation in the program plummeted, from six mother-baby pairs nationally in 2008 to three in 2009, 2010 and 2011 and only one in 2012 (Paynter et al. 2022). Before 2012 CSC did not track whether program participants were Indigenous or non-Indigenous. From 2012 to 2019, the data shows 32.8 percent of participants identified as Indigenous, although over 50 percent of people in federal prisons for women in 2021 were Indigenous (Office of the Correctional Investigator 2021). Indigenous women may be less willing than non-Indigenous women to accept ministry interference in their lives, due to the historic and ongoing overinvolvement of the state in their families and removal of their children. Indigenous women may also be more likely to be ineligible for the program because a disproportionate number of them are classified by CSC as maximum security. Finally, Indigenous women have higher rates of convictions for violent offences, many of which occur in the context of defending themselves against sexual assaults or abusive relationships, as was the case for Whitford.

The Custody Rating Scale used by CSC in security classification is both gender and race "blind," ignoring the impact of systemic discrimination in the process of criminalization. As a result, Indigenous women are disproportionately classed as higher risk. The Custody Rating Scale includes factors such as "employment, marital status, family situation, associates, social interaction, substance abuse, community functioning, personal and emotional orientation and attitude" (Miller 2017, 12). Some of these factors, such as employment, can change. Some, like a history of abuse in residential schools, cannot.

Indian Residential Schools operated for over a century in Canada, with the last finally closing in 1996. It is estimated that more than 150,000 Indigenous children were removed from their families to be sent to the facilities over that time period (*CBC News* 2021). In addition to loss of family and cultural connection, the children were subjected to sexual and physical abuse, and thousands of children died while detained at the institutions. In 2001 it was estimated that 15 to 20 percent of incarcerated Indigenous people had survived residential schools (Trevethan et al. 2001). Decades later, it is likely incarcerated people are the children of residential school survivors. The incarceration of Indigenous women is a continuation of colonial, genocidal processes in Canada such as the residential schools (Smylie and Phillips-Beck 2019).

Effectively, the systemic mistreatment of Indigenous women in the past ends up resulting in elevated classification and greater risk of mistreatment while incarcerated. The biased results of the Custody Rating Scale against Indigenous people result in restrictions in access, not only to the Mother-Child Program but also to other programs and options. These include eligibility for community-based housing alternatives to prison, which federal legislation specifies as the preferred option for Indigenous people (Canada, Department of Justice 1992). In 2018 the Supreme Court of Canada ruled that the tests commonly used in custody ratings lacked validity and were biased against Indigenous people (Ewert v. Canada 2018). Yet these invalid tests continue to be used.

CSC tracks the number of people who participate in the Mother-Child Program, but there is no information about those parents who could not participate or did not even apply, which are more common experiences. The number of minor children affected by the federal incarceration of their parents remains unknown. The number of pregnancies and births among people in federal prisons is also a mystery. Federally sentenced women are a stated priority area for the Office of the Correctional Investigator (Office of the Correctional Investigator 2016), but it does not routinely collect or publish information related to pregnancies and children. Although it makes recommendations to CSC about improving health and well-being, it lacks the authority to push those recommendations into meaningful change (Iftene 2019).

The United Nations Rules for the Treatment of Women Prisoners and Non-custodial Measures for Women Offenders (also called the Bangkok Rules) detail the minimum treatment standards for people in prisons designated for women. They were adopted unanimously by the United Nations General Assembly, including Canada, in 2010. Rule 2 stipulates that "prior to or on admission, women with caretaking responsibilities for children shall be permitted to make arrangements for those children, including the possibility of a reasonable suspension of detention, taking into account the best interests of the children." Rule 6 requires the prison administration to document each person's reproductive health history, including pregnancies and number of children, on admission (United Nations Office on Drugs and Crime 2011). In Canada this is simply not done, despite Canada signing on to the rules, because there is no body investigating compliance and no mechanism for enforcement.

Prison is nonrehabilitative. It does not change the conditions of criminalization — the trauma Indigenous women experienced as children and adults, the poverty they lived through, the violence they faced. When a sentence is over, the colonial and racist state and society are still there. Whitford was released in 2011 and broke the conditions of her parole soon after (Prince George Citizen Staff 2011). Survival crime after release is extremely common because restrictive parole conditions can set people up to fail (Cobbina 2009). It is virtually impossible to abstain from using substances when the experience of release is so traumatic; to avoid contact with people with a history of criminalization when criminalization is intergenerational and family members and close supports are also criminalized; to not participate in sex work or theft when poverty is almost certain.

Because there is so little attention paid to the children of incarcerated parents, little is known about what becomes of these children, whether they join their parent inside or not. How many parents lose or regain primary custody when their sentence is over? How healthy are the children and their parents afterwards? How many of these children experience criminalization themselves? No one knows. But we do know what prison costs. To incarcerate a woman in federal prison in Canada costs the public $83,861 per year (Office of the Parliamentary Budget Officer 2018), and to keep a child in foster care for a year costs over $40,000 (Stone 2011). Reproductive justice and prison abolition would see the redistribution of resources from carceral systems to what parents experiencing criminalization really need: income, housing, health care and safety from state surveillance, violence and control.

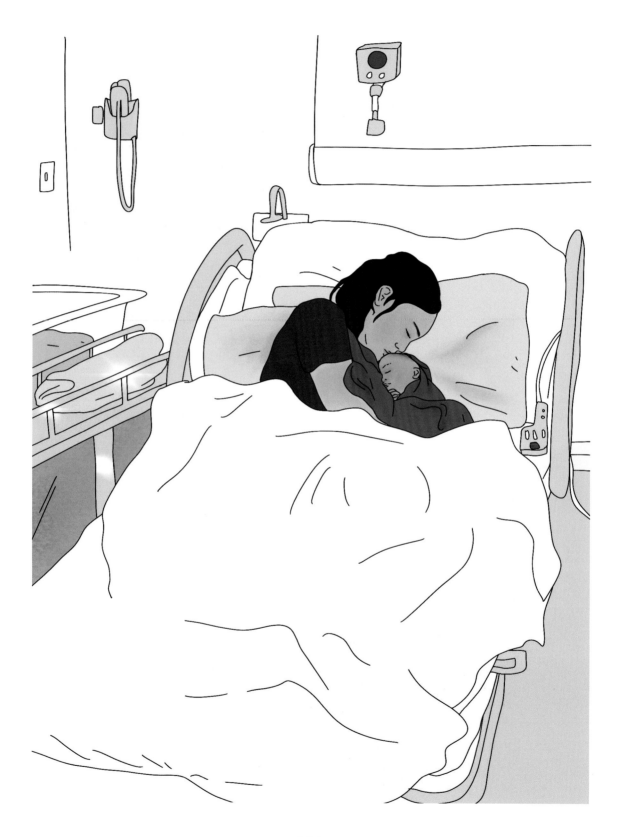

Amanda Inglis

BC was the one province where mothers in jail could keep their babies with them — that is, until 2008 when Amanda Inglis and her baby needed a spot in the program. Inglis, a Secwépemc woman, was twenty-seven years old and pregnant when she began serving a sentence at the Alouette Correctional Centre for Women in the BC town of Maple Ridge. Her son, Damien, was born several weeks early, just as the government made a sudden decision to close the facility's Mother-Baby Program. She herself had been in foster care as a child and was determined that her son would not face the same fate. "That's what your baby's need is, the love of their mother," she said. "So regardless if you're in jail or not, they need to be with their mother; right?" (Inglis v. BC 2013).

Inglis' physician, Dr. Ron Abrahams, is a well-known expert in care for people experiencing perinatal substance use, and he supported her to stay at the Fir Square unit at the BC Women's Hospital with Damien until she received parole, only seven weeks away. Rooming-in was standard practice at Fir Square and prevented the removal of children by the BC Ministry of Children and Family Development. Getting parenting support made the patients clinically healthier, whereas "women who could not keep their babies often lost hope, relapsed and went back to their old lifestyle. Women who were able to keep their babies had a sense of purpose, which aided in their efforts to recover from addiction" (Inglis v. BC 2013).

Once paroled, Inglis moved to the Phoenix transition house in Prince George. Unlike many transitional houses, Phoenix allowed Damien to stay with her and had space for them both. Transition houses may welcome babies according to policy, and even have adequate space, but if they are currently housing another person with parole conditions requiring no contact with children, it is not possible for a baby to stay. Even if a child is permitted, other circumstances could interfere with the ability to parent — for instance, if parole conditions required attendance at a daily Narcotics Anonymous meeting but the baby was not allowed to go, and the person did have any money or support people for childcare.

The closure of the program at Alouette shocked program participants and would-be participants, staff and clinical partners alike. BC had had a mother-baby residential program since 1973, beginning at Twin Maples Farm, the first minimum-security prison for women in the province. About eighty mother-baby pairs participated at Twin Maples, and the facility even had a daycare program (Inglis v. BC 2013). After Twin Maples closed in 1991, Burnaby Correctional Centre for Women started a Mother-Baby Program, and approximately thirty-five mother-baby pairs participated there before the facility closed, replaced by Alouette in 2004 (McMillan and Granger-Brown 2011). Through these iterations of the program there was no corrections policy governing its operations and no formal evaluation.

As an independent scholar, Donna MacLean conducted a 1997 survey at Burnaby Correctional Centre for Women, one of the only analyses of mother-baby programs in Canadian prisons. The facility held a mix of federally and provincially sentenced and remanded women. One-third were Indigenous and one-third had themselves been removed from their families as children by the state. Almost all reported having experienced physical, sexual or psychological abuse. Two-thirds responded they "had a drug problem." Of the 107 women surveyed, 80 were mothers, and only 26 of those mothers had ever lived with their children prior to incarceration. Almost half had had their children removed by the state. Most survey respondents approved of having children participate in a prison-based Mother-Child Program and believed it was in the best interests of the children.

To be eligible to participate in the program at Alouette, a baby had to be born while the mother was incarcerated, and the BC Ministry of Children and Family Development had to approve a mother's participation. The child could stay until two years of age. Provincial jails like Alouette hold people on remand (pretrial custody) and people with sentences up to two years less a day. At Alouette, staff were trained in infant CPR, nursing care was available from 7 a.m. to 10 p.m. and regular public health and physician visits occurred inside and outside of the jail.

"Those babies have had a better chance in their life to start off than they otherwise would have," said Dr. Ruth Elwood Martin, the prison physician at Alouette. "Once you take that baby away, you can't go back." Dr. Amy Salmon conducted research with mother-baby pairs at Alouette and found all the babies "healthy, happy, unremarkable, alert, and engaged with their environment" (Inglis v. BC 2013). She also found that staff described the program positively. For pregnant people at Alouette, the prospect of participating in the program reduced their stress. A mother in the program said, "It was everything for me. Being able to keep [baby] gave me the motivation to do something good with my life. And I — every day when I see him and we're our own little family, he's everything for me. I can't picture my life without him. I think it would be drastically different had I not had the opportunity to be with him the way that I was" (Inglis v. BC 2013).

Everything changed in 2006. Brent Merchant, assistant deputy minister for corrections, requested that Brenda Tole, the warden at Alouette, draft a policy about the Mother-Baby Program. He expected the policy to stipulate that children would be permitted at Alouette only in exceptional circumstances. Tole did draft a policy, but not with that conclusion. Then, without consulting her, the draft policy was changed by the deputy provincial director of adult custody in 2007 to read that "children will not be permitted to stay in a correctional centre" (Inglis v. BC 2013). Merchant hired a new warden in the summer of 2007 and made clear the Mother-Baby Program should be cancelled. The decision to cancel was not based on any evaluation of the program. Dr. Martin was not consulted. Thirteen pairs participated in the Alouette program over its four years of operations, and the last baby left the institution in February 2008 (Inglis v. BC 2013). The program was cancelled.

Patricia Block was pregnant when first taken into custody at Alouette in 2008. Knowing by then the Mother-Baby Program at Alouette was closed, she applied for transfer to the nearby federal prison, Fraser Valley Institution, just so she could participate in its Mother-Child Program. She faced bureaucratic delay after delay. Her application was officially rejected for failure to complete the required courses (first aid) before the baby's birth, which she was prevented from taking due to administrative hurdles. When her daughter, Amber, was born on March 19, 2009, she breastfed her and stayed up all night to not miss a moment with her. The day after Amber was born, the Ministry of Children and Family Development removed the baby from Block's care (Luk 2013). Block applied to be paroled to a treatment centre for substance use, and once Amber was three months old, the baby joined her there.

Inglis, Block and their two children launched a lawsuit against the Province of BC for violation of their Section 7 Charter rights to security of the person. Supported by the Canadian Civil Liberties Association and West Coast LEAF. The Supreme Court of BC heard volumes of expert evidence attesting to the value of the Mother-Baby Program, particularly for the breastfeeding relationship and development of healthy psychological attachment. Despite a lack of formal evaluation, BC had successfully operated mother-baby programs for over three decades. Merchant felt that babies were not the responsibility of the correctional system and that he should not be required to accommodate them. Yet the very first of the Bangkok Rules reads: "Account shall be taken of the distinctive needs of women prisoners.... Providing for such needs in order to accomplish substantial gender equality shall not be regarded as discriminatory" (United Nations Office on Drugs and Crime 2011, 8). People in prisons designated for women have different needs, such as those regarding reproductive health, that must be accommodated. Failure to do so is discriminatory.

To alleviate the impact of the program's cancellation, and recognizing the need to support attachment and breastfeeding, the leadership of Alouette stated during the trial that they increased visitation options and purchased breast pumps and breast milk storage supplies. There are no studies or statistics about breastfeeding initiation or duration for incarcerated people in Canada. However, a few hours of contact a week with the baby and a breast pump is unlikely to be adequate to sustain lactation: the stress of the prison environment and lack of physical connection to the infant impedes production of the hormones needed to produce and release milk. It is unlikely the new arrangement would provide babies with nutrition equivalent to what they would receive by being with their parent full-time, breastfeeding on demand.

Clinical experts were called as witnesses for the plaintiffs and the defence. Psychologist Dr. Peggy Koopman testified that babies would face more risk of physical and emotional harm outside of the prison than in it with their parents. Dr. Martin testified that separation increased children's risk of developmental deficits. However, psychologist Dr. Maureen Olley was concerned about the lack of regular data collection about mental illnesses among prisoners at Alouette and the potential associated risks. Dr. Michael Elterman, another psychologist, contested that the best interests of each child would have to be assessed individually.

Justice Carol Ross concluded there was no evidence that babies had experienced any harm at Alouette or had contact with contraband drugs. She found the international research supported the safety of prison nursery programs. She determined the potential for babies to experience noisy environments, to be touched by a person who was not their parent or designated babysitter or to fall asleep in bed with their parents — all likely harms suggested by the defendants — were not risks unique to Alouette. The cancellation of the program violated the Section 7 rights of both the parents and their babies. Furthermore, she found separation exacerbated the hardships incarcerated people had already endured in their lives and the ones the children had an increased likelihood of facing, discriminating against both with respect to the equality provision of Section 15. She wrote, quoting Justice Rosalie Abella, that if "state conduct widens the gap between the historically disadvantaged group and the rest of society rather than narrowing it, then it is discriminatory" (Inglis v. BC 2013).

Inglis and Block had won the case, but by that time their children were five years old. Since Alouette relaunched the Mother-Baby Program in 2014, there have only been a few participants (BC, Minister for Public Safety and Solicitor General Corrections Branch 2016). It is a challenge to convince the Ministry of Children and Family Development that parents can keep children safe in the prison after the legacy of its closure for "safety reasons." Indeed, in the first year after the program reopened, three mothers had their applications rejected by the ministry (Givetash 2016).

Both the provincial and federal programs remain deplorably underevaluated. Over 125 babies have participated in BC's Mother-Baby Programs at the Twin Maples, Burnaby and Alouette facilities, and over 133 in the federal Institutional Mother-Child Program (Paynter et al. 2022), and still no long-term research has examined the benefits (or harms) of this approach. The case of *Inglis v. BC* should have prompted action in every province and territory to address how incarceration discriminates against primary caregivers, most of whom are women, and their children. It simply did not.

There are still no operational mother-baby programs in any provincial or territorial facilities outside of BC (Paynter, Bagg and Heggie 2020). Denying some birthing people access to their newborns while others have it is decidedly unfair. However, the creation of new mother-child (or, more appropriately, parent-child) programs in facilities designated for women is fraught with ethical problems. The last major reform in the federal system, the shift from the central Prison for Women in Kingston, Ontario, to six regional facilities caused the numbers of incarcerated women to skyrocket — if you build it, they will (be forced to) come. Prison justice writer Victoria Law (2009) recounts how the Quaker-led reform to create separate prisons designated for women in the US in the late nineteenth and early twentieth centuries laid the groundwork for vast increases in the number of incarcerated people. More mother-baby programs will inevitably result in more mothers and babies being incarcerated.

Returning to Dr. Angela Davis's (2003) reminder that we need to break free of the belief in the inevitability of prisons in our society, the unequal and problematic access to mother-baby programs in prisons in Canada should prompt us not to build more of them but to insist on alternatives. What counts as an alternative must be critically assessed. Locating a mother-child program in community is insufficient if the carceral intention remains. Ethnographer Lynne Haney (2010) chronicled the intense surveillance and social control of "therapeutic communities" constructed as alternatives to incarceration for mothers serving sentences in Northern California. The result was paternalistic and pathologizing.

In May 2021 Minnesota passed legislation to allow a potentially meaningful alternative to prison nurseries and so-called therapeutic communities. The Healthy Start Act supports all pregnant mothers in state prison to apply for conditional release for the first year of their baby's life (Gaines 2021). The legislation stemmed from years of service, research and activism by the Minnesota Prison Doula Project, who observed — and objected to — the conditions of pregnant people behind bars, all of whom had to give up their infants within thirty-six hours of birth (Shlafer et al. 2015; Shlafer et al. 2021).

Mother-baby units in prisons are not immune from the institutional failures so common in the prison system, and participation in the units does not guarantee mother or baby will be safe. In September 2019 a baby was born still in a cell at the Bronzefield prison in Surrey, England, where there is a mother-baby unit on-site. Tamsin Morris, formerly the manager of a mother-baby unit at the Styal Prison in England, warned authorities the same could happen there; four months later, it did (Taylor 2020). From July 2020 to March 2021, three out of thirty-one births by prisoners in the United Kingdom happened en route to hospital (Taylor and Devlin 2021). In fall 2021, Birth Companions, a prison doula organization in the United Kingdom, issued a petition calling for a ban on all incarceration of pregnant women. Birth Companions, and the researchers and activists the group collaborates with, insist that the only way to prevent humiliating, degrading and dangerous prison births is to prevent pregnant women from ever going to prison (Birth Companions 2021).

Julie Bilotta

The United States incarcerates so many people that every year thousands of people experience pregnancy and birth in a prison or jail. At Bedford Hills Correctional Facility in New York, where the longest-standing prison nursery still operates, over two dozen children are in the nursery program at any given time (Li 2019). The dysfunctional US health insurance regime results in jail being one of the few times people experiencing poverty have access to care. In her book *Jailcare*, US obstetrician-gynecologist and medical anthropologist Dr. Carolyn Sufrin (2017, 236) concludes, "Jail care is a symptom of social failure, of abandonment of a group of people that includes poor, predominantly black women, whose reproduction has been vilified in policies and broader cultural narratives."

In Canada, carceral maternity is fortunately far less common. Saskatchewan human rights lawyer Robin Hansen submitted an access to information and privacy request about births in custody for her forthcoming book, the *Newborn's Sentence in the Colonial Shadow*. She found CSC does not track this information federally, nor does BC or Quebec provincially. In the remaining eleven provincial and territorial jurisdictions, sixty-nine births were recorded over four years, from 2011 to 2015, which is roughly seventeen per year across the country.

The flip side of the rarity of prison birth in Canada is that facilities are ill-prepared for it. This was evident when Julie Bilotta arrived at the Ottawa-Carleton Detention Centre (OCDC) in September 2012, eight months pregnant. She did not really know what it meant at first, the sick feeling, the pain. It was her first pregnancy. As it became clear what was happening, and what was going to happen, she could not believe it: she was in labour and she was going to be forced to give birth there, in a filthy jail. As the statement of claim for her subsequent civil suit against Ontario would lay out, "The Defendants had complete care and control over Ms. Bilotta and her baby. But for the Defendant's malicious and negligent actions, the shocking injuries suffered by Ms. Bilotta and her baby would not have occurred" (Bilotta v. Ontario Statement of Claim 2014).

In 2012 Julie Bilotta — now a makeup artist, writer and prison justice advocate — was twenty-six years old, in a loving relationship and, despite the entanglements she faced with the justice system, looking forward to the birth of her child. How she ended up incarcerated is not an unusual story for women who experience criminalization. Facing charges related to substance use and having broken unsustainable bail conditions, Bilotta could not secure someone else to act as her surety. Even with a doctor's note in hand attesting to her high-risk pregnancy, the court sent her to jail.

On the morning of September 29, Bilotta woke up nauseous and vomited in her bed. She could not eat anything because she felt so bad, and a guard said she would make a terrible mother since she was not even willing to eat for the health of her baby. She asked to see the nurse, and at noon the guards brought her to the health unit where a nurse gave her Tums. The guard thought she looked grey but took no action. When the contractions started, she begged for relief, the other women in her unit calling out on her behalf. Bilotta was told she was being disruptive and causing tension between the women on the unit, and was sent to a segregation cell. A guard would later describe her as "moaning and complaining throughout the afternoon about cramping, wanting to go to the hospital and wanting pain medication" (College of Nurses of Ontario 2014). Nurse Rose Gyasi went to see her and gave her a single Tylenol for the pain. Bilotta felt inside her vagina — there was a little foot in her hand. Gyasi said it was probably a mucous plug, and an accompanying guard accused Bilotta of shoving contraband inside herself. Gyasi did not perform an internal exam and when a correctional officer suggested it, she replied she "didn't do that." An internal vaginal exam is not part of standard nursing education and is considered an advanced skill learned while employed in an obstetrics or gynecology unit. Neither nurse nor correctional officer consulted with a physician or midwife. Only at 8:20 p.m., when a little leg was visibly hanging outside Bilotta's body, did the correctional officer ask for an emergency alert. Nurses and correctional staff amassed in Bilotta's cell, yet in the confusion no one called an ambulance. At 8:45, realizing no one had yet done so, the sergeant called 9-1-1. The paramedics arrived at 9:15. Gionni was born at 9:21 p.m. in the jail cell, footling breech, cord around his neck and in severe respiratory distress.

Bilotta and Gionni were separated at the hospital — she needed emergency surgery to remove the retained placenta and several blood transfusions to treat hemorrhage. After the surgery the OCDC guards shackled her to her bed. Gionni was sent to the neonatal intensive care unit, intubated, placed on a ventilator, medicated for seizures and tube-fed. It gets worse from there. Three days later, Bilotta was sent back to OCDC, the very site of the torture, unable to be near her son, who remained in critical condition for weeks. Having contracted MRSA, an antibiotic-resistant bacteria, likely in OCDC, she developed a large wound infection on her leg, requiring further surgery and leaving a scar twenty centimetres long.

Bilotta's legal advocates took her case to the press; even veterans in the field of prison justice were horrified by what she experienced. A grassroots organization called the Mom and Baby Coalition formed and staged protests outside the offices of Madeleine Meilleur, Ontario minister of community safety and correctional services (CBC News 2012a). With babies strapped to their backs, coalition members demanded Bilotta be reunited with her baby. Meilleur contested accusations of systemic barriers to health services for incarcerated people (Pedwell 2012). Ignoring Bilotta's experience, she claimed Ontario's Correctional Services had procedures in place to manage birth. "It's like if the mother was delivering at home," she said. "It's not the perfect way, it's not what is being planned but when this happens they are assisted into the delivery. The mother and the baby are taken care of and they are transferred to the hospital" (CBC News 2012b). The conflation of a planned home birth — for which there are strict clinical criteria, lifesaving supplies on hand and two trained midwives on-site — with abandonment in a prison cell is jarring and grotesque.

Bilotta was able to secure a release from jail and placement with Gionni, once he was discharged from hospital, at a halfway house managed by the Elizabeth Fry Society in Ottawa. Most criminalized women are mothers (Sawyer and Bertram 2018), and they all want to be with their children. Mother-baby accommodation arrangements can spur jealousy and sparring. Other people in the house called the Children's Aid Society to complain about Bilotta, and in February 2013 agency representatives came, with police escort, to remove Gionni from her care. Although Gionni's father is Indigenous and Bilotta had established kinship care arrangements for her son should she be again unable to care for him, he was placed in foster care with a non-Indigenous family.

Like many mothers, Bilotta decided to plead guilty to ensure a certain, short carceral sentence, which, with the assistance of the Ontario ombudsperson, she served in the Quinte Detention Centre in Napanee (Fiander 2016). Bilotta found Quinte to be easier to endure than OCDC. Once out, she worked to regain custody of Gionni from the Children's Aid Society. He had continued throughout his first year of life to have bouts of respiratory illness requiring hospitalization. On October 13, after Gionni's parents finally had regained custody of him, they found him not breathing in his crib. He was pronounced dead at the hospital, not quite thirteen months old.

In spring 2014 the College of Nurses of Ontario held a disciplinary hearing regarding the actions of nurse Rose Gyasi. She faced a complaint for professional misconduct, for failing "to adequately assess, monitor and provide appropriate nursing care" and for failing to seek assistance. She accepted all allegations. She had registered as a nurse only six months before Gionni's birth, and OCDC was her first job as a registered nurse. The ratio of prisoners to nurses at OCDC was two hundred to one (Gillis 2016). Gyasi received a five-month suspension on her licence to practise. She was the only nurse disciplined for the incident, although more senior nurses were there that day, and Gyasi's notes indicate she sought advice from them and called a physician. The physician denied being informed of the situation. The Ministry of Community Safety and Correctional Services conducted its own investigation into Bilotta's treatment and disciplined several staff, although details were never made public (Bell 2013).

In March 2016 Yasir Naqvi, who had become the minister of community safety and correctional services, appointed a task force to address overcrowding and capacity issues at OCDC. The facility has a reputation as one of the worst jails in the province. Reportedly, 22 percent of people incarcerated there will spend time in segregation (Seymour 2016). The unit designated for women is only a small part of the institution. Located in an older section of the institution, it has fifty-two beds. Overcrowding, suicide, overdose, lockdown and mistreatment by staff are frequently reported. In a study of prisoners' experiences in the jail, Laura McKendy (2018, 133) describes "a guard culture marked by the view that prisoners were sub-human," which "included the belittling and insulting of prisoners, acts of cruelty, failure to fulfill job duties, and the display of double-standards." All of this proved to be the case in how Bilotta was treated. In May 2016 she spoke in front of three hundred people at a public forum calling for change at OCDC (Johnstone 2016).

The task force recommendations included funding bail beds (spaces in supportive shelter programs that act as sureties for the charged individual), and community-based alternatives to remand; reforming bail to allow more people to be released; establishing more diversion programs for people with substance use disorders; shifting responsibility for health from Correction Services to the Ministry of Health; and conducting a review of the health care offered at the institution (Ottawa-Carleton Detention Centre Task Force 2017). Issues at OCDC continue to be met with more and more hiring of correctional officers and investment in the institution, instead of noncarceral solutions. That year, the province spent $9.5 million on body scanner technology to reduce contraband entry (Seymour 2016).

In February 2017, just months after the task force tabled its report, OCDC staff ignored a twenty-eight-year-old woman as she miscarried in her cell, bleeding heavily and screaming for help (Postmedia News 2017). The fetal remains were likely flushed down the toilet, and she was taken to hospital not in an ambulance, but a prisoner transport van. The woman had been remanded on charges of stealing $225 worth of products from Walmart. Her toddler has been killed by an impaired driver and she developed a substance use disorder trying to cope. Returned to the jail a day after this "extraordinarily traumatic and draconian way of miscarrying a child," she chose to plead guilty to her charges (Postmedia News 2017). The judged fined her $1 for each charge, arguing she had suffered enough.

Violence like what this woman and Bilotta endured is not unique to OCDC. In April 2017 Bianca Mercer was released from the Central Nova Scotia Correctional Facility in Dartmouth, at twenty-three years old and seven months pregnant. While incarcerated she had spent weeks in solitary confinement and even had her mattress confiscated (Rahr 2018). Weeks before her baby Althea was due, Bianca learned the worst: her baby had died in the womb. Bianca believed her incarceration caused this loss (CBC Radio 2019). The only explanation doctors had was the fetus had experienced distress.

In May 2017 Stephanie Albert, a thirty-year-old mother of three on remand at Fort Saskatchewan Correctional Centre, knew something was not right with her pregnancy. At almost five months, she expected to feel more fetal movement, not less. The jail physician surmised she was feeling "growing pains" and gave her Tylenol. A month later, after multiple requests, she was taken to a clinic for an ultrasound, which confirmed her fear that the pregnancy was no longer viable. Rather than being taken to hospital after the ultrasound, she was returned to jail, where she started showing signs of sepsis. She was finally taken to hospital for induction, and when the baby was born "he had been dead long enough that the skin was decomposing" (Wakefield 2018, 1).

In 2018 Julie Arseneau, twenty-one years old and about two months pregnant, started bleeding while in court in Edmundston, New Brunswick (CBC News 2018). The emergency room physician in Edmundston referred her for ultrasound, but the New Brunswick Women's Correctional Centre refused to send her. For over four weeks she bled and waited. When she was ultimately released and could seek care herself, she learned she had miscarried.

Prison is no place for a pregnant person. The risks are simply too great and the trauma too severe. Researching pregnancy in prison in the United Kingdom, Laura Abbott and colleagues (2020) have found pregnant people to be so traumatized by the experience that they go into a state of denial as a coping mechanism. Despite the fetishization of the pregnant person in society in general, in prison "the pregnancy afford[s] no special treatment" (Abbott et al. 2020, 664) — no extra space, food, care or comfort. Although prison pregnancy is understudied in Canada, what little research there is has found the babies of incarcerated pregnant people are more likely to be born prematurely and very small in size (Carter Ramirez et al. 2020).

Labour and birth are disruptive, physical, loud, organic — and prisons are designed to punish disordered behaviour. As prisoners' rights activist Alex Hundert (2013, 1) wrote, "Bilotta's pleas were not totally ignored. In fact, it was her refusal to stop crying for help that landed her in the segregation cell where she gave birth." Self-advocacy, advocacy for the baby — all will be interpreted through the carceral lens, demanding supplication.

For all she survived, Bilotta sued the Province of Ontario, and each of the nurses and correctional officers involved in the malicious and negligent treatment she and Gionni were subjected to, for $1.3 million. She settled out of court in 2018. But no settlement will bring Gionni back to her.

TOWARD REPRODUCTIVE HEALTH AND JUSTICE

As the stories in Chapter 5 make clear, ending the incarceration of pregnant people, parents and primary caregivers — of people, period — is essential for reproductive health and justice. Created and led by women of colour (Roberts 2015; Ross 2017; Ross and Solinger 2017), the movement for reproductive justice critically examines the intersecting impacts of racism, colonialism, classism, ableism, homophobia and transphobia on the right to not have children, the right to have children and the right to parent chosen children in safety. Prison abolition, a movement also led by people of colour (Davis 2003; Kaba 2021), creates space for imagination, hope and change. The depth and complexity of these movements are what tie the stories in this book together and shape the connections.

When I heard about Julie Bilotta's experience on the news, about the violence and horror of birth in a jail cell, I felt the same rage that draconian abortion restrictions first ignited in me early in my life. The rage has only amplified as the years go by. While abortion access has improved drastically in recent years, the reproductive oppression of the carceral system has expanded. More people are incarcerated in prisons designated for women, more parents are remanded before trial, more children are separated from their incarcerated parents, more parents are separated from their incarcerated children, more families are under surveillance by child "protection" services, more experiences of social marginalization are criminalized, more sentences are decided without consideration for the needs of families and communities to thrive. And around it goes.

Mother-child programs are often proposed as an alternative to forced and immediate separation of incarcerated people from their newborns, but these programs do not address the incompatibility of pregnancy with the carceral institution, the misalignment between punishment and care. While I have dedicated years to connecting incarcerated people to volunteer doula support, I am under no illusion that doula support remedies the trauma of carceral pregnancy. Doula support is a demonstration of love and solidarity; it does not change the material conditions of prison. As the stories in Chapter 5 demonstrate, for *Emily Boyle, Renee Acoby, Lisa Whitford, Amanda Inglis* and *Julie*

Bilotta, mother-child programs are a troubling "solution." They involve unequal access, increasing axes of surveillance and the incarceration and institutionalization of newborns.

There is no long-term research in Canada to attest to the harm or benefit for children (and parents) in these programs, and certainly none that compares carceral co-residence with alternatives. What if instead of calling for more care and opportunities in prison, we called for more care and opportunities outside? Instead of insisting only on the rights to parent in prison, we insisted on the rights to parent in the community? Instead of investing yet more into the prison system, we divested from it, as abolitionists urge, and put energy and funding elsewhere, to mitigate the effects of social structures that result in criminalization in the first place?

Canada has several models to build on that uphold the right to parent. Supportive care and housing programs for pregnant people who use substances and are at risk of child protection involvement, including Fir Square, Sheway, Sanctum 1.5 and others, have been developed by harm reduction advocates and demonstrate success at preventing family dissolution. Unlike in the United States, pregnant people in Canada cannot be criminalized for substance use or other actions that may affect the fetus (e.g., enduring violence, homelessness and hunger), thanks to the activism of people like *Donna George* and the Indigenous and feminist organizations that supported her legal case. This legal distinction creates space for creative solutions. But once a child is born in Canada, they become vulnerable to racist, colonial state practices of child removal like those justified through faulty for-profit *Motherisk* hair drug tests — unless these practices are recognized as such and stopped. Ending birth alerts like the one *Baby H* experienced and discriminatory child removal practices like what *Fatuma Alyaan* faced as a child and as a mother must be a priority for everyone working in reproductive rights and prison justice. Like *water protectors* Autumn Peltier and the Mi'kmaw grandmothers do for all of us, we must expose environmental racism and protect clean water for the health of children for generations to come.

Racism and control from health care professionals must also be addressed. Forced sterilization and other kinds of clinical violence divorce health services from care and strip people of the right to choose to parent. One of the reasons I wanted to write this book was for my nursing students — most of whom are white cis women — so they might understand how they can become culpable participants in coercive practices. A nurse walked *Leilani Muir* into the operating theatre for the removal of her fallopian tubes and the unnecessary removal of her appendix. Classism, racism and ableism were and are underinterrogated in reproductive health services in Canada.

Without acknowledgement of fertility as a social issue — affected, among other things, by neoliberal policies rewarding polluting resource extraction industries — the field of fertility treatment remains privatized and decidedly unjust. *Leia Picard,* the antihero in Chapter 3, was just doing what the law would let her get away with, and even when she could not get away with it any longer, the penalty she received became a positive PR stunt. Recent federal amendments to reimbursement regulations in assisted reproduction may make some headway towards reducing exploitation, but the industry requires a massive rethink if there is to be alignment between reproductive technologies and reproductive justice.

Kirsti Mathers McHenry and family made strides towards inclusive definitions of the family in the law. Organizers and activists must continue to advance the right for queer families to form. The law has significant catching up to do, as it remains decades behind the creative, adaptive, loving forms families now take. Health care providers and legal practitioners have work to do alongside, adjusting our assumptions, language and practice norms to bust out of the tired square box of the straight nuclear family.

The right to not parent — to contraception and abortion — is where Canada has most improved. The activism of many, including *Dorothea Palmer, Chantal Daigle,* the *iamkarats* campaign and the evolving team at *Clinic 554,* have pushed Canada to some of the most progressive contraception and abortion policies on the planet. While the freedom of complete decriminalization of abortion, as well as the other gains described in these pages, should be celebrated, reproductive rights in Canada remain crowded out by white feminism, by the classism and #MeFirst orientation of "vanguards" like *Dr. Emily Stowe.* Contraception and abortion are legally available, but you must have sufficient social and economic means to ensure you get timely access for yourself.

At the base of the tripod of reproductive justice principles — the right to not parent, the right to parent and the right to parent in safety — is the requirement for bodily autonomy. In Chapter 1, I traced five areas where the courage of regular people who just wanted to live — to go to school, to go to work, to go to the store, to be their very selves — brought important changes to Canadian law and understanding of bodily autonomy. *Heidi Rathjen* petitioned for safety from gun violence, a fight that continues. *Justice L'Heureux-Dubé* stood up for an unnamed teenager sexually assaulted in a job interview and firmly declared the law required clear and continuous consent. *Synthia Kavanagh,* a trans woman, asked only to get to serve her sentence in a prison designated for women. *Terri-Jean Bedford* fought paternalistic state control of her rights to govern herself as a sex worker. And *Santina Rao,* a young Black mom, would not allow herself to be abused by police without resistance.

The twenty-three stories in this book are intended to be an introductory picture of the complexity of reproductive freedom — and oppression — in Canada. Knowing what things used to be like in terms of reproductive rights, how they have changed and what they could become should direct clinical practice in reproductive health and legal reform to advance reproductive freedom. Working as clinicians in reproductive health, or even as activists for policy change, there is a danger in believing more service is enough to make things right — that an increase in funding, training or hiring in health care is enough to improve health and well-being, and that a law on paper is the same as real life. But none of these strategies are going to work without meaningful shifts in power.

Canada has made important strides in abortion access that everyone should know about and be proud of, but reproductive oppression is a grounding principle of colonialism, and it is still in vast operation in this country. It matters that abortion at Clinic 554 still goes unfunded, violation of the Canada Health Act be damned. That Indigenous and Black communities face forced sterilization, violent child removal, and police brutality. That those without citizenship status face the threat of deportation. That queer people face discrimination and aggression. That access to reproductive technologies is unequal, classist and ableist. That sex workers are criminalized and endangered. That the brave people who defend the land and water — the literal stuff our lives depend on — face state opposition. This book is intended to make practical connections between these fights in Canada. Reproductive justice creates linkages where the silos in reproductive health and law might fail to. Experiencing reproductive freedom requires social and economic equality. As the co-founder of SisterSong Loretta Ross said, "Our ability to control what happens to our bodies is constantly challenged by poverty, racism, environmental degradation, sexism, homophobia, and injustice" (Ross et al. 2002, 147).

For those of us hoping for and working to improve abortion access in health care, law and civil society, I hope we also work for prison abolition, for clean water, for a meaningful end to birth alerts and for inclusive legal definitions of parenting. I hope these are seen as connected struggles, tied to all the reproductive rights fights in between. There is so much power in working together.

ACKNOWLEDGEMENTS

I wrote the first draft of this book very quickly in the spring of 2021, but it is the product of twenty years of work in this field and collaboration with and learning from wonderful teachers, most importantly patients in Nova Scotia and people I have met inside and outside of prison spaces across the country.

Thank you to Julia Hutt, whose images make this book so beautiful. I started working with Julia on images for Wellness Within: An Organization for Health and Justice projects in 2019, and she is a visionary.

Thank you to my editor (and neighbour) Fazeela Jiwa, for inviting me into the Fernwood fold and gently pushing me through my first experience in book creation. Thank you to the Fernwood team, especially Jessica Herdman, for patience as Julia and I figured out the cover.

I thank my mother, Beth Paynter, always an excellent editor, for agreeing to be the first reader of this book, which I sent in instalments while on COVID-19 lockdown in spring 2021. Thank you to my dear Halifax friends Dr. Catherine Bryan, Claire Rillie, Lauren Matheson, Leah Pink, Lindsay McVicar, Lynn Bessoudo, Matthew Herder, Nasha Nijhawan and Rachael Borlase for their feedback and reassurance and good humour about everything. Thank you to Clark MacIntosh for suggestions to make this manuscript more gender inclusive. There is no research assistant more reliable, capable and productive than Clare Heggie. My mentors, Dr. El Jones, Dr. Francoise Baylis, Dr. Jocelyn Downie, Dr. Madine VanderPlaat and Dr. Christine Saulnier, are wise, forceful and simply stellar. Thank you for including me in your incredible work.

My PhD supervisory committee at Dalhousie University, Dr. Ruth Martin-Misener, Dr. Adelina Iftene and Dr. Gail Tomblin Murphy, were remarkably tolerant of me throwing a wrench in the form of a surprise book into the course of my dissertation. I am so grateful for your steadfast encouragement and collaboration over the past five years. Thank you to the Contraception and Abortion Research Team at the University of British Columbia, especially Dr. Wendy Norman and Dr. Sarah Munro.

I'm so glad Shari Graydon and I organized an Informed Opinions workshop in Halifax in 2011; I have been "op-ed-ing" a great deal ever since, and this book is like two dozen op-eds.

I work too much and have the absolute best coworkers at the abortion clinic, the Family Newborn unit, the School of Nursing and the Wellness Within team. Thanks for putting up with me always doing at minimum two things at once.

Nova Scotia is home to many hardworking abolitionists and prison justice advocates. I am deeply appreciative of the unwavering commitment of Darlene MacEachern, Emma Halpern, Sheila Wildeman, Ashley Avery, Ben Perryman and Hanna Garson, as well as the Coverdale, Elizabeth Fry, and East Coast Prison Justice organizations. Thank you to Senator Yvonne Boyer and the team at the Canadian Association of Elizabeth Fry Societies: Kelly Potvin, Kassandra Churcher, Emilie Coyle, Patti Tait and Jackie Omstead. You made our reproductive justice workshops happen, and they were a necessary precursor to this book.

I could not have written this book without the financial support of the Pierre Elliott Trudeau Foundation, Canadian Institutes of Health Research, Killam Foundation, Research Nova Scotia, Canadian Nurses Foundation, IWK Health Centre and Dalhousie University for my doctoral studies. Thank you to Arts Nova Scotia for funding this book as a work of art.

Thank you so much to my whole family, my mom Beth, my father Jacques, sister Emma, brother Willem and sister-in-law Erinn, for your company and love. Most of all, thank you to my partner, Johana Bearden, and our children Freyja and Agatha, astounding beauties and brilliant minds all three. I love you.

REFERENCES

Abbott, Laura, Tricia Scott, Hilary Thomas, and Kathy Weston. 2020. "Pregnancy and Childbirth in English Prisons: Institutional Ignominy and the Pains of Imprisonment." *Sociology of Health & Illness* 42, 3. doi.org/10.1111/1467-9566.13052.

Abdul, Umair. 2014. "Bedford v. Canada: Renewed Debate on the 'World's Oldest Profession.' " *CanLII Connects*, Dec. 30. canliiconnects.org/en/commentaries/35049.

Abel, Gillian, Lisa Fitzgerald, and Cheryl Brunton. 2007. *The Impact of the Prostitution Reform Act on the Health and Safety Practices of Sex Workers.* University of Otago. otago.ac.nz/christchurch/otago018607.pdf.

Aboriginal Children in Care Working Group. 2015. *Report to Canada's Premiers. First Nations Caring Society.* fncaringsociety.com/sites/default/files/Aboriginal%20Children%20in%20Care%20Report%20%28July%202015%29.pdf.

Ackerman, Katrina. 2012. "'Not in the Atlantic Provinces': The Abortion Debate in New Brunswick, 1980–1987." *Acadiensis: Journal of the History of the Atlantic Region* 41, 1.

___. 2015. "A Region at Odds: Abortion Politics in the Maritime Provinces, 1969–1988." Doctoral dissertation, University of Waterloo. uwspace.uwaterloo.ca/bitstream/handle/10012/9777/Ackerman_Katrina..pdf?sequence=1&isAllowed=y.

Action Canada for Sexual Health & Rights. 2019. "Solidarity Statement for Sex Workers' Rights." secure.actioncanadashr.org/en/solidarity-sex-workers-rights.

Ahmed, Sara. 2014. "The Problem of Perception." *Feministkilljoys.com*, Feb. 14. feministkilljoys.com/2014/02/17/the-problem-of-perception.

Alberta. 1928. The Sexual Sterilization Act, SA 1928, c 37. canlii.ca/t/53zws.

___. 1937. An Act to Amend the Sexual Sterilization Act, SA 1937, c 47. canlii.ca/t/540qt.

___. 1942. Sexual Sterilization Act, RSA 1942, c 194. canlii.ca/t/53wjj.

Allen, Bonnie. 2017. "Saskatoon Police Chief Apologizes for Refusing Young Mom a Breast Pump while in Custody." *CBC News*, June 2. cbc.ca/news/canada/saskatchewan/saskatoon-police-chief-apologizes-for-refusing-young-mom-a-breast-pump-while-in-custody-1.4141326.

AltaGas. 2021. "Alton Natural Gas Storage Project Update." altonnaturalgasstorage.ca/news/alton-natural-gas-storage-project-update.

Ambroise, Sylvie. 2021. " 'I Believe that There Is Racial Profiling': Provinces Are Slowly Banning Birth Alerts, but Not in Quebec." *APTN National News*, March 18. aptnnews.ca/national-news/birth-alerts-racial-profiling-anishnabeg-quebec.

American Psychological Association. 2008. "Postpartum Depression." apa.org/pi/women/resources/reports/postpartum-depression.

Arbour, Louise. 1996. *Commission of Inquiry into Certain Events at the Prison for Women in Kingston.* publications.gc.ca/collections/collection_2017/bcp-pco/JS42-73-1996-eng.pdf.

Ashley, Florence. 2020a. "Surgical Informed Consent and Recognizing a Perioperative Duty to Disclose in Transgender Health Care." *McGill Journal of Law and Health* 13, 1. florenceashley.com/uploads/1/2/4/4/124439164/ashley_surgical_informed_consent_and_recognizing_a_perioperative_duty_to_disclose_in_transgender_health_care.pdf.

___. 2020b. "I like genital reconfiguration surgery personally, but mostly find myself either saying simply genital surgery or the specific surgery." Twitter, Nov. 21. twitter.com/ButNotTheCity/status/13302656 05895843841?s=20.

Asian Communities for Reproductive Justice. 2005. "A New Vision." forwardtogether.org/wp-content/uploads/2017/12/ACRJ-A-New-Vision.pdf.

Bacak, Valerio, Katherine Bright, and Lauren Wilson. 2020. "Gender-Affirmative Housing in Jails and Prisons." *The Lancet* 7, 373.

Backhouse, Constance B. 1983. "Involuntary Motherhood, Abortion, Birth Control and the Law in Nineteenth Century Canada." *Windsor Yearbook of Access to Justice* 3. constancebackhouse.ca/fileadmin/publicationlist/InvoluntaryMotherhood.pdf.

___. 1991. "The Celebrated Abortion Trial of Dr. Emily Stowe, Toronto, 1879." *Canadian Bulletin of Medical History* 8, 2.

___. 2017. "Claire Heureux-Dubé: A Controversial Judge on a Controversial Court in a Controversial Time." *Revue juridique Thémis de l'Université de Montréal* 51, 2–3.

Bagley, Sarah M., Mam Jarra Gai, Joel J. Earlywine, et al. 2020. "Incidence and Characteristics of Nonfatal Opioid Overdose among Youths Aged 11 to 24 Years by Sex." *JAMA Network Open* 3, 12.

Baig, F. 2021. "Indigenous Women Still Forced, Coerced into Sterilization." *Global News*, June 3. globalnews.ca/news/7920118/indigenous-women-sterilization-senate-report.

Balfour, Gillian. 2018. "Searching Prison Cells and Prisoner Bodies: Redacting Carceral Power and Glimpsing Gendered Resistance in Women's Prisons." *Criminology and Criminal Justice* 18, 2. doi.org/10.1177/1748895817706719.

Barbra Schlifer Commemorative Clinic v. Canada, 2014 ONSC 5140. canlii.ca/t/g8wj7.

Barrera, Jorge. 2018. "Behind the Statistics: The Story of 2 Indigenous Children on the Brink of Becoming Court Wards." *CBC News*, Jan. 24. cbc.ca/news/indigenous/ottawa-indigenous-child-foster-care-1.4502217

Barretto, Jeremy. 2009. "Ten Years after R v. Ewanchuk: Confirmation that No Means No." *The Court*, Feb. 10. thecourt.ca/ten-years-after-r-v-ewanchuk-confirmed-no-means-no.

Barron, James. 1989. "Canada's Supreme Court Rejects Ex-Lover's Effort to Halt Abortion." *New York Times*, Aug. 9. nytimes.com/1989/08/09/world/canada-s-supreme-court-rejects-ex-lover-s-effort-to-halt-abortion.html.

Bartick, Melissa C., Eleanor Bimla Schwarz, Brittany D. Green, et al. 2017. "Suboptimal Breastfeeding in the United States: Maternal and Pediatric Health Outcomes and Costs." *Maternal and Child Nutrition* 13, 1. doi.org/10.1111/mcn.12366.

Battiste, Marie. 2013. *Decolonizing Education*. Vancouver: UBC Press.

Bauer, Greta, Ayden Scheim, and Siobhan Churchill. 2020. *Health and Well-Being Among Trans and Non-Binary Canadians: First Results from Trans PULSE Canada*. Trans PULSE Canada. transpulsecanada.ca/wp-content/uploads/2020/11/WPATH-2020-TPC-Health-and-Well-Being-vFINAL-FINAL-ua.pdf.

BC (British Columbia). 1933. An Act Respecting Sexual Sterilization. bclaws.gov.bc.ca/civix/document/id/hstats/hstats/1887728313.

BC (British Columbia), Minister for Public Safety and Solicitor General Corrections Branch. 2016. *Briefing note Mother Child Unit*. January 6.

Beaman, Judith. 2018. *Harmful Impacts: The Reliance on Hair Testing in Child Protection*. Report of the Motherisk Commission. www.attorneygeneral.jus.gov.on.ca/english/about/pubs/motherisk.

Beauchamp, Tom, and James Childress. 2001. *Principles of Biomedical Ethics*, 5th ed. Oxford: Oxford University Press.

Becker, Jill B., and Elena Chartoff. 2019. "Sex Differences in Neural Mechanisms Mediating Reward and Addiction." *Neuropsychopharmacology* 44, 1.

Becker, Jill B., Michele L. McClellan, and Beth Glover Reed. 2017. "Sex Differences, Gender and Addiction." *Journal of Neuroscience Research* 95, 1–2.

Bedford, Terri-Jean, Amy Lebovitch, and Valerie Scott. 2015. "Sex Work and Constitutional Reform." *Ideacity*. youtube.com/watch?v=ZSq99RBSTxM&ab_channel=ideacity.

Bell, Danielle. 2013. "Ottawa Jail Staff Disciplined over Julie Bilotta Cell Birth." *Ottawa Sun*, Aug. 13. ottawasun.com/2013/08/13/ottawa-jail-staff-disciplined-over-cell-birth.

Berman, Pam. 2021. "Halifax Police Budget with 2.7% Increase Debated by Municipal Council." cbc News, Feb. 17. cbc.ca/news/canada/nova-scotia/halifax-police-budget-with-2-7-increase-heads-to-municipal-council-1.5917305.

Bertram, Wanda, and Wendy Sawyer. 2021. "Prisons and Jails Will Separate Millions of Mothers from Their Children in 2021." *Prison Policy Initiative*, May 5. prisonpolicy.org/blog/2021/05/05/mothers-day-2021/.

Bilodeau, Johanne. 2009. "Chantal Daigle, une héroïne." *La Tribune*, Aug. 10. latribune.ca/opinions/chantal-daigle-une-heroine-babc6cbe3495fd9262561804624a5c99.

Bilotta v. Ontario. 2014. *Statement of Claim*. Superior Court of Justice (Ontario). silo.tips/download/ontario-superior-court-of-justice-7

Birth Companions. 2021. "Campaign Launch: Time to End the Imprisonment of Pregnant Women." birthcompanions.org.uk/articles/campaign-launch-time-to-end-the-imprisonment-of-pregnant-women.

Black Women for Reproductive Justice. 2012a. "Black Women on Universal Health Care Reform." bwrj.wordpress.com/category/wadrj-on-health-care-reform.

___. 2012b. "RJ Founding Mothers." bwrj.wordpress.com/2012/08/08/151.

Blackwell, Tom. 2013. "Fertility Consultant at Centre of Criminal Case Accused of Forging Egg Donor Profiles Given to Potential Clients, Documents Show." *National Post*, April 1. nationalpost.com/news/canada/fertility-consultant-at-centre-of-criminal-case-accused-of-forging-egg-donor-profiles-given-to-potential-clients-documents-show.

Blanchard, A., Laurence Bebin, Stephanie Leroux, et al. 2018. "Infants Living with Their Mothers in the Rennes, France, Prison for Women Between 1998 and 2013. Facts and Perspectives." *Archives de Pédiatrie* 25, 1.

Blatchford, Christie. 2008. "Being 'Bizarre' Might End Psychopath's Freedom." *Globe and Mail*, Sept. 23. theglobeandmail.com/news/national/being-bizarre-might-end-psychopaths-freedom/article716099/

Boe, Joshua L., Emilie Ellis, Karen Sharstrom, and Jerry Gale. 2020. "Disrupting Cisnormativity, Transnormativity, and Transmisogyny in Healthcare: Advancing Trans Inclusive Practices for Medical Family Therapists." *Journal of Feminist Family Therapy* 32, 3–4.

Bond, Toni M. 2001. "Barriers between Black Women and the Reproductive Rights Movement." *Political Environments* 8 (Winter/Spring). law.berkeley.edu/php-programs/centers/crrj/zotero/loadfile.php?entity_key=E266XDC7.

Boston Globe. 1989. "Canadian Woman's Lawyer Says She Got Boston Abortion." *Chicago Tribune*, Aug. 11. chicagotribune.com/news/ct-xpm-1989-08-11-8901030893-story.html.

Bowlby, John, and World Health Organization. 1952. *Maternal Care and Mental Health: A Report Prepared on Behalf of the World Health Organization as a Contribution to the United Nations Programme for the Welfare of Homeless Children*. 2nd ed. World Health Organization. apps.who.int/iris/handle/10665/40724.

Boyd, Susan. 2019. "Gendered Drug Policy: Motherisk and the Regulation of Mothering in Canada." *International Journal of Drug Policy* 68. doi.org/10.1016/j.drugpo.2018.10.007.

Boyer, Yvonne, and Judith Bartlett. 2017. *External Review: Tubal Ligation in the Saskatoon Health Region: The Lived Experience of Aboriginal Women*. Saskatchewan Health Authority. saskatoonhealthregion.ca/DocumentsInternal/Tubal_Ligation_intheSaskatoonHealthRegion_the_Lived_Experience_of_Aboriginal_Women_BoyerandBartlett_July_22_2017.pdf.

Brake, Justin. 2018. "Women Speak Out Against Criminalization of Land Defenders, Water Protectors." *APTN News*, Aug 3. aptnnews.ca/national-news/women-speak-out-against-criminalization-of-land-defenders-water-protectors.

Brian Sinclair Working Group. 2017. "Out of Sight." dropbox.com/s/wxf3v5uh2pun0pf/Out%20of%20Sight%20Final.pdf?dl=0.

Bridges, Stephen. 2004. "Gun Control Law (BILL C-17), Suicide, and Homicide in Canada." *Psychological Reports* 94, 3.

Bronskill, Jim. 2021. "Trudeau 'a Traitor' unless Gun Bill Overhauled, Say Families of Polytechnique Victims." *Canadian Press*, March 18. globalnews.ca/news/7705324/trudeau-gun-bill-polytechnique.

Brown, Elizabeth. 2017. "The Culture of Alcoholics Anonymous Perpetuates Sexual Abuse." *Vice*. vice.com/en/article/7x4m8q/sexual-assault-alcoholics-anonymous.

Buck, Genna. 2019. "How Birth Control Became Legal in Canada. It Starts with an Eugenicist." *Saltwire*, June 4. saltwire.com/atlantic-canada/news/canada/how-birth-control-became-legal-in-canada-it-starts-with-an-eugenicist-318363.

Burke, David. 2020a. "The Hidden Horror of Police Domestic Violence in Nova Scotia." *CBC News*, Aug. 26. cbc.ca/news/canada/nova-scotia/police-domestic-violence-abuse-halifax-regional-police-rc-mp-1.5698816.

___. 2020b. "Statistics Canada to Collect Data on Origins of Guns Used in Crime." *CBC News*, May 25. cbc.ca/news/canada/nova-scotia/gun-crime-statistics-canada-research-1.5579971.

Bushnik, Tracey, Jocelynn Cook, Edward Hughes, and Suzanne Tough. 2012. "Seeking Medical Help to Conceive." *Statistics Canada*. www150.statcan.gc.ca/n1/pub/82-003-x/2012004/article/11719-eng.htm.

Cadloff, Emily Baron. 2019. "How PEI Became One of the Most Accessible Places for Women's Health Care in Canada." *Chatelaine*. chatelaine.com/health/pei-abortion-access.

CAMH (Centre for Addiction and Mental Health). n.d. "Postpartum Depression." *CAMH*. camh.ca/en/health-info/mental-illness-and-addiction-index/postpartum-depression.

Campbell, Francis. 2020. "Alton Gas Opponents Say Documents Show Project Would Violate Fisheries Act." *Saltwire*, Feb. 11. saltwire.com/nova-scotia/news/alton-gas-opponents-say-documents-show-project-would-violate-fisheries-act-409790.

Canada (AG) v. Bedford. 2013. scc-csc.lexum.com/scc-csc/scc-csc/en/item/13389/index.do.

Canada. 2013. "Water Sources: Lakes." canada.ca/en/environment-climate-change/services/water-overview/sources/lakes.html.

___. 2017. "Water." nrcan.gc.ca/maps-tools-publications/tools/geodetic-reference-systems/water/16888.

___. 2018. "Water: Frequently Asked Questions." canada.ca/en/environment-climate-change/services/water-overview/frequently-asked-questions.html#2.

___. 2019. "Minister of Health Announces New Financial Support Program for Eligible Thalidomide Survivors." canada.ca/en/health-canada/news/2019/01/minister-of-health-announces-new-financial-support-program-for-eligible-canadian-thalidomide-survivors.html.

Canada, Department of Justice. 1982. The Constitution Act. laws-lois.justice.gc.ca/eng/Const/page-15.html.

___. 1985a. The Canada Health Act. laws-lois.justice.gc.ca/eng/acts/c-6/page-2.html.

___. 1985b. Canadian Human Rights Act. laws-lois.justice.gc.ca/eng/acts/h-6.

___. 1985c. Criminal Code. laws-lois.justice.gc.ca/eng/acts/c-46.

___. 1985d. Food and Drugs Act. laws-lois.justice.gc.ca/eng/acts/f-27/fulltext.html.

___. 1992. Corrections and Conditional Release Act. laws-lois.justice.gc.ca/eng/acts/c-44.6.

___. 1995. Firearms Act. laws-lois.justice.gc.ca/eng/acts/f-11.6.

___. 2004. Assisted Human Reproduction Act. laws-lois.justice.gc.ca/eng/acts/a-13.4.

___. 2015. "Identifying Research Gaps in the Prostitution Literature." justice.gc.ca/eng/rp-pr/csj-sjc/jsp-sjp/rr02_9/p1.html.

___. 2016. "Protecting Canadians from Unsafe Drugs Act (Vanessa's Law) Amendments to the Food and Drug Act." canada.ca/en/health-canada/services/drugs-health-products/legislation-guidelines/protecting-canadians-unsafe-drugs-act-vanessa-law-amendments-food-drugs-act.html.

___. 2017a. An Act to Amend the Canadian Human Rights Act and the Criminal Code. laws-lois.justice.gc.ca/eng/annualstatutes/2017_13/FullText.html.

___. 2017b. "Technical Paper: Bill C-36, Protection of Communities and Exploited Persons Act." justice.gc.ca/eng/rp-pr/other-autre/protect/p1.html.

___. 2019. "Reimbursement Related to Assisted Human Reproduction Regulations." laws-lois.justice.gc.ca/PDF/SOR-2019-193.pdf.

___. 2021. "Proposed Changes to Canada's *Criminal Code* relating to Conversion Therapy." justice.gc.ca/eng/csj-sjc/pl/ct-tc/index.html.

Canada, Public Health Agency. 2019. "Fertility." canada.ca/en/public-health/services/fertility/fertility.html.

Canadian Centre for Justice Statistics. 2008. "Family Violence in Canada: A Statistical Profile 2008." *Statistics Canada*. www150.statcan.gc.ca/n1/pub/85-224-x/85-224-x2008000-eng.pdf.

Canadian Femicide Observatory for Justice and Accountability. 2021. "#CallItFemicide: Understanding Sex/Gender Related Killings of Women and Girls in Canada, 2020." femicideincanada.ca/callitfemicide2020.pdf.

Canadian Fertility & Andrology Society. 2016. "ART Live Birth Rates – Media Releases." cfas.ca/canadian-art-register.html.

Canadian Friends Service Committee. 2018. "Considering the Best Interests of the Child When Sentencing Parents in Canada." *Quaker Service.* quakerservice.ca/wp-content/uploads/2018/12/Considering-the-Best-Interests-of-the-Child-when-Sentencing-Parents-in-Canada.pdf.

Canadian Institute for Health Information. 2019. "Inpatient Hospitalization, Surgery, Newborn, Alternate Level of Care and Childbirth Statistics, 2017–2018." secure.cihi.ca/free_products/dad-hmdb-childbirth-quick-stats-2017-2018-snapshot-en-web.pdf.

——. 2021. "National Health Expenditure Trends." cihi.ca/en/national-health-expenditure-trends.

Canadian Judicial Council to the Minister of Justice. 2017. *Canadian Judicial Council Inquiry into the Conduct of the Honourable Robin Camp.* cjc-ccm.ca/sites/default/files/documents/2019/2017-03-08%20Report%20to%20Minister.pdf.

Canadian Medical Hall of Fame. 2018. "Emily Stowe, MD." cdnmedhall.ca/laureates/emilystowe.

Canadian Nurses Association. 2017. "Code of Ethics for Registered Nurses." hl-prod-ca-oc-download.s3-ca-central-1.amazonaws.com/CNA/2f975e7e-4a40-45ca-863c-5ebf0a138d5e/UploadedImages/documents/Code_of_Ethics_2017_Edition_Secure_Interactive.pdf.

Canadian Paediatric Society. 2008. "Harm Reduction: An Approach to Reducing Risky Health Behaviours in Adolescents." *Paediatrics & Child Health* 13, 1.

Canadian Press. 2011. "The Millennium Scoop: Native Children in Care Surpass Residential School Era." *McGill Newsroom.* mcgill.ca/newsroom/channels/news/canadian-press-millenium-scoop-native-children-care-surpass-residential-school-era-176814.

Canadian Public Health Association. 2014. "Sex Work in Canada: The Public Health Perspective." cpha.ca/sites/default/files/assets/policy/sex-work_e.pdf.

Canadian Stamp News. 2015. "Emily Stowe Born in Ontario." canadianstampnews.com/emily-stowe-born-in-ontario.

Canadian Thalidomide Survivors Support Program. n.d. "Canadian Thalidomide Survivors Support Program." tsspcanada.ca/index.html.

Canadian Women's Foundation. n.d. "The Facts about Sexual Assault and Harassment." canadianwomen.org/the-facts/sexual-assault-harassment.

——. 2018. "Gun Control & Violence Prevention." canadianwomen.org/wp-content/uploads/2018/07/Canadian-Womens-Foundation-Submission-to-SECU-re-Bill-C-71.pdf.

Canadian Women's Health Network. 1997. "Why the Supreme Court Should Rule against Mandatory Treatment: Five Good Reasons." cwhn.ca/en/node/39765.

Cardinal, Colleen. 2018. *Ohpikiihaakan-ohpihmeh (Raised Somewhere Else).* Halifax and Winnipeg: Fernwood.

Cardoso, Tom. 2020. "Bias behind Bars: A Globe Investigation Finds a Prison System Stacked against Black and Indigenous Inmates." *Globe and Mail*, Oct. 24. theglobeandmail.com/canada/article-investigation-racial-bias-in-canadian-prison-risk-assessments.

Carson, Rachel. 1962. *Silent Spring.* Boston: Houghton Mifflin.

Carter Ramirez, Alison, Jessica Liauw, Dustin Costescu, Laura Holder, Hong Lu, and Fiona Kouyoumdjian. 2020. "Infant and Maternal Outcomes for Women Who Experience Imprisonment in Ontario, Canada: A Retrospective Cohort Study." *Journal of Obstetrics and Gynaecology Canada* 42, 4.

Carter Ramirez, Alison, Jessica Liauw, Alice Cavanagh, Dustin Costescu, Laura Holder, Hong Lu, and Fiona Kouyoumdjian. 2020. "Quality of Antenatal Care for Women Who Experience Imprisonment in Ontario, Canada." *JAMA Network Open* 3, 8.

Cascio, Justin. 2003. "Origins of the Real-Life Test." *Transhealth.* trans-health.com/2003/real-life-test.

CATIE. 2018. "Why Has HIV in Saskatchewan Become More Harmful for Some People?" *CATIE News.* catie.ca/en/catienews/2018-08-14/why-has-hiv-saskatchewan-become-more-harmful-some-people.

CBC News. 2000. "Daigle Testifies About Violent Relationship." April 19. cbc.ca/news/canada/daigle-testifies-about-violent-relationship-1.238997.

___. 2004. "Stan Koebel Gets 1 Year in Jail, Frank 9 Months House Arrest." Dec. 20. cbc.ca/news/canada/stan-koebel-gets-1-year-in-jail-frank-9-months-house-arrest-1.485905.

___. 2009. "N.B. Court of Appeal Paves Way for Morgentaler's Lawsuit." May 21. cbc.ca/news/canada/new-brunswick/n-b-court-of-appeal-paves-way-for-morgentaler-s-lawsuit-1.825955.

___. 2010a. "Woman in Fetus Rights Case Speaks Out." Dec. 15. cbc.ca/news/canada/manitoba/woman-in-fetus-rights-case-speaks-out-1.943242.

___. 2010b. "Highlights of the Walkerton Inquiry Report." May 10. cbc.ca/news/canada/highlights-of-the-walkerton-inquiry-report-1.867604.

___. 2012a. "Parents, Babies Protest Ottawa Jailhouse Birth." Oct. 17. cbc.ca/news/canada/ottawa/parents-babies-protest-ottawa-jailhouse-birth-1.1172839.

___. 2012b. "Inmates Right's Allegedly Violated in Jailhouse Birth." Oct. 10. cbc.ca/news/canada/ottawa/inmate-s-rights-allegedly-violated-in-jailhouse-birth-1.1142465.

___. 2012c. "Mother Reunited with Baby Born in Ontario Jail." Oct. 18. cbc.ca/news/canada/ottawa/mother-reunited-with-baby-born-in-ontario-jail-1.1146314.

___. 2013. "Morgentaler's Death Puts N.B. Abortion Lawsuit in Limbo." May 30. cbc.ca/news/canada/new-brunswick/morgentaler-s-death-puts-n-b-abortion-lawsuit-in-limbo-1.1369360.

___. 2014. "Abortion Service on P.E.I. Would Have Saved Money: Report." Oct. 20. cbc.ca/news/canada/prince-edward-island/abortion-service-on-p-e-i-would-have-saved-money-report-1.2803587.

___. 2015a. "P.E.I. Doctor Apologizes for Abortion Care, 'I Communicated Poorly.'" Aug. 20. cbc.ca/news/canada/prince-edward-island/p-e-i-doctor-apologizes-for-abortion-care-i-communicated-poorly-1.3197187.

___. 2015b. "P.E.I. Woman Who Used Abortion Drug Unhappy with ER Care." May 22. cbc.ca/news/canada/prince-edward-island/p-e-i-woman-who-used-abortion-drug-unhappy-with-er-care-1.3084304.

___. 2016. "Mother Files Complaint Against Saskatoon Police After Being Refused Breast Pump." March 3. cbc.ca/news/canada/saskatoon/mother-files-complaint-after-refused-breast-pump-1.3474593.

___. 2018. "Woman Learns of Miscarriage After Jail Denies Her Ultrasound." Nov. 19. cbc.ca/news/canada/new-brunswick/julie-arseneau-ultrasound-miscarriage-miramichi-jail-1.4926332.

___. 2019. "Black People in Halifax 6 Times More Likely to Be Street Checked than Whites." March 27. cbc.ca/news/canada/nova-scotia/street-checks-halifax-police-scot-wortley-racial-profiling-1.5073300.

___. 2020. "Review Finds No Evidence Birth Alerts Improve Child Safety, Manitoba Families Minister Says." Jan. 30. cbc.ca/news/canada/manitoba/birth-alerts-manitoba-child-welfare-1.5446706.

___. 2021. "Your Questions Answered about Canada's Residential School System." June 4. cbc.ca/news/canada/canada-residential-schools-kamloops-faq-1.6051632.

CBC *Radio*. 2017. "'We Could All Be Dying.' Grassy Narrows, Ont., Youth Suffer Mercury Poisoning Consequences." *The Current*, Sept. 12. cbc.ca/radio/thecurrent/the-current-for-september-12-2017-1.4284337/we-could-all-be-dying-grassy-narrows-ont-youth-suffer-mercury-poisoning-consequences-1.4284359.

___. 2018. "The Millenium Scoop: Indigenous Youth Say Care System Repeats Horrors of the Past." *The Current*, Jan. 25. cbc.ca/radio/thecurrent/a-special-edition-of-the-current-for-january-25-2018-1.4503172/the-millennium-scoop-indigenous-youth-say-care-system-repeats-horrors-of-the-past-1.4503179.

___. 2019. "This Documentary About Women in Prison Handed the Cameras to the Inmates Themselves." *The Current*, Nov. 29. cbc.ca/radio/thecurrent/the-current-for-nov-29-2019-1.5378009/this-documentary-about-women-in-prison-handed-the-cameras-to-the-inmates-themselves-1.5378026..

Centre for Suicide Prevention. n.d. "Transgender People and Suicide." mentalhealthcommission.ca/sites/default/files/2019-05/Transgender%20people%20and%20suicide%20fact%20sheet.pdf.

Ceulemans, Michael, Angela Lupattelli, Hedvig Nordeng, et al. 2019. "Women's Beliefs About Medicines and Adherence to Pharmacotherapy in Pregnancy: Opportunities for Community Pharmacists." *Current Pharmaceutical Design* 25, 5.

Chan, Laurie, Malek Batal, Tonio Sadik, et al. 2019. FNFNES *Final Report for Eight Assembly of First Nations Regions: Draft Comprehensive Technical Report*. Assembly of First Nations, University of Ottawa, Université de Montréal. fnfnes.ca/docs/FNFNES_draft_technical_report_Nov_2__2019.pdf.

Chapin, Angelina. 2016. "Writing a Love Letter Instead of a Police Report: Why Victims Contact Sex Attackers." *The Guardian*, Feb. 13 theguardian.com/world/2016/feb/13/jian-ghomeshi-trial-sexual-assault-victims-response.

Chapman, Chris, Allison C. Carey, and Liat Ben-Moshe. 2014. "Reconsidering Confinement: Interlocking Locations and Logics of Incarceration." In *Disability Incarcerated,* edited by Liat Ben-Moshe, Chris Chapman, and Allison C. Carey. New York: Palgrave Macmillan.

Chapman, Chris, and A.J. Withers. 2019. *A Violent History of Benevolence.* Toronto: University of Toronto Press.

Chandler, Feleshia. 2021. "Nova Scotia Ends Use of Controversial Birth Alerts but Calls for Change Persist." *CBC News*, Nov. 30. cbc.ca/news/canada/nova-scotia/nova-scotia-ending-birth-alerts-1.6268029.

Cheung, Christopher. 2019. "Inside One First Nation's Long Water Crisis." *The Tyee*, Oct. 15. thetyee.ca/News/2019/10/15/First-Nations-Water-Crisis.

Chiu, Elizabeth. 2020. "Man Hired to Observe SIRT Investigation into Woman's Arrest Slams Result." *CBC News*, Oct. 9. cbc.ca/news/canada/nova-scotia/tony-smith-sirt-investigation-santina-rao-halifax-police-1.5756087.

Clarke, Jennifer, and Rachel Simon. 2013. "Shackling and Separation: Motherhood in Prison." *AMA Journal of Ethics Policy Forum* 15, 9. doi.org/10.1001/virtualmentor.2013.15.9.pfor2-1309.

Coalition for Gun Control. 2018. "Women's Safety and Gun Violence." guncontrol.ca/issues-and-facts/womens-safety-and-gun-violence/.

Cobbina, Jennifer. 2009. "From Prison to Home: Women's Pathways in and out of Crime." Doctoral dissertation, University of Missouri–St. Louis. ojp.gov/pdffiles1/nij/grants/226812.pdf.

Cohen, Steven. 2020. "Canada Class Action Alleges Forced Aboriginal Sterilization." Top Class Actions. ca.topclassactions.com/civil-rights/canada-class-action-alleges-forced-aboriginal-sterilization/.

Cole, Desmond. 2020. *The Skin We're In.* New York: Penguin Random House.

Coletta, Amanda. 2021. "Canadian Police Discriminated against Mother of Slain Indigenous Man, Watchdog Says." *Washington Post*, March 22. washingtonpost.com/world/the_americas/canada-rcmp-indigenous-discrimination/2021/03/22/66accca0-8a58-11eb-9423-04079921c915_story.html.

Collard, Juliane. 2015. "Into the Archive: Vancouver's Missing Women Commission of Inquiry." *Society and Space* 33, 5.

College of Nurses of Ontario. 2014. "Discipline Committee of the College of Nurses of Ontario: College of Nurses of Ontario and Rose Gyasi." cno.org/globalassets/2-howweprotectthepublic/ih/decisions/fulltext/pdf/2014/rose-gyasi-12491047-may-7-2014.pdf.

Collins, Patricia Hill, and Sirma Bilge. 2020. *Intersectionality*, 2nd ed. Cambridge: Polity.

Conor, Patricia, Sophie Carrière, Suzanne Amey, et al. 2020. "Police Resources in Canada, 2019." *Statistics Canada.* www150.statcan.gc.ca/n1/pub/85-002-x/2020001/article/00015-eng.htm.

Cook, Katsi. 2007. "Environmental Justice: Woman Is the First Environment." In *Reproductive Justice Briefing Book; A Primer on Reproductive Justice and Social Change.* Pro-Choice Public Education Project. protectchoice.org/downloads/Reproductive%20Justice%20Briefing%20Book.pdf.

Cooke, Alex. 2021. "N.B. One of Last Canadian Provinces to End Controversial Birth Alert Practice." *Global News*, Oct. 29. globalnews.ca/news/8335469/nb-ends-birth-alerts.

Cox, Kevin. 2000. "The Walkerton Tragedy: 2-Year-Old Victim Laid Quietly to Rest." *Globe and Mail*, June 1. theglobeandmail.com/news/national/the-walkerton-tragedy-2-year-old-victim-quietly-laid-to-rest/article1040388.

Cox, Sue. 1993. "Strategies for the Present, Feminist Resistance to New." *Canadian Women's Studies* 13, 2.

Craig, Elaine. 2018. *Putting Trials on Trial.* Montreal, Toronto: McGill-Queen's University Press.

Craig, Elaine, and Alice Woolley. 2015. "Myths and Stereotypes: Some Judges Still Don't Get It." *Globe and Mail*, Nov. 9. theglobeandmail.com/opinion/myths-and-stereotypes-some-judges-still-dont-get-it/article27164326/.

Crenshaw, Kimberlé. 1989. "Demarginalizing the Intersection of Race and Sex: A Black Feminist Critique of Antidiscrimination Doctrine, Feminist Theory and Antiracist Politics." *University of Chicago Legal Forum* 1.

Critical Resistance. 2004. "The Abolitionist Toolkit." criticalresistance.org/resources/the-abolitionist-toolkit/.

CSC (Correctional Services Canada). 2013. "Coroner's Inquest Touching the Death of Ashley Smith." csc-scc.gc.ca/publications/005007-9009-eng.shtml.

___. 2017. "Commissioner's Directive 800-5: Gender Dysphoria." csc-scc.gc.ca/lois-et-reglements/800-5-gl-eng.shtml.

___. 2020. "Commissioner's Directive 768: Institutional Mother-Child Program." csc-scc.gc.ca/politiques-et-lois/768-cd-en.shtml#4.

CTV News. 2006. "Mother of Marc Lepine Finally Breaks Her Silence." Sept. 25. web.archive.org/web/20070318031547/http:/www.ctv.ca/servlet/ArticleNews/print/CTVNews/20060925/lepine_mother_060925/20060925.

___. 2021. "Saskatchewan Ending Controversial Birth Alerts." Jan. 25. regina.ctvnews.ca/sask-ending-controversial-birth-alerts-1.5281706.

Culbert, Lori, and Gerry Bellett. 2008. "Baby Stays with Jailed Mom." *Vancouver Sun*, Feb. 8. pressreader.com/canada/vancouver-sun/20080208/281487862037896.

Cunningham, Alison, and Linda Baker. 2007. "Little Eyes, Little Ears: How Violence against a Mother Shapes Children as They Grow." *Centre for Children and Families in the Justice System*. canada.ca/content/dam/phac-aspc/migration/phac-aspc/sfv-avf/sources/fem/fem-2007-lele-pypo/pdf/fem-2007-lele-pypo-eng.pdf.

Currie, Brooklyn. 2021. "High School Student Speaks Out about Suspension After Calling Out Rape-Themed T-Shirt." CBC *News*. cbc.ca/news/canada/nova-scotia/suspension-rapey-tshirt-west-kings-district-high-1.5983454.

Daoud, Nihaya, Marcelo L. Urquia, Patricia O'Campo, et al. 2012. "Prevalence of Abuse and Violence before, during, and after Pregnancy in a National Sample of Canadian Women." *American Journal of Public Health* 102, 10.

Davis, Angela. 1981. *Women, Race and Class.* New York: Random House.

___. 2003. *Are Prisons Obsolete?* New York: Seven Stories Press.

de la Cour, Lykke. 2017. "Eugenics, Race and Canada's First-Wave Feminists: Dis/Abling the Debates." *Atlantis* 38, 2.

Deachmen, Bruce. 2020. "That Was Then: Ottawa Activist Dorothea Palmer Charged in Landmark Birth-Control Case." *Ottawa Citizen*, Sept. 14. ottawacitizen.com/news/local-news/that-was-then-ottawa-activist-dorothea-palmer-charged-in-landmark-birth-control-case.

Delacourt, Susan. 2009. "Long-Gun Registry Politics Taint Service for Victims." *Toronto Star*, Dec. 5. thestar.com/news/canada/2009/12/05/longgun_registry_politics_taint_service_for_the_victims.html.

Democracy Now. 2021. "Just Out of Jail, Winona LaDuke Decries Militarized Crackdown on Enbridge Line 3 Pipeline Protests." July 23. democracynow.org/2021/7/23/protests_line_3_pipeline_minnesota.

Denison, Jacqueline, Colleen Varcoe, and Annette J. Browne. 2014. "Aboriginal Women's Experiences of Accessing Health Care When State Apprehension of Children Is Being Threatened." *Journal of Advanced Nursing* 70, 5.

Desjardins, Stephanie. 2021. "P.E.I. Ends Controversial Birth Alert Practice." CBC *News*, Feb. 1. cbc.ca/news/canada/prince-edward-island/pei-birth-alert-banned-1.5896854.

Devet, Robert. 2020. "Protesters Rally at Walmart in Support of Santina Rao." *The NS Advocate*, Jan 17. nsadvocate.org/2020/01/17/protesters-rally-at-walmart-in-support-of-santina-rao.

Dhanraj, Travis. 2019. "Walkerton Residents Worry about Ford Government's Bill 66." *Global News*, Jan. 10. globalnews.ca/news/4835648/walkerton-ford-government-66.

Dieterich, Christine, Julia P. Felice, Elizabeth O'Sullivan, and Kathleen M. Rasmussen. 2013. "Breastfeeding and Health Outcomes for the Mother-Infant Dyad." *The Pediatric Clinics of North America* 60, 1.

DiNovo, Cheri. 2015. Bill 137, Cy and Ruby's Act (Parental Recognition), 2015. *Legislative Assembly of Ontario.* ola.org/en/legislative-business/bills/parliament-41/session-1/bill-137.

Dobson (Litigation Guardian of) v. Dobson, 1999 2 SCR 753. scc-csc.lexum.com/scc-csc/scc-csc/en/item/1716/index.do.

Dodd, Dianne. 1985. "The Canadian Birth Control Movement: Two Approaches to the Dissemination of Contraceptive Technology." *Scientia Canadensis* 9, 1.

Dubovicky, Michal, Kristína Belovicova, Kristína Csatlosova, and Eszter Bogi. 2017. "Risks of Using SSRI / SNRI Antidepressants during Pregnancy and Lactation." *Interdisciplinary Toxicology* 10, 1.

Duffin, Jacalyn. 1992. "The Death of Sarah Lovell and the Constrained Feminism of Emily Stowe." *Canadian Medical Association Journal* 146, 6.

Dyck, Erika. 2013a. *Facing Eugenics: Reproduction, Sterilization, and the Politics of Choice*. Toronto: University of Toronto Press.

___. 2013b. "Sterilization and Birth Control in the Shadow of Eugenics: Married, Middle-Class Women and Catholics on the Prairies." *Canadian Bulletin of Medical History* 31, 1.

Edmonds, Alan. 1965. "He's Too Rich to Be Cautious, Too Popular to Be Fired." *Macleans*, June 19. archive. macleans.ca/article/1965/6/19/hes-too-rich-to-be-cautious-too-popular-to-be-fired.

Égale Canada. n.d. "Sex Reassignment Surgery (SRS) Backgrounder." egale.ca/awareness/sex-reassignment-surgery-srs-backgrounder.

___. 2020. "National Action Plan for LGBTQI2S Rights in Canada." egale.ca/wp-content/uploads/2020/01/Egale-Canada-National-LGBTQI2S-Action-Plan-Full_Web_Final.pdf.

Emily Stowe Public School. n.d. "School and Contact Information." emilystowe.kprdsb.ca/About%20Us/School%20Information.

Erskine, Michael. (2019). "Wiikwemkoong's Water Warrior Autumn Peltier Speaks at UN Climate Summit." *Manitoulin Espositor*, Oct. 2. manitoulin.com/wiikwemkoongs-water-warrior-autumn-peltier-speaks-at-un-climate-summit.

Ewert v. Canada. 2018 SCC 30. scc-csc.lexum.com/scc-csc/scc-csc/en/item/17133/index.do.

Federation of Medical Women of Canada. n.d. "Thank you, Emily Stowe." fmwc.ca/thank-you-emily-stowe/.

Felitti, Vincent J., Robert F. Anda, Dale Nordenberg, et al. 1998. "Relationship of Childhood Abuse and Household Dysfunction to Many of the Leading Causes of Death in Adults. The Adverse Childhood Experiences (ACE) Study." *American Journal of Preventive Medicine* 14, 4.

Fiander, Sarah. 2016. "Pregnancy, Birth, and Mothering Behind Bars: A Case Study of One Woman's Journey Through the Ontario Criminal Justice and Jail Systems." Master's dissertation, Wilfred Laurier University. scholars.wlu.ca/cgi/viewcontent.cgi?article=2980&context=etd&httpsredir=1&referer=.

Findlay, Barbara. 1999. "Transsexuals in Canadian Prisons: An Equality Analysis." Conference presentation. barbarafindlay.com/uploads/9/9/6/7/9967848/199906_transsexuals_in_canadian_prisons_-_an_equality_analysis.pdf.

Fine, Sean. 2016. "The Robin Camp Transcript: 'Keep Your Knees Together' and Other Key Passages." *Globe and Mail*, Sept. 9. theglobeandmail.com/news/national/the-robin-camp-transcript-keep-your-knees-together-and-other-keypassages/article31807105.

Foster, Robin. 2021. "California to Pay Reparations to Victims of Forced Sterilization." *U.S. News & World Report*, July 8. usnews.com/news/health-news/articles/2021-07-08/california-to-pay-reparations-to-victims-of-forced-sterilization.

Fraser, Laura. 2019. "Halifax Police Chief Apologizes for Street Checks and Historical 'Mistreatment.'" *CBC News*, Nov. 29. cbc.ca/news/canada/nova-scotia/halifax-police-chief-apology-street-checks-black-males-1.5376868.

Fraser, Marian Botsford. 2010. "Does Canada's Penal System Create Dangerous Offenders?" *The Walrus*, March. thewalrus.ca/life-on-the-instalment-plan.

___. 2013. "Forgotten Woman." *The Walrus*, Nov. thewalrus.ca/forgotten-woman.

Friedersdorf, Conor. 2014. "Police Have a Much Bigger Domestic-Abuse Problem than the NFL Does." *The Atlantic*, Sept 19. theatlantic.com/national/archive/2014/09/police-officers-who-hit-their-wives-or-girlfriends/380329.

Fulford, Sarah. 2017. "Redefining the Nuclear Family: Changes to Ontario Law Reflect Our Society's Evolving Notion of Parenthood." *Toronto Life*, Dec. 20. torontolife.com/life/redefining-nuclear-family.

Gaard, Greta. 2010. "Reproductive Technology, or Reproductive Justice? An Ecofeminist, Environmental Justice Perspective on the Rhetoric of Choice." *Ethics and the Environment* 15, 2. jstor.org/stable/10.2979/ete.2010.15.2.103.

Gaines, Patrice. 2021 "One State Is Trying to Make Pregnancy in Prison Slightly More Bearable." *NBC News*, Aug. 4. nbcnews.com/news/nbcblk/one-state-trying-make-pregnancy-prison-slightly-bearable-rcna1578.

Gerster, Jane, and Krista Hessey. 2019. "Why Some First Nations Still Don't Have Clean Drinking Water — despite Trudeau's Promise." *Global News*, Sept. 18. globalnews.ca/news/5887716/first-nations-boil-water-advisories.

Gillis, Megan. 2016. "New Details on Jail Birth in Nurse's Discipline Decision." *Ottawa Citizen*, June 12. ottawacitizen.com/news/local-news/new-details-on-jail-birth-in-nurses-discipline-decision.

Gilmore, Rachel. 2019. "Few Canadian Women Own Guns, but Are Twice as Likely to Be Attacked with One: Analysis." *CTV News*, Apr. 10. ctvnews.ca/politics/few-canadian-women-own-guns-but-are-twice-as-likely-to-be-attacked-with-one-analysis-1.4374216.

Gilmore, Ruth Wilson. 2005. "Mothers and Prisoners in the Post-Keynesian California Prison Landscape." In *Global Lockdown*, edited by Julia Sudbury. Oxfordshire: Routledge.

___. 2007. *Golden Gulag*. Berkeley: University of California Press.

Givetash, Linda. 2016. "Jail Program Gives Moms a New Start, Helps Babies Develop, Advocates Say." *CTV News*, July 17. ctvnews.ca/canada/jail-program-gives-moms-a-new-start-helps-babies-develop-advocates-say-1.2990230.

Glass, Nancy, Kathryn Laughon, Jacquelyn Campbell, et al. 2008. "Non-Fatal Strangulation Is an Important Risk Factor for Homicide of Women." *The Journal of Emergency Medicine* 35, 3.

Globe and Mail. 2021. "Since 1977, Ottawa Has Spent Billions Trying – And Failing – to Bring Clean Water to Every Reserve." March 5. theglobeandmail.com/opinion/editorials/article-since-1977-ottawa-has-spent-billions-trying-and-failing-to-bring-clean.

Gonzales, Maribel, and Elizabeth Mandelman. 2009. "Small Arms and Domestic Violence: The Situation in Canada." *The Ploughshares Monitor* 30, 3 (Autumn). ploughshares.ca/pl_publications/small-arms-and-domestic-violence-the-situation-in-canada.

Goodwin, Michelle. 2020. *Policing the Womb*. Cambridge: Cambridge University Press.

Googoo, Maureen. 2019. "Nova Scotia Mi'kmaw Water Protectors Arrested at Alton Gas Site for Violating Court Injunction." *Kukukwes News*, Apr. 11. kukukwes.com/2019/04/11/nova-scotia-mikmaw-water-protectors-arrested-at-alton-gas-site-for-violating-court-injunction.

Grant, Taryn. 2020. "Former Child Refugees Abdoul and Fatouma Abdi Sue N.S. for Alleged Abuse in Care." *CBC News*, Sept 2. cbc.ca/news/canada/nova-scotia/abdi-lawsuit-children-in-care-nova-scotia-home-for-colored-children-1.5709163.

Green, Ben, Rachel Suzanne Oeppen, Dave W. Smith, and Peter A. Brennan. 2017. "Challenging Hierarchy in Healthcare Teams – Ways to Flatten Gradients to Improve Teamwork and Patient Care." *British Journal of Oral and Maxillofacial Surgery* 55, 5.

Greenfield, Shelly F., Sudie E. Back, Katie Lawson, and Kathleen T. Brady. 2010. "Substance Abuse in Women." *The Psychiatric Clinics of North America* 33, 2.

Grekul, Jana. 2008. "Sterilization in Alberta, 1929–1972: Gender Matters." *Canadian Review of Sociology* 44, 3.

Grekul, Jana, Arvey Krahn, and Dave Odynak. 2004. "Sterilizing the 'Feeble-Minded': Eugenics in Alberta, Canada, 1929–1972." *Journal of Historical Sociology* 17, 4.

Greschner, Donna. 1990. "Abortion and Democracy for Women: A Critique of Tremblay v. Daigle." *McGill Law Journal* 35, 3.

Gunderman, Richard. 2021. "Francis Galton Pioneered Scientific Advances in Many Fields – but also Founded the Racist Pseudoscience of Eugenics." *The Conversation*, Jan. 15. theconversation.com/francis-galton-pioneered-scientific-advances-in-many-fields-but-also-founded-the-racist-pseudo-science-of-eugenics-144465.

Ham, Julie. 2011. "Moving Beyond 'Supply and Demand' Catchphrases: Assessing the Uses and Limitations of Demand-Based Approaches in Anti-Trafficking." *Global Alliance Against Traffic of Women*. gaatw.org/publications/MovingBeyond_SupplyandDemand_GAATW2011.pdf.

Hampshire, Gareth. 2016. " 'Something Wrong' with Alberta's Child Welfare System for Indigenous Families: Advocate." *CBC News*, July 19. cbc.ca/news/canada/edmonton/something-wrong-with-alberta-s-child-welfare-system-for-indigenous-families-advocate-1.3685268.

Haney, Lynne. 2010. *Offending Women*. Berkeley: University of California Press.

Hannah-Mofffat, Kelly. 2001. *Punishment in Disguise*. Toronto: University of Toronto Press.

Hansen, Robin. Forthcoming. *The Newborn's Sentence in the Colonial Shadow*. University of Regina Press.

Harris, Kathleen. 2017. "In Historic 1st, Transgender Inmate Wins Transfer to Women's Prison." *CBC News*, July 21. cbc.ca/news/politics/fallon-aubee-transgender-inmate-1.4215594.

___. 2020. "Just 257 Pardons Granted for Pot Possession in Program's 1st Year." *CBC News*, Aug. 9. cbc.ca/

news/politics/cannabis-record-suspension-pardon-pot-1.5678144.

Harris, Kim. 2018. "Liberals Pitch New Rules on Payments for Surrogates, Sperm Donors." *CBC News*, Oct. 26. cbc.ca/news/politics/assisted-reproduction-surrogate-sperm-1.4879572.

Hayes, Crystal M., Carolyn Sufrin, and Jamila B. Perritt. 2020. "Reproductive Justice Disrupted: Mass Incarceration as a Driver of Reproductive Oppression." *American Journal of Public Health* 110, S1.

Hayman, Stephanie. 2006. *Imprisoning Our Sisters*. Montreal: McGill-Queen's University Press.

Health Canada. 2015. "Regulatory Decision Summary: Mifegymiso." *Government of Canada*. hpr-rps.hres. ca/reg-content/regulatory-decision-summary-detail.php?lang=en&linkID=RDS00294.

___. 2017. "Health Canada Updates Prescribing and Dispensing Information for Mifegymiso." *Government of Canada*. healthycanadians.gc.ca/recall-alert-rappel-avis/hc-sc/2017/65034a-eng.php.

___. 2020. "Social Determinants of Health and Health Inequalities." *Government of Canada*. canada.ca/en/public-health/services/health-promotion/population-health/what-determines-health.html.

Hennessy, Trish. 2015. "Assessing the Common Sense Revolution, 20 Years Later." *On Policy" The Long Shadow of Mike Harris*. Canadian Centre for Policy Alternatives. policyalternatives.ca/sites/default/files/uploads/publications/Ontario%20Office/2015/06/Ontario%20Policy%20magazine%20-%20Summer%202015-%20final.pdf.

Herder, Matthew, Elaine Gibson, Janice Graham, et al. 2014. "Regulating Prescription Drugs for Patient Safety: Does Bill C-17 Go Far Enough?" *CMAJ* 186, 8.

Hippocrates of Cos. n.d. "The Oath." *Loeb Classic*. doi.org/10.4159/DLCL.hippocrates_cos-oath.1923.

Hirsh, Alana. 2020. "Addressing Trauma in Substance Use Disorder: A Critical Gap in Service Amplified by COVID-19." *Canadian Family Physician*, July 15. cfp.ca/news/2020/07/15/07-15.

Hoover, Elizabeth, Katsi Cook, Ron Plain, et al. 2012. "Indigenous Peoples of North America: Environmental Exposures and Reproductive Justice." *Environmental Health Perspectives* 120, 12.

Houpt, Simon. 2015. "CBC Executives Let Go as Third-Party Jian Ghomeshi Investigation Released." *Globe and Mail*, Apr. 16. theglobeandmail.com/news/national/cbc-ghomeshi-investigation/article23985409/.

Howells, Laura. 2020. "Ontario to End Practice of Birth Alerts that's Led to Babies Being Seized from New Mothers." *CBC News*, July 14. cbc.ca/news/canada/toronto/ontario-ends-birth-alerts-1.5648940.

Human Rights Watch. 2016. "Make It Safe: Canada's Obligation to End the First Nations Water Crisis." *Human Rights Watch*, June 7. hrw.org/report/2016/06/07/make-it-safe/canadas-obligation-end-first-nations-water-crisis.

Hundert, Alex. 2013. "Down in a Hole: Imprisoned Activist Alex Hundert on Incarceration and Solitary Confinement." *Briarpatch Magazine*, March 22. briarpatchmagazine.com/articles/view/down-in-a-hole.

Hunt, Jerome, and Aisha Moodie-Mills. 2012. "The Unfair Criminalization of Gay and Transgender Youth: An Overview of the Experiences of LGBT Youth in the Juvenile Justice System." *Center for American Progress*. cdn.americanprogress.org/wp-content/uploads/issues/2012/06/pdf/juvenile_justice.pdf.

Iacobucci, Frank, and Graeme Hamilton. 2010. "The Goudge Inquiry and the Role of Medical Expert Witnesses." *Canadian Medical Association Journal* 182, 1.

Ibrahim, Hadeel. 2020. "Clinic 554 and Abortion Access: 5 Key Questions Answered." *CBC News*, Sept. 10. cbc.ca/news/canada/new-brunswick/clinic-554-abortion-access-new-brunswick-election-1.5713098.

Iftene, Adelina. 2019. *Punished for Aging: Vulnerability, Rights, and Access to Justice in Canadian Penitentiaries*. Toronto: University of Toronto Press.

Indigenous Services Canada. 2021. "Reducing the Number of Indigenous Children in Care." *Government of Canada*. sac-isc.gc.ca/eng/1541187352297/1541187392851.

Inglis v. BC, 2013 BCSC 2309. bccourts.ca/jdb-txt/SC/13/23/2013BCSC2309.htm.

Janigan, Mary. 1998. "Ryan vs. His Mom." *Maclean's*, Dec. 21. archive.macleans.ca/article/1998/12/21/ryan-vs-his-mom.

Jenish, D'Arcy. 1989. "Abortion on Trial." *Maclean's*, July 31. archive.macleans.ca/article/1989/7/31/abortion-on-trial.

Johnson, Genevieve Fuji, Mary Burns, and Kelly Porth. 2017. "A Question of Respect: A Qualitative Text Analysis of the Canadian Parliamentary Committee Hearings on the Protection of Communities and

Exploited Persons Act." *Canadian Journal of Political Science* 50, 4.

Johnson, Rebecca. 2008. "Mothers, Babies and Jail." *University of Maryland Law Journal of Race, Religion, Gender and Class* 8, 1.

Johnstone, Hillary. 2016. "Julie Bilotta Calls for 'Serious Change' at Public Forum on OCDC Conditions." CBC *News*, May 13. cbc.ca/news/canada/ottawa/ocdc-public-forum-julie-bilotta-conditions-1.3580390.

Jones, El. 2019. "Photos of Trudeau in Blackface Don't Surprise Black People; We Live This Racist Reality." *The Halifax Examiner*, Sept. 20. halifaxexaminer.ca/featured/trudeaublackface.

___. 2020. "There Was No Care." *The Halifax Examiner*, Sept. 2. halifaxexaminer.ca/featured/there-was-no-care.

Josef v. Ontario Minister of Health, 2013 ONSC 6091. canlii.ca/t/g0r4k.

Just Detention International. n.d. "Sexual Abuse in Prison: A Global Human Rights Crisis." *Just Detention International*. justdetention.org/wp-content/uploads/2015/11/International_Summary_English.pdf.

Kaba, Mariame. 2021. *We Do This Till We Free Us*. Chicago: Haymarket Books.

Kavanagh v. Canada (Attorney General), 2001 CanLII 8496 (CHRT). canlii.ca/t/1g946.

Kennedy, Merrit. 2016. "Lead-Laced Water in Flint: A Step-by-Step Look at the Makings of a Crisis." NPR, *The Two-Way*, Apr. 2. npr.org/sections/thetwo-way/2016/04/20/465545378/lead-laced-water-in-flint-a-step-by-step-look-at-the-makings-of-a-crisis.

Kendall, Mikki. 2020. *Hood Feminism*. New York: Viking.

Kenny, Kathleen, Andrea Krüsi, Clare Barrington, et al. 2021. "Health Consequences of Child Removal Among Indigenous and Non-Indigenous Sex Workers: Examining Trajectories, Mechanisms and Resiliencies." *Sociology of Health & Illness* 43, 8. doi.org/10.1111/1467-9566.13364.

Khazan, Olga. 2019. "The Suffragists Who Opposed Birth Control." *The Atlantic*, July 16. theatlantic.com/health/archive/2019/07/did-suffragists-support-birth-control/593896.

Knockwood, Isabelle. 2015. *Out of the Depths*. Halifax: Fernwood.

Kok-Choi, Cheng, Lee Hee-Ming, Shum S.F. Bobby, and Yip C.P. David. 1990. "A Fatality Due to the Use of Cantharides from Mylabris Phalerata as an Abortifacient." *Medicine, Science, and the Law* 30, 4.

Kolla, Gillian, Zoe Dodd, Jen Ko, Nick Boyce, and Sarah Ovens. 2019. "Canada's Overdose Crisis: Authorities Are Not Acting Fast Enough." *The Lancet* 4, 4. thelancet.com/journals/lanpub/article/PIIS2468-2667(19)30040-4/fulltext.

Koskie Minsky LLP. 2018. "Koskie Minsky Brings Class Action against Government of Alberta for Coerced Sterilization of Indigenous Women." *Cision*, Dec. 19. newswire.ca/news-releases/koskie-minsky-brings-class-action-against-government-of-alberta-for-coerced-sterilization-of-indigenous-women-703158991.html.

Kouyoumdjian, Fiona, Andrée Schuler, Flora I. Matheson, and Stephen W Hwang. 2016. "Health Status of Prisoners in Canada: Narrative Review." *Canadian Family Physician* 62, 3.

LaDuke, Winona. 2020. *To Be a Water Protector*. Halifax and Winnipeg: Fernwood.

Lalonde, Marc. 1974. *A New Perspective on the Health of Canadians*. Government of Canada. phac-aspc.gc.ca/ph-sp/pdf/perspect-eng.pdf.

Lang, Susan. 2015. "Report of the Motherisk Hair Analysis Independent Review." *Ontario Ministry of the Attorney General*. attorneygeneral.jus.gov.on.ca/english/about/pubs/lang.

Law, Victoria. 2009. *Resistance behind Bars*. Oakland: PM Press.

LEAF (Women's Legal Education and Action Fund). n.d. "Reproductive Justice." leaf.ca/issue-area/reproductive-justice-2.

Lee, Jennifer. 2018. "At up to $20K per Round, IVF Is out of Reach for a Growing Number of Alberta Couples, Fertility Doctor Says." CBC *News*, May 4. cbc.ca/news/canada/calgary/alberta-ivf-cost-1.4647224.

Leeder, Jessica. 2021. "One Doctor's Fight to Provide Abortion Care in New Brunswick." *The Walrus*, Aug. 3. thewalrus.ca/one-doctors-fight-to-provide-abortion-care-in-new-brunswick

Lewis, Alicia. 2014. "Time for Change: Quantitative & Qualitative Analyses of Women's Desires to Improve Access to Abortion Services on Prince Edward Island." Doctoral dissertation, University of Prince Edward Island. islandscholar.ca/islandora/object/ir:13084.

Lewis, Robert. n.d. "What Is a Truckhouse?" *Stop Alton Gas*. stopaltongas.wordpress.com/whyoppose/treaties.

Lexchin, Joel. 2018. "U of T Expert on Why We Need Answers to the Thalidomide Tragedy to Ensure

Drug Safety Now." *University of Toronto News.* utoronto.ca/news/u-t-expert-why-we-need-answers-thalidomide-tragedy-ensure-drug-safety-now.

Li, Johanna. 2019. "Inside the Prison Where Babies Serve Time with Their Incarcerated Mothers." *Inside Edition.* insideedition.com/inside-the-prison-where-babies-serve-time-with-their-incarcerated-mothers-50207.

Liddell, Jessica, and Sarah Kington. 2021. " 'Something Was Attacking Them and Their Reproductive Organs': Environmental Reproductive Justice in an Indigenous Tribe in the United States Gulf Coast." *International Journal of Environmental Research and Public Health* 18, 2.

Lim, Charles. 2020. "New Zealand Sex Worker Gets Six Figure." *Business Times*, Dec. 14. btimesonline.com/articles/143675/20201214/new-zealand-sex-worker-awarded-six-figures-after-winning-harassment-case.htm.

Lindsay, Bethany. 2021. "Non-profit Supporting Sex Workers Ends Partnership with vpd over Officer's Abuse, Alleged Police Harassment." cbc News, Feb. 11. cbc.ca/news/canada/british-columbia/bc-living-in-community-vancouver-police-department-1.5909709.

Ling, Justin. 2018. "Governments Have Failed Canada's Sex Workers — and They're Running Out of Patience." *Maclean's*, Sept. 6. macleans.ca/news/canada/governments-have-failed-canadas-sex-workers-and-theyre-running-out-of-patience.

____. 2021. "Houses of Hate: How Canada's Prison System Is Broken." *Maclean's*, Feb. 28. macleans.ca/news/canada/houses-of-hate-how-canadas-prison-system-is-broken.

Loreto, Nora. 2020. *Take Back the Fight.* Halifax and Winnipeg: Fernwood.

Luck, Shaina. 2019. "Abdoul Abdi's Case Changes N.S. Policies on Children in Care." *cbc News*, Jan. 22. cbc.ca/news/canada/nova-scotia/abdoul-abdi-child-welfare-nova-scotia-policy-change-1.4979208.

Luk, Vivian. 2013. "Rights of Imprisoned Moms with Babies at Stake in B.C. Supreme Court Case." *Globe and Mail*, May 22. theglobeandmail.com/news/british-columbia/rights-of-imprisoned-moms-with-babies-at-stake-in-bc-supreme-court-case/article12169463/.

Lumsden, Stephanie. 2016. "Reproductive Justice, Sovereignty, and Incarceration: Prison Abolition Politics and California Indians." *American Indian Culture and Research Journal* 40, 1.

MacDonald, Michael. 2018. "3 Adults in Polyamorous Relationship Declared Legal Parents by N.L. Court." *cbc News*, June 14. cbc.ca/news/canada/newfoundland-labrador/polyamourous-relationship-three-parents-1.4706560.

MacDonald, J. Michael, and Jennifer Taylor. 2019. "NS Human Rights Commission — Independent Legal Opinion on Street Checks." *Nova Scotia Human Rights Commission* humanrights.novascotia.ca/sites/default/files/editor-uploads/independent_legal_opinion_on_street_checks.pdf.

MacDonald, Nancy. 2016. "Canada's Prisons Are the 'New Residential Schools.'" *Maclean's*, Feb. 18. macleans.ca/news/canada/canadas-prisons-are-the-new-residential-schools/.

MacKinnon, Mark, and Keith Lacey. 2001. "Bleak House." *Globe and Mail*, August 18.

MacQuarrie, Colleen, Jo-Ann MacDonald, and Cathrine Chambers. 2014. "Trials and Trails of Accessing Abortion in PEI: Reporting on the Impact of PEI's Abortion Policies on Women." *University of Prince Edward Island.* projects.upei.ca/cmacquarrie/files/2014/01/trials_and_trails_final.pdf

Makin, Kirk. 2002. "Gatecrashing the Old Boys' Club." *Globe and Mail*, May 2. theglobeandmail.com/news/national/gatecrashing-the-old-boys-club/article4134439/.

Malone, Kelly Geraldine. 2021. "Number of Canadian Police Shootings in 2021 Remain Too High, Experts Say." *Global News*, Dec. 27. globalnews.ca/news/8475396/canada-police-shootings-2021.

Manitoba Law Reform Commission. 2014. *Assisted Reproduction: Legal Parentage and Birth Registration.* manitobalawreform.ca/pubs/pdf/additional/assisted_reproduction-legal_parentage_and_birth_registration.pdf.

Martens, Kathleen. 2019. "Birth Alerts Are 'Race-Based Genocide' Says Mi'kmaw Lawyer." *aptn News*, July 27. aptnnews.ca/national-news/birth-alerts-are-raced-based-genocide-says-mikmaw-lawyer/.

Mathers McHenry, Kirsti. n.d. "Cy and Ruby's Law: Parental Recognition for Female Same-Sex Partners in Ontario." *Legal Aid Ontario.* legalaid.on.ca/2019/10/16/cy-and-rubys-law-parental-recognition-for-female-same-sex-partners-in-ontario/.

Matheson, Kate, and Alec Stratford. 2018. "Our Children Deserve Better: Reflections on How the System Failed Abdoul Abdi." *Nova Scotia College of Social Workers.* nscsw.org/our-children-deserve-better-reflections-on-how-the-system-failed-abdoul-abdi/.

Maynard, Robyn. 2017. *Policing Black Lives*. Halifax: Fernwood.

McClearn, Matthew. 2017. "Unsafe to Drink." *Globe and Mail*, Feb. 20. theglobeandmail.com/news/water-treatment-plants-fail-on-reserves-across-canada-globe-reviewfinds/article34094364.

McClelland, Alexander, and Alex Luscombe. 2020. "Policing the Pandemic: Tracking the Policing of COVID-19 across Canada." *Scholars Portal Dataverse*. doi.org/10.5683/SP2/KNJLWS.

McCoy, Ted. 2017. "Emily's Maternal Ideal: Pregnancy, Birth, and Resistance at Kingston Penitentiary." *Journal of the Canadian Historical Association* 27, 1.

___. 2019. *Four Unruly Women: Stories of Incarceration and Resistance from Canada's Most Notorious Prison*. Vancouver: UBC Press.

McGregor, Deborah. 2015. "Indigenous Women, Water Justice and *Zaagidowin* (Love)." *Canadian Woman Studies* 30, 2–3. cws.journals.yorku.ca/index.php/cws/article/view/37455.

McHardie, Daniel. 2016. "New Brunswick Will Now Cover Gender-Confirming Surgeries." *CBC News*, June 3. cbc.ca/news/canada/new-brunswick/gender-confirming-surgeries-1.3614766.

McHugh, R. Kathryn, Elise E. DeVito, Dorian Dodd, et al. 2013. "Gender Differences in a Clinical Trial for Prescription Opioid Dependence." *Journal of Substance Abuse Treatment* 45, 1.

McKendy, Laura. 2018. "The Pains of Jail Imprisonment: Experiences at the Ottawa-Carleton Detention Centre." Doctoral dissertation, Carleton University. curve.carleton.ca/system/files/etd/96758ed0-204e-46b3-8f31-6df3d1650c99/etd_pdf/2e742199235341711df8cd065e6b2133/mckendy-thepain-sofjailimprisonmentexperiencesatthe.pdf.

McKenna, Kate. 2018. *No Choice: The 30-Year Fight for Abortion on Prince Edward Island*. Halifax: Fernwood.

McKenzie, Anna. 2021. "Birth Alerts Banned in BC, but Trust Still a Barrier for Indigenous Parents." *Toronto Star*, Feb. 3. thestar.com/news/canada/2021/02/03/birth-alerts-banned-in-bc-but-trust-still-a-barrier-for-indigenous-parents.html.

McLellan, Anne A. 1990. "Abortion Injunction Vacated." *Constitutional Forum* 2.

McLeod, Carolyn, and Sue Sherwin. 2000. "Relational Autonomy, Self-Trust, and Health Care for Patients Who Are Oppressed." *Philosophy Publications* 345.

McClung, John. 1999. "Suicide Remark Was 'Included as a Facetious Chide to the Judge.' " *National Post*, Mar. 2. people.stu.ca/~oregan/mcclung2.html.

McMillan, Elizabeth. 2020. "Former N.S. Lieutenant-Governor Says Racial Profiling 'Alive and Well.' " *CBC News*, Jan. 21. cbc.ca/news/canada/nova-scotia/mayann-francis-racial-profiling-santina-rao-arrest-1.5434509.

McMillan, Jennifer, and Alison Granger-Brown. 2011. "On Mothering in Prison." *Journal of Prisoners on Prisons* 20, 1.

McMullen, Sarah. 2003. "Dr. Emily Howard Jennings Stowe: A Battle Half Won." *McMaster University Medical Journal* 1, 1

McNamara, Adam. 2020. " 'End Racial Profiling': Protesters Rally at Halifax Store Where Woman Was Arrested." *The Signal*, Jan 18. signalhfx.ca/end-racial-profiling-protesters-rally-at-halifax-store-where-woman-was-arrested.

McPhedran, Samara, and Gary Mauser. 2013. "Lethal Firearm-Related Violence against Canadian Women: Did Tightening Gun Laws Have an Impact on Women's Health and Safety?" *Violence Victims* 28, 5.

McQuaig, Linda. 1980. "Ten Years Later, the Bad News Gets Worse." *Macleans*, July 14. archive.macleans.ca/article/1980/7/14/ten-years-later-the-bad-news-gets-worse.

McTavish, Lianne. 2015. "Abortion in New Brunswick." *Acadiensis* 44, 2.

MDR v. Ontario (Deputy Registrar General) 2006, 270 D.L.R. (4th) 90. mccarthyco.ca/wp-content/uploads/MDR-and-mps.pdf.

Mehler Paperny, Anna. 2017. "Exclusive: New Data Shows Race Disparities in Canada's Bail System." *Reuters*, Oct. 19. reuters.com/article/domesticNews/idCAKBN1CO2RD-OCADN?edition-redirect=ca.

Mendleson, Rachel. 2018. "Motherisk Hair Testing 'Unfair and Harmful' to the Poorest and Most Vulnerable Ontario Families." *Toronto Star*, Feb. 26. thespec.com/news/ontario/2018/02/26/motherisk-hair-testing-unfair-and-harmful-to-the-poorest-and-most-vulnerable-ontario-families.html.

Mergler, Donna, Judy DaSilva, Myriam Fillion, and Aline Philibert. 2019. "The Legacy of Mercury Poisoning in Grassy Narrows First Nation." Presentation at First Nations Food, Nutrition and Environment Forum Ottawa, Nov. 5. afn.ca/wp-content/uploads/2019/12/Judy-DaSilva-and-Myriam-Fillion-Presentation-Compressed.pdf.

Miller, Kayliah. 2017. "Canada's Mother-Child Program and Incarcerated Aboriginal Mothers: How and Why the Program Is Inaccessible to Aboriginal Female Offenders." *Canadian Family Law Quarterly* 37, 1.

Minson, Shona. 2020. *Maternal Sentencing and the Rights of the Child.* London: Palgrave Macmillan.

Moed, Lisa, Tor A. Shwayder, and Mary Wu Chang. 2001. "Cantharidin Revisited: A Blistering Defense of an Ancient Medicine." *Archives of Dermatology* 137, 10.

Mombourquette, Angela. 2018. "Why PEI Didn't Provide Abortions for 35 years." *Broadview.* broadview.org/why-p-e-i-didnt-provide-abortions-for-35-years.

Moore, Dawn. 2020. "Why Domestic Violence Victims Often Feel Retraumatized by Police." *The Conversation*, Dec. 20. halifaxtoday.ca/local-news/why-domestic-violence-victims-often-feel-retraumatized-by-police-3176183.

Moore, Elizabeth R., Nils Bergman, Gene C. Anderson, and Nancy Medley. 2016. "Early Skin-to-Skin Contact for Mothers and Their Healthy Newborn Infants." *Cochrane Library* 11, 25.

Morin, Brandi. 2020. "Pipelines, Man Camps and Murdered Indigenous Women in Canada." *Al Jazeera*, May 5. aljazeera.com/features/2020/5/5/pipelines-man-camps-and-murdered-indigenous-women-in-canada.

Motherisk Commission. n.d. "Our Restorative Process." archives.gov.on.ca/en/e_records/motheriskcommission/our_restorative_process.html.

Motluk, Alison. 2014. "First Prosecution under Assisted Human Reproduction Act Ends in Conviction." *Canadian Medical Association Journal* 186, 2.

___. 2016. "After Pleading Guilty for Paying Surrogates, Business Is Booming for This Fertility Matchmaker." *Globe and Mail*, Feb. 28. theglobeandmail.com/life/health-and-fitness/health/business-is-booming-for-fertility-matchmaker-leia-swanberg/article28930242.

Muir v. Alberta. 1996. 132 D.L.R. (4th) 695. eugenicsnewgenics.files.wordpress.com/2014/01/muir-v-alberta.pdf.

Muir, Leilani. 2014. *A Whisper Past: Childless after Eugenic Sterilization in Alberta.* Altona: FriesenPress.

National Collaborating Centre on Determinants of Health. n.d. "Upstream/downstream." nccdh.ca/glossary/entry/upstream-downstream.

National Inquiry into Missing and Murdered Indigenous Women and Girls. 2019. *Reclaiming Power and Place: Final Report of the National Inquiry into Missing and Murdered Indigenous Women and Girls.* mmiwg-ffada.ca/final-report.

Native Women's Association of Canada. 2017. "Indigenous Women in Solitary Confinement: Policy Backgrounder." nwac.ca/wp-content/uploads/2017/07/NWAC-Indigenous-Women-in-Solitary-Confinement-Aug-22.pdf.

New Brunswick. 1984. "Medical Services Payment Act." laws.gnb.ca/en/ShowPdf/cr/84-20.pdf.

___. n.d. "Gender Confirming Surgery." www2.gnb.ca/content/gnb/en/departments/health/patientinformation/content/GenderConfirmingSurgery.html.

No Notoriety. n.d. "No Notoriety Media Protocol." nonotoriety.com.

Norman, Wendy V., and Jocelyn Downie. 2017. "Abortion Care in Canada Is Decided Between a Woman and Her Doctor, Without Recourse to Criminal Law." *British Medical Journal* 356, J1506.

Nova Scotia. 2019. *Accountability Report 2018 to 2019: Department of Community Services.* beta.novascotia.ca/sites/default/files/documents/1-1880/accountability-report-2018-19-department-community-services-en.pdf.

Nova Scotia, African Nova Scotian Affairs n.d. "African Nova Scotians Today." ansa.novascotia.ca/sites/default/files/inline/documents/ansa-stats-research-2014-11.pdf.

Nova Scotia Home for Colored Children Restorative Inquiry. 2019. *Journey to Light: A Different Way Forward – Final Report.* restorativeinquiry.ca.

O'Connor, Dennis. 2002a. *Part One: Report of the Walkerton Inquiry.* Queens Press Ontario. archives.gov.on.ca/en/e_records/walkerton/index.html.

___. 2002b. *Part Two: Report of the Walkerton Inquiry A Strategy for Safe Drinking Water.* Queens Press

Ontario. archives.gov.on.ca/en/e_records/walkerton/report2/index.html.

Odynak, David. 2004. "Sterilizing the 'Feeble-minded': Eugenics in Alberta, Canada, 1929–1972." *Journal of Historical Sociology* 17, 4.

Office of the Correctional Investigator. 2016. "Federally Sentenced Women." oci-bec.gc.ca/cnt/priorities-priorites/women-femmes-eng.aspx.

___. 2020. "Indigenous People in Federal Custody Surpasses 30%." oci-bec.gc.ca/cnt/comm/press/press20200121-eng.aspx.

___. 2021. "Proportion of Indigenous Women in Federal Custody Nears 50%:

Correctional Investigator Issues Statement." oci-bec.gc.ca/cnt/comm/press/press20211217-eng.aspx.

Office of the Parliamentary Budget Officer. 2013. "Expenditure Analysis of Criminal Justice in Canada." pbo-dpb.gc.ca/web/default/files/files/files/Crime_Cost_EN.pdf.

___. 2018. "Update on Costs of Incarceration." pbo-dpb.gc.ca/web/default/files/Documents/Reports/2018/Update%20Incarceration%20Costs/Update%20on%20Costs%20of%20Incarceration_EN.pdf.

Olff, Miranda. 2017. "Sex and Gender Differences in Post-Traumatic Stress Disorder: An Update." *European Journal of Psychotraumatology* 8, supp 4. ncbi.nlm.nih.gov/pmc/articles/PMC5632782.

Omstead, Jordan. 2018. "After Decades of Silence, Canada's One-Time Most Dangerous Woman Slams Justice System." *cbc News*, Aug. 10. cbc.ca/news/canada/edmonton/edmonton-lisa-neve-canada-dangerous-offender-1.4779821.

Ontario. 2002. Safe Drinking Water Act c. 32 - Bill 195. ontario.ca/laws/statute/s02032.

___. 2006. Clean Water Act. ontario.ca/laws/statute/06c22.

___. 2012. Toby's Act (Right to Be Free from Discrimination and Harassment Because of Gender Identity or Gender Expression) 2012, S.O. 2012, c. 7 - Bill 33. ontario.ca/laws/statute/s12007.

___. 2016. "All Families Are Equal Act (Parentage and Related Registrations Statute Law Amendment), 2016, S.O. 2016, c. 23 - Bill 28." ontario.ca/laws/statute/s16023.

Ontario Human Rights Commission. 2018. "Interrupted Childhoods: Over-Representation of Indigenous and Black Children in Ontario Child Welfare." ohrc.on.ca/sites/default/files/Interrupted%20childhoods_Over-representation%20of%20Indigenous%20and%20Black%20children%20in%20Ontario%20child%20welfare_accessible.pdf.

Oppal, Wally T. 2012. *Forsaken: The Report of the Missing Women Commission of Inquiry*. missingwomen.library.uvic.ca/wp-content/uploads/2010/10/Forsaken-ES-web-RGB.pdf.

Ottawa-Carleton Detention Centre Task Force. 2017. *Action Plan*. documentcloud.org/documents/2850149-Ottawa-Carleton-Detention-Centre-Task-Force.

Owusu-Bempah, Akwasi, Maria Jung, Firdaous Sbai, et al. 2021. "Race and Incarceration: The Representation and Characteristics of Black People in Provincial Correctional Facilities in Ontario, Canada." *Race and Justice*. doi.org/10.1177/21533687211006461.

Owusu-Bempah, Akwasi, and Alex Luscombe. 2021. "Race, Cannabis and the Canadian War on Drugs: An Examination of Cannabis Arrest Data by Race in Five Cities." *International Journal on Drug Policy* 91.

Palacious, Lena. 2016. "Challenging Convictions: Indigenous and Black Race-Radical Feminists Theorizing the Carceral State and Abolitionist Praxis in the United States and Canada." *Meridians: Feminism, Race, Transnationalism* 15, 1.

Paradis, Catherine. 2018. "Vous êtes toutes une gang de féministes, j'haïs les féministes." *La Riposte* 39, 5.

Paynter, Martha. 2021. *Reproductive (In)justice in Canadian Federal Prisons for Women*. Canadian Association of Elizabeth Fry Societies. ac935091-bf76-4969-8249-ae3a107fca23.filesusr.com/ugd/d2d30e_13d22f66c3eb41449c2e52c519913b35.pdf.

Paynter, Martha, M. Leslie Bagg, and Clare Heggie. 2020. "Invisible Women: Carceral Facilities for Women and Girls across Canada and Proximity to Maternal Health Care." *International Journal of Prisoner Health* 17, 2. doi.org/10.1108/IJPH-06-2020-0039.

Paynter, Martha, Keisha Jefferies, and Leah Carrier. 2020. "Nurses for Police and Prison Abolition." *Public Health Nursing* 37, 4.

Paynter, Martha, Keisha Jefferies, Leah Carrier, and Laurie Goshin. 2021. "Feminist Abolitionist Nursing." *Advances in Nursing Science*. Advanced online publication. doi.org/10.1097/ANS.0000000000000385.

Paynter, Martha, Keisha Jefferies, Shelley McKibbon, et al. 2020. "Mother Child Programs for Incarcerated Mothers and Children and Associated Health Outcomes: A Scoping Review." *Nursing Leadership* 33,

1. doi.org/10.12927/cjnl.2020.26189.

Paynter, Martha, Ruth Martin-Misener, Adelina Iftene, and Gail Tomblin Murphy. 2022. "The Correctional Services Canada Institutional Mother Child Program: A Look at the Numbers." *The Prison Journal*. Forthcoming.

Pedwell, Terry. 2012. "Pregnant Woman's Treatment in Ottawa Jail Has Mothers Calling for Inquiry." *Globe and Mail*, Oct. 17. theglobeandmail.com/news/national/pregnant-womans-treatment-in-ottawa-jail-has-mothers-calling-for-inquiry/article4619179.

Pelletier, Francine. 2019. "Chantale et Jean-Guy." *Le Devoir*, July 17. ledevoir.com/opinion/chroniques/558824/chantal-et-jean-guy.

Pemberton, Sarah. 2013. "Enforcing Gender: The Constitution of Sex and Gender in Prison Regimes." *Signs* 39, 1.

Peterson, Jillian, and James Densley. 2021. "Why Mass Shootings Stopped in 2020 — and Why They Are Roaring Back Now." *Wisconsin State Journal*, May 27. madison.com/wsj/opinion/column/jillian-peterson-and-james-densley-why-mass-shootings-stopped-in-2020-and-why-they-are/article_087e40a0-0451-5ce4-9b5c-130e87ca9341.html.

Phare, Merrell-Ann. 2009. *Denying the Source: The Crisis of First Nations Water Rights*. Calgary: Rocky Mountain Books.

Philibert, Aline, Myriam Fillion, and Donna Mergler. 2020. "Mercury Exposure and Premature Mortality in the Grassy Narrows First Nation Community: A Retrospective Longitudinal Study." *The Lancet* 4, 4. thelancet.com/journals/lanplh/article/PIIS2542-5196(20)30057-7/fulltext.

Phipps, Alison. 2020. *Me, Not You: The Trouble with Mainstream Feminism*. Manchester: Manchester University Press.

Picard, Leia. n.d. "Leia Picard." *Yummymummyclub*. yummymummyclub.ca/users/leia-picard.

Pictou, Sherry. 2017. "Decolonizing Mi'kmaw Memory of Treaty: L'sitkuk's Learning with Allies in Struggle for Food and Lifeways." Master's dissertation, Dalhousie University. dalspace.library.dal.ca/bitstream/handle/10222/72811/PICTOU-SHERRY-IDPHD-APRIL%202017.pdf%20.pdf.

Planned Parenthood. 2021. "Choice vs. Access: Defining Reproductive Justice." *Planned Parenthood of the Pacific Southwest blog*, Jan. 28. plannedparenthood.org/planned-parenthood-pacific-southwest/blog/choice-vs-access-defining-reproductive-justice.

Poitras, Jacques. 2021. "New Brunswick Being Sued Over Abortion Access." *CBC News*, Jan. 7. cbc.ca/news/canada/new-brunswick/abortion-new-brunswick-lawsuit-civil-liberties-association-medicare-1.5864555.

Pollack, Shoshanna. 2000. "Dependency Discourse as Social Control." In *An Ideal Prison? Critical Essays on Women's Imprisonment in Canada*, edited by Kelly Hannah-Mofffat and Margaret Shaw. Halifax: Fernwood.

Postmedia News. 2017. "Ottawa Inmate Who Had Miscarriage in Cell Says Her Cries for Help Were Ignored for up to 15 Minutes." *National Post*, Feb 3. nationalpost.com/news/canada/ottawa-inmate-who-had-miscarriage-in-cell-says-her-cries-for-help-were-ignored-for-up-to-15-minutes.

Poulette, Dale, and Rachael Greenland-Smith. 2019. *The Alton Gas Project: The Fight to Save the Shubenacadie River and Countering a Flawed Project Approval Process*. nsadvocate.org/wp-content/uploads/2019/10/Final-Executive-Summary-the-fight-to-save-the-Shubenacadie-River-and-countering-a-flawed-project-approval-process-Rachael-and-Dale.pdf.

Prentiss, Mairin. 2019. "Worker Charged with Sex Offence at Truro Youth Treatment Facility." *CBC News*, Apr. 18. cbc.ca/news/canada/nova-scotia/government-youth-worker-charged-with-sexual-exploitation-1.5100226.

Press, Alex. 2018. "#MeToo Must Avoid 'Carceral Feminism.'" *Vox*, Feb. 1. vox.com/the-big-idea/2018/2/1/16952744/me-too-larry-nassar-judge-aquilina-feminism.

Price, Kimala. 2010. "What Is Reproductive Justice? How Women of Color Activists Are Redefining the Pro-Choice Paradigm." *Meridians: Feminism, Race, Transnationalism* 10, 2.

Prince Edward Island. 1988. "Resolution No. 17." *Journal of the Legislative Assembly of Prince Edward Island*, 57th Parliament, 3rd Session, 90–91. peildo.ca/islandora/object/leg%3A3295#page/84/mode/2up

Prince George Citizen Staff. 2011. "Local Federal Offender Wanted Canadawide." *Prince George Citizen*, June 8. princegeorgecitizen.com/local-news/local-federal-offender-wanted-canadawide-3706309.

Prison Research Education Action Project. 1976. *Instead of Prisons: A Handbook for Abolitionists*. prison-policy.org/scans/instead_of_prisons/index.shtml.

Pro-Choice Action Network. n.d. "A Legal History of Abortion in Canada." prochoiceactionnetwork-canada.org/abortioninfo/history.shtml.

___. 2007. "Abortion History – Chronology of Events." arcc-cdac.ca/wp-content/uploads/2020/06/Abortion-Chronology.pdf.

Proctor, Jason. 2021. "B.C. Judge Orders Second Mother Declared a Third Parent to Child of Polyamorous Trio." *CBC News*, April 26. cbc.ca/news/canada/british-columbia/polyamorous-parents-birth-certificate-judge-1.6002991.

Public Safety Canada. 2019. *Corrections and Conditional Release Statistical Overview 2018*. publicsafety.gc.ca/cnt/rsrcs/pblctns/ccrso-2018/index-en.aspx.

___. 2020. *Corrections and Conditional Release Statistical Overview 2019*. publicsafety.gc.ca/cnt/rsrcs/pblctns/ccrso-2019/ccrso-2019-en.pdf.

Puentes, Chase. 2021. "Dr. Sherry Pictou on Indigeneity, Feminism, and Resource Extraction." *Currents: A Student Blog*, Feb. 4. smea.uw.edu/currents/dr-sherry-pictou-on-indigeneity-feminism-and-resource-extraction.

Puljak, Katarina. 2015. "Canada's New Residential School: Exploring the Impact of Cultural Racism on Federally Imprisoned Aboriginal Women." *Revue YOUR Review (York Online Undergraduate Research)* 2.

Quebec Coroner's Office. 1990. *Rapport d'investigation du coroner concernant le massacre à l'École polytechnique de l'Université de Montréal*. bibliotheque.assnat.qc.ca/DepotNumerique_v2/AffichageFichier.aspx?idf=147445.

___. 1991. *Report of Coroner's Investigation Part 2*. web.archive.org/web/20160303180531/http://www.diarmani.com/Montreal_Coroners_Report.pdf.

Quon, Alexander, Aya Al-Hakim, and Jesse Thomas. 2020. "Charges against Santina Rao in connection with violent arrest dropped." *Global News*, July 6. globalnews.ca/news/7145103/charges-against-santina-rao-dropped.

R. v. Ewanchuk. 1999. 1 SCR 330. scc-csc.lexum.com/scc-csc/scc-csc/en/item/1684/index.do.

R. v. Morgentaler. 1988. 1 SCR 30. scc-csc.lexum.com/scc-csc/scc-csc/en/item/288/index.do.

R. v. Picard and Canadian Fertility Consulting Limited. *Agreed Statement of Facts*. cdn.dal.ca/content/dam/dalhousie/pdf/sites/noveltechethics/AHRA_Facts.pdf.

Radio Canada. 2019. "Chantal Daigle et le droit à l'avortement." *Radio Canada*, Aug. 7. ici.radio-canada.ca/nouvelle/1250388/affaire-chantal-daigle-droits-femme-avortement-canada-archives.

Rahr, Maggie. 2018. "A Prison Pregnancy." *The Deep Magazine*. thedeepmag.ca/aprisonpregnancy.

Rao, Ankita. 2019. "Indigenous Women in Canada Are Still Being Sterilized without Their Consent." *Vice*, Sept. 9. vice.com/en/article/9keaev/indigenous-women-in-canada-are-still-being-sterilized-without-their-consent.

Rao, Santina. 2020. "Is a Black Woman's Voice and Presence Threatening? Santina Rao Responds to the SIRT Report." *Halifax Examiner*, Oct. 10. halifaxexaminer.ca/featured/s-a-black-womans-voice-and-presence-threatening-santina-rao-responds-to-the-sirt-report.

Rathjen, Heidi, and Charles Montpetit. 1999. *December 6: From the Montreal Massacre to Gun Control: The Inside Story*. Toronto: McClelland & Stewart.

RCMP (Royal Canadian Mounted Police). 2014. *Missing and Murdered Aboriginal Women: A National Operational Overview*. rcmp-grc.gc.ca/wam/media/460/original/0cbd8968a049aa0b44d343e76b4a9478.pdf.

___. n.d. "History of Firearms in Canada." rcmp-grc.gc.ca/en/history-firearms-canada.

Rebick, Judy. 2008. "Morgentaler at 20: An Activist Reflects." *TheCourt.ca*, Jan. 7. thecourt.ca/morgentaler-at-20-an-activist-reflects.

Redden, Molly. 2017. " 'A Third of People Get Major Surgery to Be Born': Why Are C-Sections Routine in the US?" *The Guardian*, Oct. 4. theguardian.com/lifeandstyle/2017/oct/04/one-in-three-us-births-happen-by-c-section-caesarean-births.

Renke, Wayne N. 1995. "Case Comment: Lisa Neve, Dangerous Offender." *Alberta Law Review* 33, 3. canlii.ca/t/sl47.

Renzetti, Elizabeth. 2014. "Abortion in New Brunswick: The Vise Tightens, and Activists Push Back." *Globe and Mail*, July 4. theglobeandmail.com/opinion/new-brunswicks-abortion-vise-tightens/article19571563.

Resolute FP Canada Inc. v. Ontario (Attorney General). 2019. Court of Appeal for Ontario. SCC 60. scc-csc.ca/case-dossier/cb/2019/37985-eng.pdf.

Revie, Linda. 2006. "More than just Boots! The Eugenic and Commercial Concerns behind A.R. Kaufman's Birth Controlling Activities." *Canadian Bulletin of Medical History* 23, 1.

Richardson, Chinué Turner. 2006. "Environmental Justice Campaigns Provide Fertile Ground for Joint Efforts with Reproductive Rights Advocates." *Guttmacher Institute.* guttmacher.org/gpr/2006/03/environmental-justice-campaigns-provide-fertile-ground-joint-efforts-reproductive.

Riddle, John. 1994. *Contraception and Abortion from the Ancient World to the Renaissance.* Cambridge: Harvard University Press.

Ridgen, Melissa. 2019. "Baby H Taken Again as Living Arrangement Collapses." *APTN News*, June 28. aptnnews.ca/national-news/baby-h-taken-again-as-living-arrangement-collapses.

Ritchie, Andrea. 2017. *Invisible No More.* Boston: Beacon Press.

Ritchie, Beth. 2012. *Arrested Justice.* New York: NYU Press.

Ritland, Lisa, Victoria Thomas, Kate Jongbloed, et al. 2021. "The Cedar Project: Relationship between Child Apprehension and Attempted Suicide among Young Indigenous Mothers Impacted by Substance Use in Two Canadian Cities." *PlosOne* 16, 6. doi.org/10.1371/journal.pone.0252993.

Roberts, Dorothy. 1997. *Killing the Black Body.* Pantheon Books.

___. 2015. "Reproductive Justice, Not Just Rights." *Dissent.* dissentmagazine.org/article/reproductive-justice-not-just-rights.

___. 2020. Abolishing Policing also Means Abolishing Family Regulation. *Imprint News*, June 16. imprint-news.org/child-welfare-2/abolishing-policing-also-means-abolishing-family-regulation/44480.

Roe v. Wade, 410 U.S. 113 (1973). supreme.justia.com/cases/federal/us/410/113.

Ross, Loretta. 2006a. "The Color of Choice: White Supremacy and Reproductive Justice." In *Color of Violence: The INCITE! Anthology*, edited by INCITE! Women of Color Against Violence. Durham: Duke University Press.

___. 2006b. "Understanding Reproductive Justice." *Sistersong Women of Color Reproductive Health Collective newsletter*, April. d3n8a8pro7vhmx.cloudfront.net/rrfp/pages/33/attachments/original/1456425809/Understanding_RJ_Sistersong.pdf?1456425809.

___. 2006c. "Understanding Reproductive Justice: Transforming the Pro-Choice Movement." *Off Our Backs* 36, 4.

___. 2017. "Reproductive Justice as Intersectional Feminist Activism." *Souls* 19, 3.

Ross, Loretta, Sarah Brownlee, Dazon Dixon Diallo, et al. 2002. "Just Choices: Women of Color, Reproductive Health, and Human Rights." *Policing the National Body*, edited by Jael Silliman and Anannya Bhattacharjee. Cambridge, MA: South End Press.

Ross, Loretta, and Rickie Solinger. 2017. *Reproductive Justice: An Introduction.* Berkeley: University of California Press.

Rotenberg, Cristine. 2016. "Prostitution Offences in Canada: Statistical Trends." *Statistics Canada.* www150.statcan.gc.ca/n1/en/pub/85-002-x/2016001/article/14670-eng.pdf.

___. 2017. "From Arrest to Conviction: Court Outcomes of Police-Reported Sexual Assault in Canada, 2009 to 2014." *Statistics Canada.* www150.statcan.gc.ca/n1/pub/85-002-x/2017001/article/54870-eng.htm.

Roth, Rachel. 2017. " 'She Doesn't Deserve to Be Treated Like This': Prisons as Sites of Reproductive Injustice." *Radical Reproductive Justice: Foundations, Theory, Practice, Critique*, edited by Loretta J. Ross, Lynn Roberts, Erika Derkas, Whitney Peoples, and Pamela Bridgewater Toure. New York: The Feminist Press. prisonpolicy.org/scans/Roth%202017%20Prisons%20Reproductive%20Injustice.pdf.

Royal Commission on New Reproductive Technologies. 1991. *What We Heard: Issues and Questions Raised During Public Hearings.* publications.gc.ca/site/eng/9.895466/publication.html.

___. 1994. *Final Report.* publications.gc.ca/Collection-R/LoPBdP/MR/mr124-e.htm.

Rubin, Rita. 2021. "Pregnant People's Paradox — Excluded from Vaccine Trials despite Having a Higher Risk of COVID-19 Complications." *JAMA: The Journal of the American Medical Association* 325, 11.

Rutgers, Julia-Simone. 2019. " 'A Long Way to Go': Indigenous Water Protectors Speak Up at Treaty Day Rally in Halifax." *Toronto Star*, Oct 1. thestar.com/halifax/2019/10/01/a-long-way-to-go-indigenous-water-protectors-speak-up-at-treaty-day-rally-in-halifax.html.

Ryan, Haley. 2020. "Halifax Woman's Walmart Arrest Should 'Never Have Happened': Lawyer." CBC *News*, Feb 19. cbc.ca/news/canada/nova-scotia/halifax-mother-walmart-arrest-santina-rao-court-1.5468752.

___. 2021. "Alton Gas Project Cancelled after Years of Opposition." CBC *News*, Oct. 22. cbc.ca/canada/nova-scotia/alton-gas-project-cancelled-after-years-of-opposition-1.6221165.

Saltwire Network. 2017. "Man Raised in Halifax Fights Deportation to Somalia Once Prison Sentence Ends." Oct. 23. saltwire.com/atlantic-canada/news/man-raised-in-halifax-fights-deportation-to-somalia-once-prison-sentence-ends-156968/.

Save Clinic 554. 2021. "Your daily reminder that the repeal of Reg 84-20 does not require legislation." Twitter, Oct. 24. twitter.com/SaveClinic554/status/1452401427821830149?s=20.

Sawyer, Wendy, and Wanda Bertram. 2018. "Jail Will Separate 2.3 Million Mothers from Their Children This Year." *Prison Policy Initiative*, May 13. prisonpolicy.org/blog/2018/05/13/mothers-day-2018.

Scala, Francesca. 2019. "Should We Publicly Fund IVF in Canada?" *Policy Options*, April 30. policyoptions.irpp.org/magazines/april-2019/publicly-fund-ivf-canada.

Scharper, Stephen. 2016. "Grassy Narrows Mercury Disaster a Form of Environmental Racism." *Toronto Star*, June 29. thestar.com/opinion/commentary/2016/06/29/grassy-narrows-mercury-disaster-a-form-of-environmental-racism.html.

Schrek, Paula, and Julie Lothamer. 2016. *Breastfeeding & Lead Exposure*. Michigan Breastfeeding Network. michigan.gov/documents/flintwater/Final_Breastfeeding_and_Lead_Exposure_003_516600_7.pdf.

Schulich Medicine and Dentistry. n.d. "Dr. Emily Stowe." Western University. schulich.uwo.ca/meds66/sculpture/honoured_physicians/Dr.%20Emily%20Stowe.html.

Schwartz, Michael. 2021. "Canadian Permanent Resident Deported Due to Serious Criminality after Serving Sentence." CIC *News*, March 28. cicnews.com/2021/03/canadian-permanent-resident-deported-due-to-serious-criminality-after-serving-sentence-0317590.html.

Senate of Canada. 2017. "Life on the Inside: Human Rights in Canada's Prisons." sencanada.ca/en/sencaplus/news/life-on-the-inside-human-rights-in-canadas-prisons.

Serving Life 25: One Guard's Story. 2021. "Synthia Kavanagh." Facebook, March 22. facebook.com/1502228986754345/posts/synthia-kavanghwhile-i-might-be-the-last-person-to-shed-a-tear-for-the-passing-o/2728887404088491.

Sethna, Christabelle, and Steve Hewitt. 2009. "Clandestine Operations: The Vancouver Women's Caucus, the Abortion Caravan, and the RCMP." *Canadian Historical Review* 90, 3.

Seymour, Andrew. 2016. "Revealed in Photos: Take a Tour inside Ottawa's Notorious Jail." *Ottawa Citizen*, Oct 27. ottawacitizen.com/news/local-news/inside-the-ottawa-jail-tour-of-the-ocdc.

Shakur, Assata. 1988. *Assata: An Autobiography*. Chicago: Lawrence Hill Books.

Shlafer, Rebecca, Rachel R. Hardeman, and Elizabeth A. Carlson. 2019. "Reproductive Justice for Incarcerated Mothers and Advocacy for Their Infants and Young Children." *Infant Mental Health Journal* 40. doi.org/10.1002/imhj.21810.

Shlafer, Rebecca, Wendy L. Hellerstedt, Molly Secor-Turner, et al. 2015. "Doulas' Perspectives about Providing Support to Incarcerated Women: A Feasibility Study." *Public Health Nursing* 32, 4. doi.org/10.1111/phn.12137.

Shlafer, Rebecca, Jennifer B. Saunders, Christy M. Boraas, et al. 2021. "Maternal and Neonatal Outcomes among Incarcerated Women Who Gave Birth in Custody." *Birth* 48, 1. doi.org/10.1111/birt.12524.

SickKids. 2019. "Motherisk." sickkids.ca/en/news/motherisk.

Silliman, Jael, Marlene Gerber Fried, and Loretta Ross. 2016. *Undivided Rights: Women of Color Organizing for Reproductive Justice*. Chicago: Haymarket Books.

Singer, Joel, Laura Sauve, Fatima Kakkar, et al. 2020. "Vertical Transmission in Canada: Canadian Perinatal HIV Surveillance Program." CAHR. cahr-acrv.ca/wp-content/uploads/2020/04/EPHP4.10-Vertical-Transmission-in-Canada-Canadian-Perinatal-HIV-Surveillance-Program.pdf.

SisterSong. n.d. "Reproductive Justice." sistersong.net/reproductive-justice.

Smellie, Sarah. 2021. "Data Shows Sexual Assault Conviction of N.L. Police Officer Not the Norm." CBC

News, May 17. cbc.ca/news/canada/newfoundland-labrador/snelgrove-conviction-sexual-assault-data-1.6030117.

Smith. Emma. 2021. "Calls to Ban Birth Alerts Grow Louder as Other Provinces End Controversial Practice." *CBC News*, Feb. 8. cbc.ca/news/canada/nova-scotia/birth-alerts-mothers-babies-child-welfare-indigenous-women-1.5904676.

Smylie, Janet, and Wanda Phillips-Beck. 2019. "Truth, Respect and Recognition: Addressing Barriers to Indigenous Maternity Care." *Canadian Medical Association Journal* 191, 8. doi.org/10.1503/cmaj.190183.

Somos, Christy. 2021. "Residential School Graves 'Totally Pushed to the Wayside' in Shadow of Election, Indigenous Leaders Say." *CTV News*, Aug. 17. ctvnews.ca/politics/federal-election-2021/residential-school-graves-totally-pushed-to-the-wayside-in-shadow-of-election-indigenous-leaders-say-1.5550433.

Stanley, Darcy, Nicole Sata, Julia Chinyere Oparah, and Monica R. McLemore. 2015. "Evaluation of the East Bay Community Birth Support Project, a Community-Based Program to Decrease Recidivism in Previously Incarcerated Women." *Journal of Obstetric, Gynecological & Neonatal Nursing* 44, 6.

Stasiuk, Melissa. 2020. "IVF Was My Last Hope to Have a Baby. All Canadians Deserve That Hope, Too." *Globe and Mail*, Feb 15. theglobeandmail.com/opinion/article-ivf-was-my-last-hope-to-have-a-baby-all-canadians-deserve-that-hope.

Statistics Canada. 2005. "Induced Abortion." /www150.statcan.gc.ca/n1/en/pub/82-223-x/82-223-x2008000-eng.pdf?st=T46cYyig.

___. 2016. "Census Profile, 2016. Dryden, City." www12.statcan.gc.ca/census-recensement/2016/dp-pd/prof/details/page.cfm?Lang=E&Geo1=CSD&Code1=3560027&Geo2=CD&Code2=3560&Data=Count&SearchText=dryden&SearchType=Begins&SearchPR=01&B1=All&TABID=1.

___. 2017. "Same-Sex Couples in Canada in 2016." www12.statcan.gc.ca/census-recensement/2016/as-sa/98-200-x/2016007/98-200-x2016007-eng.cfm.

___. 2018. "Canadian Classification of Functions of Government." www150.statcan.gc.ca/n1/daily-quotidien/181128/dq181128b-eng.htm.

___. 2019a. "Gender-Based Violence and Unwanted Sexual Behaviour in Canada, 2018: Initial Findings from the Survey in Public and Private Spaces." www150.statcan.gc.ca/n1/daily-quotidien/191205/dq191205b-eng.htm.

___. 2019b. "Diversity of the Black Population in Canada: An Overview." www150.statcan.gc.ca/n1/pub/89-657-x/89-657-x2019002-eng.htm

___. 2019c. "At a Glance: Government Revenues from the Sale of Cannabis, March 2019." www150.statcan.gc.ca/n1/daily-quotidien/190619/dq190619e-eng.htm.

___. 2020. "Sex at Birth and Gender: Technical Report on Changes for the 2021 Census." www12.statcan.gc.ca/census-recensement/2021/ref/98-20-0002/982000022020002-eng.cfm.

Stephenson, Bill. 1957. "The Great Birth Control Trial." *Macleans*, Nov. 23. archive.macleans.ca/article/1957/11/23/the-great-birth-control-trial.

Stewart, Dave. 2016. "Anne-tagonizing Posters Connect Icon to P.E.I. Abortion Debate." *Saltwire*, Jan. 28. saltwire.com/prince-edward-island/news/local/anne-tagonizing-posters-connect-icon-to-pei-abortion-debate-101014/.

Stickney, R. 2011. "Prison Sentence for Attorney in Black-Market Baby Selling Ring." *NBC San Diego*, Dec. 2. nbcsandiego.com/news/local/prison-sentence-for-attorney-in-black-market-baby-selling-ring/1912712.

Stone, Laura. 2011. "Babies behind Bars: Mother-Child Program Little Used Despite Support." *Winnipeg Free Press*, Oct. 15. winnipegfreepress.com/opinion/fyi/babies-behind-bars-131910023.html.

Stortz, Gerald, and Murray Eaton. 1983. " 'Pro Bono Publico': The Eastview Birth Control Trial." *Atlantis* 8, 2.

Stote, Karen. 2012. "The Coercive Sterilization of Aboriginal Women in Canada." *American Indian Culture and Research Journal* 36, 3.

Sufrin, Carolyn. 2017. *Jailcare*. Berkeley: University of California Press.

Sufrin, Carolyn, Alexa Kolbi-Molinas, and Rachel Roth. 2015. "Reproductive Justice, Health Disparities and Incarcerated Women in the United States." *Perspectives on Sexual and Reproductive Health* 47, 4. doi.org/10.1363/47e3115.

Sufrin, Carolyn, Lauren Beal, Jennifer Clarke, et al. 2019. "Pregnancy Outcomes in US Prisons, 2016–2017." *American Journal of Public Health* 109, 5.

Sunrise Group. n.d. "About Us." en.sunriseltd.ca/about-us.

Taillieu, Tamara L., and Douglas A. Brownridge. 2010. "Violence against Pregnant Women: Prevalence, Patterns, Risk Factors, Theories, and Directions for Future Research." *Aggression and Violent Behavior* 15, 1.

Tait, Caroline. 2002. "Pregnant Addicted Women in Manitoba." *Canadian Women's Health Network* 4–5, 4–1.

Task Force on Federally Sentenced Women. 1990. *Creating Choices: Report on the Task Force on Federally Sentenced Women.* csc-scc.gc.ca/women/092/002002-0001-en.pdf.

Taylor, Brooke. 2021. "Trans Health Care in Canada Needs Major Improvements, Advocates Say." CTV *News*, May 22. ctvnews.ca/health/trans-health-care-in-canada-needs-major-improvements-advocates-say-1.5439295.

Taylor, Diane. 2020. "Cheshire Prison Worker Warned of Problems before Deatho Baby." *The Guardian*, July 27. theguardian.com/society/2020/jul/27/cheshire-prison-worker-warned-of-problems-before-death-of-baby.

Taylor, Diane, and Hannah Devlin. 2021. "Fear of More Baby Deaths as Ministers Stand Firm on Jailing Pregnant Women." *The Guardian*, Sept. 23. theguardian.com/society/2021/sep/23/fear-of-more-baby-deaths-as-ministers-stand-firm-on-jailing-pregnant-women.

Thalidomide Victims Association of Canada. n.d. "The Tragedy of Thalidomide in Canada." thalidomide.ca/en/the-canadian-tragedy.

Thumath, Meaghan, David Humphreys, Jane Barlow, et al. 2021. "Overdose among Mothers: The Association between Child Removal and Unintentional Drug Overdose in a Longitudinal Cohort of Marginalised Women in Canada." *International Journal on Drug Policy* 91.

Times Colonist. 2008. "Killer Mom to Raise Baby in Prison." Feb. 8. pressreader.com/canada/times-colonist/20080208/281608121122279.

Toronto Star. 2015. "No Still Means No: Editorial." Nov. 13 thestar.com/opinion/editorials/2015/11/13/no-still-means-no-editorial.html.

Toth, Katie. 2018. "Nightmare at Wood Street." *The Coast.* thecoast.ca/halifax/nightmare-at-wood-street/Content?oid=15149314.

Trevethan, Shelley, Sarah Auger, John-Patrick Moore, Michael MacDonald, and Jennifer Sinclair. 2001. *The Effect of Family Disruption on Aboriginal and Non-Aboriginal Inmates.* Correctional Services Canada. csc-scc.gc.ca/research/092/r113-eng.pdf.

Trudeau Foundation. n.d. "Wade MacLauchlan." trudeaufoundation.ca/member/wade-maclauchlan.

Truth and Reconciliation Commission. 2015. *Calls to Action.* www2.gov.bc.ca/assets/gov/british-columbians-our-governments/indigenous-people/aboriginal-peoples-documents/calls_to_action_english2.pdf.

Tuttle, Myrna. 2020. "Transgender Inmates in Prison." *LawNow.* lawnow.org/transgender-inmates-in-prison.

Tyndall, Mark. 2020. "A Safer Drug Supply: A Pragmatic and Ethical Response to the Overdose Crisis." *Canadian Medical Association Journal* 192, 34.

Tyndall, Mark, and Dodd, Zoë. 2019. "How Structural Violence, Prohibition, and Stigma Have Paralyzed North American Responses to Opioid Overdose." *AMA Journal of Overdose* 22, 8. doi.org/10.1001/amajethics.2020.723.

Ubel, Peter A., Karen A. Scherrkmath, and A. Fagerlin. 2017. "Empowerment Failure: How Shortcomings in Physician Communication Unwittingly Undermine Patient Autonomy." *American Journal of Bioethics* 17, 11.

Union of Nova Scotia Mi'kmaq. n.d. "Jordan's Principle." unsm.org/dept/jordans-principle.

Union of Ontario Indians. 2013. *An Overview of the Indian Residential School System.* anishinabek.ca/wp-content/uploads/2016/07/An-Overview-of-the-IRS-System-Booklet.pdf.

United Nations. 2015. *Eliminating Discrimination and Inequalities in Access to Water and Sanitation.* unwater.org/publications/eliminating-discrimination-inequalities-access-water-sanitation.

United Nations General Assembly. 1989. "Convention on the Rights of the Child." *United Nations.* ohchr.

org/en/professionalinterest/pages/crc.aspx.

___. 1993. "Declaration on the Elimination of Violence against Women." *United Nations.* ohchr.org/en/professionalinterest/pages/violenceagainstwomen.aspx.

United Nations Office on Drugs and Crime. 2011. *The Bangkok Rules.* unodc.org/documents/justice-and-prison-reform/Bangkok_Rules_ENG_22032015.pdf.

United Nations Population Fund. 2014. *Programme of Action of the International Conference on Population Development.* unfpa.org/sites/default/files/pub-pdf/programme_of_action_Web%20ENGLISH.pdf.

Vafaei, Homeira, Sara Ajdari, Kamran Hessami, et al. 2020. "Efficacy and Safety of Myrrh in Patients with Incomplete Abortion: A Randomized, Double-Blind, Placebo-Controlled Clinical Study." *BMC Complementary Medicine and Therapies* 20, 1.

Van Dusen, Lisa. 1989. "The Final Appeal." *Maclean's*, Aug 14. archive.macleans.ca/article/1989/8/14/the-final-appeal.

Vancouver Prisoner Justice Day Committee. 2007. "Transgender Prisoners in Canada." vcn.bc.ca/august10/downloads/trans_prisoners_july2007.pdf.

Vasilakopoulos, Reah. 2020. "Putting Aside Moral Judgment and Making Room for Care: Reproductive Justice and Harm Reduction." *NARAL Pro-Choice MD.* prochoicemd.medium.com/putting-aside-moral-judgment-and-making-room-for-care-reproductive-justice-and-harm-reduction-56c1cab247cb.

Vescera, Zak. 2021. "Sanctum Gets Funding Boost for High-Risk Expectant Moms." *Saskatoon StarPhoenix*, Apr. 13. thestarphoenix.com/news/saskatchewan/sanctum-gets-funding-boost-for-high-risk-expectant-moms.

Victora, Cesar G., Rajiv Bahl, Aluísio Barros, et al. 2016. "Breastfeeding in the 21st Century: Epidemiology, Mechanisms, and Lifelong Effect." *The Lancet (British Edition)* 387.

Vikander, Tessa, and Bailey Marelj. 2021. "Several Canadian Provinces Still Use Birth Alerts, Deemed 'Unconstitutional and Illegal' in BC." *APTN National News*, Jan. 15. aptnnews.ca/national-news/provinces-continue-birth-alerts.

Wahlsten, Douglas. 1997. "Leilani Muir versus the Philosopher King: Eugenics on Trial in Alberta." *Genetica* 99, 2. doi.org/10.1007/BF02259522

Wakefield, Jonny. 2018. "Former Alberta Inmate Carried Stillborn Baby for Weeks after Seeking Help from Staff." *Edmonton Journal*, Mar. 26. edmontonjournal.com/news/local-news/former-alberta-inmate-carried-stillborn-baby-for-weeks-after-seeking-help-from-staff.

Waldron, Ingrid. 2018. *There's Something in the Water: Environmental Racism in Indigenous and Black Communities.* Black Point, Winnipeg: Fernwood.

Walkem, Ardith. 2004. "Indigenous Peoples Water Rights: Challenges and Opportunities in an Era of Increased North American Integration." uvic.ca/research/centres/globalstudies/assets/docs/publications/IndigenousPeoplesWaterRights.pdf.

Wall-Wieler, Elizabeth, Kathleen Kenny, Janelle Lee, et al. 2019. "Prenatal Care among Mothers Involved with Child Protection Services in Manitoba: A Retrospective Cohort Study." *Canadian Medical Association Journal* 191, 8.

Wall-Wieler, Elizabeth, Leslie L. Roos, James Bolton, et al. 2017. "Maternal Health and Social Outcomes after Having a Child Taken into Care: Population-Based Longitudinal Cohort Study Using Linkable Administrative Data." *Journal of Epidemiology and Community Health* 71, 12.

Wall-Wieler, Elizabeth, Leslie L. Roos, Marni Brownell, et al. 2018. "Suicide Attempts and Completions among Mothers Whose Children Were Taken into Care by Child Protection Services: A Cohort Study Using Linkable Administrative Data." *Canadian Journal of Psychiatry* 63, 3.

Wallace, Bruce, Lisa Van Dusen, and Glen Allen. 1989. "Abortion Agony." *Maclean's*, Aug. 21. archive.macleans.ca/article/1989/8/21/abortion-agony.

Warner, Elizabeth, Robert Walker, and Peter Friedmann. 2003. "Should Informed Consent Be Required for Laboratory Testing for Drugs Used in Medical Settings?" *American Journal of Medicine* 115, 1.

Washington, John. 2016. "At Least 24,000 Inmates Have Staged Coordinated Protests in the Past Month. Why Have You Not Heard of Their Actions?" *The Nation*, Oct. 14. thenation.com/article/archive/at-least-24000-inmates-have-staged-coordinated-protests-in-the-past-month-why-have-you-not-heard-of-their-actions.

WAVAV Rape Crisis Centre. 2018. "To the Sex Worker Community — We Owe You an Apology." wavaw.ca/

to-the-sex-worker-community-we-owe-you-an-apology.

Wells, Karin. 2020. *The Abortion Caravan: When Women Shut Down Government in the Battle for the Right to Choose.* Toronto: Second Story Press.

Werb, Dan, R.N. Bluthenal, G. Kolla, C. Strike, A.H. Kral, A. Uusküla, and D. Des Jarlais. 2018. "Preventing Injection Drug Use Initiation: State of the Evidence and Opportunities for the Future." *Journal of Urban Health* 95. doi.org/10.1007/s11524-017-0192-8.

Whiffen, Glen. 2021. "Newfoundland and Labrador Putting an End to Controversial Birth-Alerts." *Saltwire*, June 28. saltwire.com/atlantic-canada/news/newfoundland-and-labrador-putting-an-end-to-controversial-birth-alerts-100605546.

White, Pamela M. 2016. "Hidden from View: Canadian Gestational Surrogacy Practices and Outcomes, 2001–2012." *Reproductive Health Matters* 24, 47.

Williams, Vanessa. 2019. "Why Black Women Issued a Public Demand for 'Reproductive Justice' 25 Years Ago." *The Washington Post*, Aug. 16. washingtonpost.com/nation/2019/08/16/reproductive-justice-how-women-color-asserted-their-voice-abortion-rights-movement.

Willingham, A.J., and Carma Hassan. 2016. "Judge to Woman in Rape Case: 'Why Couldn't You Just Keep Your Knees Together?'" *CNN*, Sept. 13. cnn.com/2016/09/12/world/robin-camp-rape-comments-trnd/index.html.

Wilson, Robert A. 2019. "Eugenics Undefended." *Monash Bioethics Review* 37, 68.

Women's College Hospital Foundation. n.d. "The Emily Stowe Society." wchf.convio.net/site/PageNavigator/EmilyStoweSociety_Home.html.

Woodward, Jon. 2008. "Newborn Goes to Prison in B.C. First." *CTV News*, Feb. 6. bc.ctvnews.ca/newborn-goes-to-prison-in-b-c-first-1.275064.

World Health Organization. 2005. *Trihalomethanes in Drinking-Water.* who.int/water_sanitation_health/dwq/chemicals/THM200605.pdf.

___. 2020. "Infertility." who.int/news-room/fact-sheets/detail/infertility.

___. 2021. "Lead Poisoning." who.int/news-room/fact-sheets/detail/lead-poisoning-and-health.

Wortley, Scot. 2019. *Halifax, Nova Scotia: Street Checks Report.* Nova Scotia Human Rights Commission. humanrights.novascotia.ca/sites/default/files/editor-uploads/halifax_street_checks_report_march_2019_0.pdf.

York University. n.d. "Emily Stowe Memorial Scholarship." sfs.yorku.ca/scholarships/award-search?awardID=024

Yuzpe, A. Albert. 2019. "A Brief Overview of the History of In Vitro Fertilization in Canada." *Journal of Obstetrics and Gynaecology Canada* 41, S2.

Zakaria, Rafia. 2021. *Against White Feminism: Notes on Disruption.* New York: W.W. Norton.

Zingel, Avery. 2019. "Indigenous Women Come Forward with Accounts of Forced Sterilization, Says Lawyer." *CBC News*, April 18. cbc.ca/news/canada/north/forced-sterilization-lawsuit-could-expand-1.5102981.

INDEX